Transforming Classroom Culture

Transforming Classroom Culture

Inclusive Pedagogical Practices

Edited by
Arlene Dallalfar
Esther Kingston-Mann
and
Tim Sieber

palgrave
macmillan

TRANSFORMING CLASSROOM CULTURE

Copyright © Arlene Dallalfar, Esther Kingston-Mann, and Tim Sieber, 2011.

First published in 2011 by
PALGRAVE MACMILLAN®
in the United States—a division of St. Martin's Press LLC,
175 Fifth Avenue, New York, NY 10010.

Where this book is distributed in the UK, Europe and the rest of the world,
this is by Palgrave Macmillan, a division of Macmillan Publishers Limited,
registered in England, company number 785998, of Houndmills,
Basingstoke, Hampshire RG21 6XS.

Palgrave Macmillan is the global academic imprint of the above companies
and has companies and representatives throughout the world.

Palgrave® and Macmillan® are registered trademarks in the United States,
the United Kingdom, Europe and other countries.

ISBN: 978–0–230–11191–2

Library of Congress Cataloging-in-Publication Data

Transforming classroom culture : inclusive pedagogical practices /
edited by Arlene Dallalfar, Esther Kingston-Mann, and R. Timothy Sieber.
p. cm.
ISBN 978–0–230–11191–2 (hardback)
1. College teaching—United States. 2. Effective teaching—United
States. I. Dallalfar, Arlene, 1955– II. Kingston-Mann, Esther. III. Sieber, R.
Timothy. IV. Title.

LB2331.T725 2011
378.1′250973—dc22   2011005460

A catalogue record of the book is available from the British Library.

Design by Newgen Imaging Systems (P) Ltd., Chennai, India.

First edition: September 2011

10 9 8 7 6 5 4 3 2 1

Transferred to Digital Printing in 2012

Dedicated to

Paula Rothenberg
Micah Sieber
John Horton

Contents

Microcosms of Hope: A Foreword

Hubie Jones

The contributors to this book form part of a thriving and increasing number of college and university faculty committed to research and pedagogy that focuses on diversity and inclusion. I have joyfully supported their courageous and difficult work to move these issues to center stage. Acknowledging their own diverse backgrounds, they engage in a collaborative student/faculty pedagogy that requires them to learn from their students. In this process, these scholar-teachers contribute to our understanding of issues that extend far beyond the classroom. They provide opportunities for their students to engage in deep reflection and study of how we move as a people from segregation, to mere coexistence, to a solid integration of racial and ethnic groups. In so doing, they address one of the great challenges of our times.

As I see it, one cannot truly be a fully educated person unless he or she appreciates the cultural gifts of all people and knows how to weave them into a rich mosaic in a beloved community. It is inspiring that the educators represented in this collection of essays recognize their own limitations and personal challenges but remain committed to pedagogical strategies that empower students to take responsibility for their own learning. They are truly a band of sisters and brothers united in advancing teaching, learning, and research on diversity and inclusion. Through their work, they are living up to the noblest purposes of the academy in a democracy.

In my own teaching, I recall a time when a student stopped a seminar in its tracks by asking, "Has anybody here ever had an experience that would let them know what it would be like to live in an ideal society?" After a moment or two, her fellow students and I began to reflect aloud on the experience of being—no matter how briefly—in a community where each person was accepted and embraced on the basis of their human attributes, regardless of race, ethnicity, social class, disability, and sexual orientation.

As we learned from each other, we began to understand that diversity was a source of collective strength. In that seminar, I learned a great deal from my students. The seminar itself became a venue for deep and authentic learning and—equally important—a microcosm of an ideal society.

In their pedagogical practice, many contributors to this book build such ideal societies in their own classrooms. Their mission is to transform these venues into places where teachers and students work collaboratively in an atmosphere of mutual respect. In this process, they are preparing a new and more culturally competent generation to be participants in a democracy that extends beyond the classroom. The contributors to this volume represent a widening circle of the committed, those who live and breathe this diversity vision. This is not ancillary work; it forms an important part of our core definition of an educated human being and authentic citizen. Engaged in the daunting task of making the academy all that it should be, their stories reveal how difficult and rewarding it can be to open up a respectful civil dialogue about our history, our values, and our fate. In so doing, they confront one of the most important challenges of our time.

Acknowledgments

The journey in conceiving and preparing this book has truly been transformative for all involved: students, faculty, and administrators. It began over eight years ago at a conference organized by Esther Kingston-Mann on inclusive teaching at the University of Massachusetts Boston (UMB). Support from the Ford Foundation and the vision of Esther Kingston-Mann led to the creation of a New England Center for Inclusive Teaching (NECIT). We wish to thank the late Edgar Beckham and Gertrude Fraser for their unwavering support. The Foundation's funding allowed us as scholar-teachers to examine how we engage in inclusive teaching and the different ways we connect with students from diverse cultural/linguistic/ ethnic and class backgrounds. We thank Rajini Srikanth, Vivian Zamel, Caroline Brown, Jay Dee, and Karen Suyemoto for their efforts in helping to carry NECIT forward over the years. Chancellor Keith Motley and Provost Winston Langley have also been essential supporters of our efforts. We also want to thank the anonymous reviewers and others at Palgrave Macmillan who recognized the importance of these first-person narratives and the value added in reviewing differing personal experiences to illustrate the challenges of engaging in inclusive teaching practices.

As contributors and editors, we navigated multiple roles as we organized potlucks, group meetings, and individual sessions to work with contributors on their chapters, many of whom are publishing for the first time in this interdisciplinary field of the scholarship of teaching. We the editors would like to thank our contributors for their steadfastness in our years of collective dialogues over inclusive teaching, culminating in the present volume.

The idea of this book initially grew out of Arlene Dallalfar's experiences at Lesley University as the faculty seminar leader and NECIT liaison. The powerful and dynamic exchanges in the weekly Lesley seminar opened up many spaces for invigorating and difficult conversations about power dynamics, vulnerabilities, and challenges in teaching and empowering students. At Lesley, Arlene would like to thank Provost Martha McKenna for her support of the NECIT seminar. In addition to the Lesley faculty who have chapters in this book, she would also like to thank Katherine Barone, Solange Lira, and Eleanor Roffman for their continual encouragement to address the hard questions in challenging oneself to improve and engage all students in the classroom; Jenn Walker for always trying her best to find extra work-study support; and Kat Rubio for her help with the bibliography. Also, Arlene thanks her colleague and husband, Fereydoun Safizadeh, who continues to inspire her in his generosity and intellectual clarity.

For Esther Kingston-Mann, Paula Rothenberg and Hubie Jones have been consistent and inspirational supporters of her individual and collaborative work over the course of many years, and she values the early and steadfast UMB support that her work received from Sherry Penney and Edmund Toomey. Esther also thanks John Wooding and (as always) Jim Mann and Larisa Mann.

Tim Sieber would like to thank many people for their encouragement, support, and inspiration over the years during this project, including his coeditors Arlene and Esther, Natalicia Tracy, Donaldo Macedo, Sherry Penney, Denise Patmon, Judy Zeitlin, Vivian Zamel, Diane D'Arrigo, Andrea Klimt, Andrew Gordon, Angela Cacciarru, Lin Zhan, Mariah Sixkiller, and Micah Sieber.

ARLENE DALLALFAR, ESTHER KINGSTON-MANN, AND TIM SIEBER
Boston, Massachusetts, December 8, 2010

Faculty Collaboration and Inclusive Pedagogical Practice: An Introduction

Tim Sieber, Esther Kingston-Mann, and Arlene Dallalfar

This book is the result of collaboration among the contributors over four years of seminars, conferences, book meetings, and sustained conversation about what constitutes good teaching. Supported by external funding, the authors have participated in semester-long, faculty-led teaching seminars on our own campuses and shared insights with colleagues at other New England–area colleges and universities at intercollegiate gatherings. Although our campuses, academic fields, and cultural backgrounds differ, our common experience of collaboration has convinced us that sharing information and teaching strategies among colleagues fosters improvements in student learning. Our experiences have taught us that this goal can be reached by introducing collaborative approaches into the classroom and into our relationships with students. These help define the classroom as a learning community and foster reflective student engagement with texts and writing.

As contributors, we consider ourselves to be scholar-teachers and reflective practitioners who understand the importance of raising questions of epistemology in our individual teaching practice. Convinced that in many cases, knowledge creation and critical intellectual engagement are as much a collective as an individual process, our contributors document how the teaching-learning encounter can become a catalyst for transforming individual students and the wider learning community. Faculty are also participants in these learning communities. As a consequence, our contributors are able to illuminate teaching practice and inclusive pedagogy from both student and faculty perspectives.

Our volume builds on a wide array of valuable earlier scholarship.[1] At the same time, it moves in a new direction by paying particular attention to the role that collaborative work and self-reflection by faculty play in creating a positive environment for learning. We agree with bell hooks that the learning of faculty and of students and, indeed, the broader self-actualization of each are intertwined and reciprocal processes (hooks 1994). Faculty gain teaching expertise from a continual process of practice, reflection, and learning. They do not know how to teach simply because they possess specialized knowledge. Becoming a good teacher is not an intuitive matter; it is a skill that is learned through an ongoing process of trial and error that involves making mistakes, reflecting on them, and drawing lessons from experience. Our contributors have also found that the support of faculty colleagues and administrators plays a very significant role in the improvement of teaching. By acknowledging and analyzing what is involved in this process of faculty learning, our volume tries to fill a gap in the literature on higher education pedagogy.

It is sometimes forgotten that the classroom is not the only pedagogical space in the university where significant learning takes place. Within the academy, collaboration may occur in one-on-one meetings between faculty and students and among the faculty who do not shut their doors but open them instead to the insights of colleagues from their own and other institutions. It should be noted as well that the practice of collaboration—or the absence of collaboration—profoundly affects the relationship between faculty and administrators. Successful teaching may be powerfully fostered or hindered by the style of institutional leadership deployed by university and college administrators.

Knowledge and Civic Engagement

Many educators are already aware that effective teaching and learning require both students and professors to consider how they construct knowledge as an intellectual matter. In the chapters that follow, it will become evident that our contributors also view the classroom as a socially constructed space where identity and power are subject to negotiation between teacher and student and among students themselves. The classroom may become an arena of agency and self-empowerment for faculty and students alike—a public space, a site for social activism, and a sphere of struggle for social justice. A more inclusive pedagogy may then become the basis for a democratic and civic engagement by students and teachers with many of the most critical public and global issues of our day.

Diversity and Identity in Today's College Classrooms

In this volume, our contributors lay bare the excitement, struggles, challenges, and minefields that faculty of diverse backgrounds encounter when they teach in classrooms that are both mixed and homogeneous. As we see it, it takes a certain amount of courage to write honestly about teaching and to recognize the personal vulnerabilities that faculty often experience, but rarely receive permission to acknowledge. The act of teaching is a complex, creative, and sometimes even heroic professional and personal achievement. The chapters in this book constitute a response to the challenges that all faculty face—challenges that are particularly intense for those who come from diverse racial and ethnic backgrounds. Our authors document in detail the wide array of strategies devised by faculty who have developed productive learning encounters in racially homogeneous institutions where they may be the only visible representative of diversity in the classroom. Some of their narratives show that some make a deliberate effort to disrupt students' expectations, for example, that a South Asian professor should focus on an Asia-centered topic instead of teaching the traditional canon. Some provide important insights into the ways that their teaching can be affected by the demoralizing impact of invisibility and/or hypervisibility that may occur when they engage in departmental-, college-, and university-wide committees and institutional initiatives.

Including Diverse Faculty and Diverse Voices

Our contributors are discipline-trained faculty whose fields of study range from studio art, history, anthropology, education, art history, counseling, sociology, women's studies, social work, psychology, to writing composition. They are scholar-teachers from colleges and universities that range from PhD-granting institutions to community colleges, both public and private. They bring their own diverse cultural identities and backgrounds to the teaching enterprise: five contributors came to the United States as immigrants, all but three are women, four are African American, and their social origins range from upper middle class to working class. In this respect, they accurately mirror the changing face of today's professoriate, with a social profile more diverse than ever.

No matter how long they have been teaching, it is important for professors to know and to believe that they can change their practice. Although many faculty are pessimistic about this possibility, the experiences recounted by our authors argue for optimism and hope. They show that over time, professors can become better at creating a classroom environment that generates a kind of learning that transforms both parties to the teaching-learning encounter. Students raise questions that faculty have not considered before and cause them to reexamine their approach to teaching; faculty may inspire in students a love of learning, and awaken their confidence in their own analytical and critical skills, and propel them into never-before-imagined intellectual terrain.

The New England Center for Inclusive Teaching

These initiatives moved beyond the University of Massachusetts Boston through the creation of a regional New England Center for Inclusive Teaching (NECIT) that has been headquartered at the University of Massachusetts Boston for a decade. These grassroots faculty initiatives could not have come into being without the support of enlightened, supportive administrators at the university and external foundation grants (see Kingston-Mann 1992). The Ford Foundation funded the creation of the University of Massachusetts Boston's Center for the Improvement of Teaching (CIT) and supported the establishment of semester-long faculty-development seminars at seven New England–area higher education institutions under the auspices of NECIT. These seminars eventually became a catalyst for the emergence of an intercampus faculty network dedicated to the reflection and dialogues that inspired our contributors to engage in the scholarship of inclusive teaching reflected in this book.

In our work together, the editors and contributors have discovered that despite the differences among our campus histories and missions, faculty encounter dilemmas and challenges that are in important respects quite similar. Equally important, the same pedagogical principles and teaching practices have turned out to work in strikingly diverse academic settings. The chapters that follow are thus broadly consistent in message even though they represent faculty experiences at five different institutions (institutional descriptions are given at the end of this chapter).

Our book is a direct product of several years of intercampus regional faculty meetings in which over 150 professors have focused on inclusive pedagogy, innovative instructional strategies, and the similarities and differences between teaching experiences in varying institutional contexts. In all of these efforts, we have found collegial collaboration and interfaculty dialogue to be powerful tools for the promotion of reflective teaching practice and improvements in student learning. These interactions have resulted in the production of valuable contributions to the scholarship of inclusive teaching.

Part I: Setting the Stage—
Institutional Contexts of Innovation and Change

The first set of chapters offers a cross-institutional examination of pedagogical issues surrounding inclusion in today's colleges and universities and makes clear that the individual professor does not and cannot act alone. As we see it, the shape that teaching takes anywhere is dependent on far more than the acts and intentions of individual professors in their own classrooms. Whether they acknowledge it or not, faculty belong to and are influenced by collegial communities. This collection in particular tells the story of how building regional and campus-based grassroots organizations at the University of Massachusetts Boston led to the creation of sophisticated and skilled faculty development communities at other universities in the New England region. In this process, institutional context and history and varying administrative arrangements exerted a significant influence in defining challenges and possibilities for individual academics facing the students in their classrooms.

"Academic Integrity and Academic Inclusion: The Mission of the 'Outsider Within'" traces Esther Kingston-Mann's odyssey as both a successful and often frustrated leader in initiatives to foster multicultural curriculum change, original student research, and the improvement of teaching. She points out that collective efforts, movements, and grassroots faculty leadership are always key factors in promoting an innovative pedagogical practice. Transformations at the classroom level can result from change at the institutional level, in faculty identity, roles, new practice standards, and growth of a "culture of teaching." Kingston-Mann's account of several decades as an activist faculty leader also reminds us that faculty must take a "long view" of what is required to change institutional culture and to foster teaching transformation. In her view, successful change initiatives build on the achievements of their predecessors and eventually themselves become the basis for new projects.

Tim Sieber's "A History Lived and Lessons Learned: Collaboration, Change, and Teaching Transformation," documents the use of collaborative work as a catalyst for teaching transformation at both individual and institutional levels throughout the history of University of Massachusetts Boston's CIT. Sieber presents abundant evidence that demonstrates that such grassroots faculty-led initiatives were a response to wider social historical changes in U.S. higher education during the second half of the twentieth century. Their success owed much to support from faculty colleagues and from enlightened administrators who made use of collaboration in their own management styles.

Denise Patmon's "Pedagogy for the Professoriate: The Personal Meets the Political" takes us inside the workings of a faculty teaching development seminar. It shows how a seminar's leader draws on the personal teaching/learning histories and pedagogical aspirations of its participants to encourage a productive sharing of problem-solving strategies among colleagues. Her narrative description of a faculty development seminar reveals the power and the promise of honest, open faculty dialogues on issues of pedagogy. When questions of intercultural communication and inclusion are discussed, they invariably involve professors as well as students. In many respects, the collegial and mentoring relations that arise within a faculty development seminar resemble the learning environment that faculty are attempting to create in their own classrooms.

Part II: Faculty Identity as a Resource for Effective Teaching

The second cluster of chapters focuses on the diverse and particular ways that faculty draw on varying disciplinary and philosophical inspirations and on insights linked to personal identity to shape their understanding of teaching and learning and their instructional strategies. By engaging holistically with their own experience as scholars and as human beings, faculty model an honest, critical intellectual stance that then becomes more accessible and permissible for students themselves. When identity is acknowledged in this manner, self-insight as well as empathy can be the result.

In Vivian Poey's "Imaging the Spaces between Art and Inclusive Pedagogy," for example, the author explains how important it is to reveal her own creative process and her engagement with issues of her Latino identity and culture to model what it means to be an artist and a teacher of art. This is an essential step for her students, who are themselves art teachers in public schools, who in turn have their own students to inspire as producers of art.

Rajini Srikanth, in her "Inexplicable Desire, Pedagogical Compulsion: Teaching the Literatures of the Middle East," draws on her own background as a native of South Asia, but not to claim authority over the subject matter of her course on Middle Eastern literature. Instead, her background experiences provoke a deep curiosity about the material, and a willingness to risk being a relative beginner in the field, as her students are. She reveals the always-close reciprocity between learning and teaching in our work as college professors and shows that faculty's own vulnerabilities as people and as learners, if honestly acknowledged, can yield the type of modeling and mentoring that guides and inspires.

These accounts thus situate personal cultural identity as an important element in creative and intellectual engagement for both teacher and student.

In a class on "Women's Lives: Global Perspectives," described in "Teaching Women's Lives: Feminist Pedagogy and the Sociological Imagination," Arlene Dallalfar offers her students the example of her own complex identity and so challenges essentialist notions of the cultural "Other." Dallalfar's teaching enhances students' awareness of how their epistemological position and lived experiences impact their understanding of the "Other," so that their education can lead to transformative learning experiences both inside and outside the classroom. She encourages students to critically examine assigned readings about global women, so that they can discover in that context unexpected and challenging diversities that have been present in their own family histories.

Sunanda Sanyal, in his chapter "Teaching Art History at an Art School: Making Sense from the Margin," documents not only a struggle with teaching art history to sometimes uninterested studio artists but also the necessity that he deal with the way that his own Indian identity affects his pedagogical efforts. By interrupting students' stereotypes, he challenges their assumption that someone who looks like him should be a specialist in Asian instead of European art. He is only one of many contributors who as professors feel, at the same time, hypervisible and invisible in the classroom.

In these chapters, faculty from art history, education, sociology, and literature focus on cultivating an awareness of otherness and subjectivity by exploring epistemological limits, and most importantly, by critically examining representations of otherness in popular culture, arts, media, and literature. Each chapter addresses the theory and pedagogy that informs its author's teaching practice and more specifically how particular texts, strategies, and formats work to enhance the teaching-learning dynamic as well as teacher-student engagement.

Part III: Engaging Students in Learning—Inclusive Pedagogical Practices and the Classroom as Learning Community

Pedagogical engagement and the critical reflection that it invites are the bedrock of emerging work in the "Scholarship of Teaching," and the insights that can be gained are well revealed in the last set of chapters. This final section of the book assembles case studies of particular professors in their specific classroom situations and the pedagogies they use to engage students in dialogue, critical reflection, and learning. Contributors' fields vary from psychology, counseling, and composition, to human services.

The writers draw on different intellectual and professional sources for the inspiration that shapes their pedagogical approaches to students, though content and learning exercises among the classes naturally differ.

Nonetheless, remarkable confluences arise. The authors explain how pedagogical clarity and versatility, and the resulting social and intellectual experience they foster in their classrooms, permit students to envision new horizons for themselves as they strengthen their capacity for empathy, collaboration, ethical action and judgment, participatory democracy, civil debate, and compassion.

In "Teaching Ethics through Multicultural Lenses," Janel Lucas emphasizes the importance of students' competence in compassion as a skill that will help them in their subsequent work in a counseling role toward others. She focuses on the close links between counseling and pedagogy in her classroom process, as well as in her own training. Her narrative demonstrates that the outcomes of education are not limited to intellectual learning alone but have profound, long-term effects in life and in professional practice. Lucas suggests that the special "lens" that she as an African American brings to her thinking and teaching helps her to meet the complex pedagogical challenge of enhancing students' ethical competence.

In the chapter titled "The Whole Person in Front of Me: Toward a Pedagogy of Empathy and Compassion," Robin Robinson presents a fascinating series of classroom exercises that involve mock trials and role playing that are intended to provide her students with meaningful opportunities for practicing empathy and discovering their capacity for it in their own personal histories. In a real sense, these contributions show how much education is, above all, an exercise in community building, how much the classroom connects with other communities in participants' lives, and finally how much the classroom truly can be a preparation for life, especially in its civic dimensions.

For many students, the practice and tutoring they receive in written and spoken language also emerge as valuable elements of the voice, agency, and inclusion they exercise within the learning community and more broadly. This is especially evident in Marjorie Jones's "Building Agency Through Writing," an essay that lays out her methodical plan to build writing confidence and performance in often-discouraged adult learners who are returning to school after long breaks. Jones makes clear that fostering a classroom learning community and individual struggle supported by that community are both essential to this process.

Carol Panofsky's and Lesley Bogad's "Hearing Students' Silence: Issues of Identity, Performance, and Recognition in College Classrooms" grapples with the cynicism and alienation students can feel in relation to the educational process, their reluctance to engage, and the power of the voice that can emerge when professors break through students' hesitance. The piece powerfully reveals how much college-level teaching must focus on helping students overcome the hidden injuries of class and take themselves seriously as learners.

Our contributors suggest that a classroom community can offer a safe, comfortable arena for discovering and practicing civic responsibility with one's peers and professors. The resulting self-discovery and development may be as transformative for the professors as for the students. Professors' own personal disappointments and anger, struggles with marginality and exclusion, and need for hope can be salved in the intense give and take, excitement, serendipity, and mutual discovery that characterize the engaged classroom. This theme is displayed in Phyliss Brown's "Exploring and Exploding the Boundaries of Inclusive Teaching: Social Class Confronts Race and Gender." Discouraged and pessimistic about her career as an African American woman at a mostly white school where she felt increasingly out of place, Brown took a summer assignment working with youth in a middle-school remedial program and found inspiration and a sense of professional renewal in her work with this unlikely group of disadvantaged white boys.

Finally, the enormous power of sensitive listening to one's students, and willingness to be open to new learning about their hidden capabilities, is revealed in Richard Pepp's "Words Matter: Vocabulary in a Diverse Precollege-Level Writing Class." Pepp shows how acknowledging one's own imperfections as an educator, being willing to change preconceptions, and holding true to major teaching objectives are all essential to improving as a pedagogue. Pepp's account describes the often-surprising responses to his questions from students, who can often be the best teachers that faculty have when they challenge us to reexamine our own assumptions.

Conclusion

In the same collaborative and collegial spirit in which the authors have worked together these many years, we offer this collection of work to all our colleagues who will read this book. Our hope is that you will find our insights and strategies useful and be inspired to go on to create your own, based on your own institutional context. There is no one better than you to do that, and we hope that you will have the help of your colleagues in this process of pedagogical reflection and transformation that has more power to change institutional practices when it is a collective effort. We also encourage you to consider recording your reflections and experiences in written form, so that they can be better shared both within and outside your institution and thus add to the growing corpus of knowledge in today's scholarship of teaching.

Colleges and Universities Cited in This Book

The New England region is especially rich in the number and diversity of its higher educational institutions, many of them among the nation's oldest. Five of the institutions that were part of NECIT project will come under discussion in the following chapters.

The University of Massachusetts Boston is the urban campus within the state-wide University of Massachusetts system and the only public university among Boston's rich panoply of more than twenty-five colleges and universities. With six colleges and two graduate schools, the university offers undergraduate and graduate study to 15,000 students in more than 150 fields. Known for its considerable ethnic, class, and age diversity, the student body at the school is almost half students of diverse ethnic/racial backgrounds as well as international students.

Lesley University, an 8,000-student, multisite university, educates women and men in the fields of education, humanities, human services, environmental sciences, and the arts. The university is divided into four colleges and institutes. Lesley College offers a four-year, residential college experience for undergraduate students in the arts, sciences, humanities, education, social sciences, human services, management, and the environment. The Art Institute of Boston is a college of visual arts whose mission is to educate and train artists, designers, and art historians. Lesley's Center for the Adult Learner serves adults on and off campus. All students in Lesley College can enroll in courses across divisions bringing together a variety of ages, experiences, and professional interests in interdisciplinary courses. The School of Education is committed to education reform, research, and providing lifelong learning for educators. Offered through the Creative Arts and Learning Division, Lesley's Integrated Teaching through the Arts is a master's program based in Massachusetts and offered across the country in twenty-three states. The university's enrollment includes 18 percent students and 14 percent faculty of diverse racial/ethnic backgrounds.

Rhode Island College was established in 1854 as the state's first academic institution for preparing teachers, and Rhode Island College became a comprehensive institution of higher education in 1959. With an enrollment predominantly from Rhode Island and nearby Massachusetts and Connecticut, it has a history of serving as a "College of Opportunity" for first-generation college students, who continue to account for the majority of its undergraduates. Being the oldest public institution of higher education in the state, the college now serves approximately 9,000 students in courses and programs both on and off campus: of these, 85 percent are undergraduates, and 12.8 percent are students from historically underrepresented groups.

The University of Massachusetts Dartmouth, part of the statewide university system, offers liberal arts, science, and professional academic programs for more than 9,000 students. As a public university, its mission is to provide a high-quality and personalized education for its students and to serve as an intellectual catalyst for the economic, social, and cultural development of its region and beyond. The university is best known for quality programs in engineering, nursing, marine science, business, visual and performing arts, and business and is host to one of the nation's most extensive interdisciplinary programs in Portuguese studies. The University of Massachusetts Dartmouth also includes, as of 2010, the state's only public law school. The student body contains 13 percent students of diverse ethnic/racial backgrounds and many first-generation college students. Given the region's immigration history, many University of Massachusetts Dartmouth students are of Portuguese, Brazilian, and Cape Verdean heritage.

Massasoit Community College is a comprehensive community college that serves students in southeastern Massachusetts, from the southern tier of Boston to the edge of Cape Cod. Founded in 1966, its main campus is located in the old industrial city of Brockton. Massasoit enrolls almost 8,000 students in transfer and career programs. Over a quarter of them are students aged thirty years or older; 30 percent identify themselves with a particular ethnic minority group, and many of these are immigrants and the children of immigrants.

Notes

1. Some of these earlier foundational texts that have inspired our work include the following: Francisco Rios, *Teaching Thinking in Cultural Contexts* (1996); Parker Palmer, *A Tenth Anniversary Celebration of the Courage to Teach and the Work of Parker Palmer* (2007); Carmelita Rosie Castenada, *Teaching and Learning in Diverse Classrooms: Faculty Reflections on Their Experiences and Pedagogical Practice of Teaching Diverse Populations* (2004); JoAnn Moody, *Faculty Diversity: Problems and Solutions* (2004); and Esther Kingston-Mann and Tim Sieber, eds., *Achieving against the Odds* (2001).

PART I

The Institutional Contexts of Innovation and Change

CHAPTER 1

Academic Integrity and Academic Inclusion: The Mission of the "Outsider Within"[1]

Esther Kingston-Mann

In the intensely entrepreneurial world that we live in today, the more economics-minded among us might find it hard to credit the story I propose to tell—of a diverse faculty, deeply committed to teaching, scholarship, and the life of the university, who freely invested large quantities of labor over the course of eighteen years and transformed the culture and practices of the University of Massachusetts Boston (UMB) and other institutions as well. Their work challenges the stereotype of faculty as lazy and conservative, reluctant to invest time or energy in teaching unless compelled to do so by top-down administrative sanctions and rewards. Although we have all encountered faculty who fit this description, the "feckless professor" may well represent something of a caricature of faculty behavior and potential. In the counternarrative that follows, a Russian historian emerges as a leader of diverse colleagues—they in turn become campus activists and successfully foster inclusive pedagogy, curriculum change, and scholarship at UMB and beyond.

Successes

Since 1989, I have been a leader, participant, and beneficiary of (1) a successful faculty/student/staff initiative that won acceptance for a university-wide diversity curriculum requirement (1990); (2) the work of UMB's Center for the Improvement of Teaching (CIT), whose semester-long pedagogy seminars focused on issues of diversity and inclusion (1991–2000); (3) a successful effort to shift the funding priorities of the Ford Foundation to include urban commuter as well as private academic institutions (1991); (4) a diversity research initiative that invited undergraduates to learn research skills by making use of the university as the site of inquiry into issues of diversity (1997–1999); (5) a New England Center for Inclusive Teaching, Learning, Curriculum Change and Scholarship (NECIT 2003); and (6) a New England–area Students as Scholars program that celebrates student contributions to diversity/inclusion scholarship (2004 to present; see www.km-awards.umb.edu). Frequently, veterans of the first two initiatives have been participants in subsequent projects.

There is no single explanation for our hard-won successes. A very diverse student body, a relatively diverse faculty, a personnel process that values teaching, and initial access to generous internal and external support were all significant factors (Kingston-Mann and Sieber 2001). Nevertheless, however crucial these factors were as building blocks for change, the discussion that follows will focus on the peculiar combination of academic self-interest and justice-seeking that inspired these projects and moved them forward. It turned out, for example, that many diverse faculty at UMB found themselves empowered by the struggle for an inclusive curriculum, one that fulfilled intellectual standards that far exceeded conventional academic norms. In contrast to previous academic experiences of isolation and alienation, we hoped to build at UMB a collaborative community that valued our productive efforts. Above all, we were inspired by a passion to spare our students the experience of intellectual and academic exclusion that we had ourselves survived, often at significant personal cost. For all of us, these were important priorities, although the more romantic among us regretted that—for better or for worse—these commitments were not forever and permanently at the top of everyone's agenda.

It turned out that for some CIT veterans, the opportunity to lead a prestigious, top-down, administration-sponsored task force on faculty development would be far more appealing than collaborative grassroots efforts. However, it turned out that the CIT community survived and grew, while the administratively driven initiative did not. The CIT veterans eventually returned, the administration's task force faded from view, and the Ford Foundation continued its support for the continuation of the CIT seminars. Over the years, whenever the university was led by administrators who placed a low priority on diversity/inclusion issues, tensions between executive and grassroots faculty leadership invariably reemerged. In the latter context, faculty loyalty to colleagues was repeatedly tested.

From the outset, our most persistent core change agents tended to be outsiders within the world of academe. Many—like myself—began as more or less naïve believers in the story that the academic world tells of itself: that we had entered a world of knowledge and wisdom that fostered the learning of all of its members. Having ourselves struggled mightily to gain entry to the academy, we turned out to be particularly receptive to collaborative initiatives that aimed at narrowing the gap between promise and reality that we ourselves had faced.

In Search of Greater Academic Excellence

As the first generation of my working-class, Eastern European Jewish family to attend college, I was thrilled to be entering an academic institution—a place my unschooled parents had taught me to envision as a world of reason and wisdom. Although some of my lofty expectations were realized, I discovered quite early on that despite its many cultural rewards and challenges, an elite research university was in some respects an intellectually narrow world. As an undergraduate at the University of Michigan, a History of the Modern World turned out to be a narrative of middle-class white males in Western Europe and the United States, while an Introduction to Psychology focused exclusively on "white males and white rats." Later, as a graduate student at Johns Hopkins University, I noticed that the repression and invalidation of particular bodies of evidence extended from the non-Western world to women, minority racial groups, and working-class people within and outside the West. (The only exception to this general rule was the occasional appearance of the latter groups in cameo roles as tragic victims of one or another notable modern trend.)

Throughout most of the twentieth century—and in many colleges and universities even today—students have been routinely required to repeat back to their teachers the patently untrue proposition that the experience of the West and of particular social groups was equivalent to the experience of the world. So much intellectual certainty, such an intellectually narrow focus, such a wide array of intellectual exclusions—was there really no place in the academy for the hundreds of millions who have—in Eduardo Galeano's words—"been standing on line for centuries to get into history"? (quoted in Espada 1999, 86). Like many newcomers to the academic world, the experience of studying history was like looking into a mirror and seeing nothing (Takaki 1993).

As a beginning graduate student, I was reluctant to question the professors who chose these exclusionary texts, lectured about their universal significance and applicability, and delighted most in students who accepted the invitation to explore more deeply the narrow track of understanding they had laid out. Drawn into a struggle that has led outsiders before and after me to abandon the world of academe, I feared that my frustration was simply proof that I lacked the dispassionate temperament required of a scholar. Better, I thought, to remain silent and bide my time until I could find a place to speak more freely—at my first scholarly conference, for example. Or at least so I thought then.

Initiation

Having learned from my unschooled parents that the world of academe was a Promised Land of rational discourse and dialogue, I arrived at my first scholarly conference with the highest of expectations. As a fast-talking, dark-haired, working-class woman of Eastern European Jewish background, I hoped against hope that there was nothing about my style or manner that would signal to this predominantly male, Anglo and middle-class gathering in a luxury hotel that I did not belong.[2]

At my first conference session, I sat at the back of the room, intimidated by the camaraderie of the panel of men in dark suits and ties who nodded casually to people they knew and joked among themselves, as if standing in a position of authority before an audience of scholars was nothing special. I listened intently, and was relieved to find the presentations easy to follow and not very challenging.

The moderator opened the discussion by calling on the men he knew by their first names. The spirited repartee that followed was exclusively male. We [the women] did not meet each other's eyes; a few raised their hands but eventually gave up and lowered them. But I, enraged at such injustice in my newfound world of Reason continued to wave my hand in the air. The moderator looked at me blankly, and proceeded to call on several more men. Then, glancing to the right and left to survey the audience and seeing no other male hands raised, he slowly nodded in my direction. By this time, I was incoherent with anger and could not even manage to formulate my question.

Not an auspicious debut. My contribution to the conference session was to reinforce whatever stereotypes those present may have already had about the irrational and unsocialized lower-class women in their midst. I doubt if anyone saw a connection between my incoherence and the structure of that workshop session. Although I had always been praised for my verbal skills, it had taken less than an hour for a conference workshop to teach me how to become incoherent and inarticulate. However, my deficiencies were not inborn; they were site specific.

It took three years before I was willing to try again—much better defended this time and accompanied by a supportive colleague. Nevertheless, my initiation into the world of scholars seared into my heart and brain a lesson that inspired most of the diversity work that I later undertook at UMB. I came to believe that the exclusionary practices that prevented outsiders from participating productively in traditional academic settings were intertwined with the intellectual exclusions of the conventional university curriculum. The conference presenters' assumption that people from particular social groups were more worth listening to than others seemed to me inextricably linked to the traditional scholarly assumption that the voices of people from particular social groups and geographic locations were more significant than others.

Since I was myself the product of an intellectually narrow curriculum and a student of research-oriented faculty whose commitment to teaching was—with few exceptions—extremely modest, I had much to learn if I was to provide my students with a learning experience that differed from my own. If my students were to learn to respect and develop their intellectual powers and to claim their places in a wider world without inordinate pain and suffering, I would have to become something of an autodidact on diversity as both a pedagogical and content issue. Neither my working-class origins nor my activism in civil rights, antiracist, and antiwar organizations prepared me either to teach about diversity or to teach diverse students.

After I came to teach Russian and introductory history courses at UMB, I was soon recognized by my department as a good teacher who received positive course evaluations from students accustomed to lectures and appreciative—or at least tolerant—of my youth and enthusiasm. I reached out to students on an individual basis, experimented with course content, constructed classroom research projects, and was able to convince my department that at least one non-Western history course should be mandatory for history majors. At the same time, it was frustrating to be so frequently called upon to justify the study of women, "minorities," working-class and non-Western peoples, and to redress the inaccuracies reinforced by a curriculum that marginalized these groups. Matters came to a head in 1988, when a lively class became much less so when we reached the Africa unit of a modern world history course. I asked a white male student a question about the readings, and after a silence, he asked, "Why do we need to learn this? Why learn about Africa, for God's sake!" When I asked other students to comment, several defended him, noting that mine was the only course that required study of a non-Western culture. "If it's so important," students asked, "then why aren't other faculty teaching about it?" After a flash of anger, I was able to calmly observe that a modern world history class that left out many of the world's peoples did not make much sense. This was a new and attractive idea to some, but it was by no means a solution to the problem that had surfaced in my class. But what about the possibility of a university-wide diversity curriculum requirement that legitimized the study of diverse peoples and regions of the world—that, I thought, might be a giant step in the right direction!

Creating a More Intellectually Honest Curriculum: A Collaborative Effort

Serendipitously, in 1989, I received a letter that transformed my professional life and helped me to achieve this goal. I was invited to direct UMB's CIT, an organization that coordinated semester-long, faculty-led pedagogy seminars in the College of Liberal Arts. In a simple exchange of letters, the former codirectors (with whom I was never to meet) transferred leadership of the organization to me. As they saw it, my "outstanding" reputation as a teacher at UMB was more than sufficient to qualify me for leadership. Since I possessed little leadership experience, I was not at all sure they were right to choose me (and later events would demonstrate that there were aspects of leadership for which I was woefully unprepared). On the other hand, I was excited by the possibility that CIT might become a venue for faculty efforts to eliminate the exclusionary curriculum that then existed at UMB. I decided to take some risks: with support from the Ford Foundation, I was able to extend CIT's semester-long seminars to include all of the university's five colleges, focus them on the topic of teaching about differences, and orient CIT's seminars and workshops toward the creation of a grassroots initiative to establish a university-wide diversity curriculum requirement. It cannot be overemphasized that in its early stages—before the initiative had won wide support—external funding was essential.

I began by bringing together a dozen interested teachers and students. Among the first to join were the African American chair of the Black Studies Department, the director of the Student Disabilities Center, the first faculty member in the Department of English ever to teach a course on homosexuality in Western literature, a music student of Irish working-class background, an Asian American faculty member in the American Studies program, and an African American economics major.

Inclusion as a Political/Intellectual Strategy: Confronting "Justified Suspicions"

Although the ad hoc Diversity Working Group (DWG) that emerged from our early meetings was open to all members of the university community, we soon learned that the greatest obstacle to building faculty support for our initiative was not "unjustified suspicion" but "justified suspicion." In order to build connections with those who felt unheard and unvalued, and fed up with committee work that produced little discernible or positive change, we needed to find a way to demonstrate that our project was different. Recalling my earlier experience of initiation into the world of scholarship, I made a conscious decision to create a structure and set of expectations that contradicted it. My task was made easier by the spontaneous enthusiasm of initial group members, by the participation of individuals with more organizing experience than I, and by the general enthusiasm for identifying and implementing the practical tasks that would move the project forward. To ensure that our effort would not be viewed as the work of a "radical elite," critics of the project—and there were many—received verbal and then written invitations to join the group. (It is worth noting that none of them ever responded.) To foster consistency between our inclusive goals and our organizational practice, I made it a priority to ensure that all of our forums and panels comprised diverse students and faculty, and that student voices were well represented in our decision-making process. All of our meetings ended with a deliberate "check in" to provide an opportunity for anyone who had not yet spoken. This rule was particularly enforced when any group decision had to be reached.

Strategies for Success

Between 1989 and 1991, with the help of the DWG, CIT organized two campus-based conferences and thirty-five faculty/student forums on different aspects of teaching about differences. After a year of enthusiastic volunteer effort by students, faculty, and staff, we were able to gain the support of UMB's chancellor and provost. Our expenses were extremely minimal, because faculty drew on their own scholarship and experience and volunteered their own time in presenting workshops on such topics as "Helping Diverse Students Improve Quantitative Skills" and "Anguish as a Second Language." It turned out to be surprisingly easy to find faculty and student speakers and workshop leaders. In the words of one African American student, "I've been waiting all my life for someone to ask me to talk about this!" By the fall of 1990, more than 300 faculty, students, and staff were participating in the diversity curriculum initiative.

Students, who are usually objects rather than shapers of curriculum reform, turned out to be particularly good at educating their teachers about how much their learning was limited and damaged by the absence of exposure to academic work on race, class, gender, sexual orientation, disability, age, and culture. A group of students worked with the director of the Women's Studies Program to produce a video entitled "Acknowledge the Other One: Diversity Issues at UMB." The pain and honesty of student testimonies moved many previously uncommitted faculty members to recognize that an intellectually narrow curriculum was at odds with the university's commitment to high academic standards. Many of us learned from students about how such a curriculum limited the range of student learning and made it more difficult for them to feel at home in a university setting. By the fall of l990, a student-run Center for Educational Rights had gathered 600 student signatures in favor of the diversity requirement.

The curriculum proposal that eventually emerged from the DWG deliberately focused on academic values. In the unambiguous words of the chair of the Black Studies Program: "If I wanted lessons in sensitivity or appreciation, I would go to church!...This is not about giving students good feelings; it's about giving them the best knowledge."

Our definition of diversity was inclusive: we argued that each of us possess a number of cultures; we are members of a particular generational cohort, social class, race, and gender and possess a particular sexual orientation and degree of ability or disability. In different settings, one or more of these cultures may come into play. As we then saw it, such a definition would make clear to the university community that diversity was not a program advocated by a minority of "others"; it was an intellectually honest recognition of the range of differences shared by members of the university community. No particular perspective on diversity was mandated or required by our proposal—we argued instead that a wide range of disciplinary approaches, theoretical viewpoints, and subjects were both essential and appropriate.

Faculty responses to the diversity curriculum initiative were varied and distinctly unpolemical. Critics argued that a requirement was unnecessary and questioned the wisdom of imposing still another academic requirement upon an already burdened student body. We continued to invite naysayers to participate in the revising and rewriting of the diversity proposal and tried very hard to meet any concern that we legitimately could. Although some of our discussions and debates were heated, our worst fears did *not* materialize. At a time when the media was filled with reports on the "multiculturalism crisis" in higher education, UMB critics of the diversity requirement proposal did not ever accuse their reform-minded colleagues of political correctness. But some administrators continued to describe our initiative as a "civility requirement" rather than an intellectually grounded curriculum change.

By the end of 1990, a wide range of traditional and nontraditional faculty had come to agree that diversity and multiculturalism should be a requirement rather than an option in the university's course offerings. After two years of outreach, and consultations with faculty governance committees and the deans of all of the university's five colleges, the diversity requirement proposal won the approval of the university's highest governing body by a 10–2 vote and became operational in September 1992. Our countless midnight conversations, weekend meetings, endless discussions and decisions, "amateur" student and faculty presentations, and sustained outreach eventually produced a transformation in the academic experience of every student at UMB. From within the DWG, a number of faculty emerged as campus-level experts and contributors to the scholarship of teaching and learning. On a personal level, it was exciting to discover for the first time at middle age that I possessed a gift for bringing people together and articulating a vision for change that a wide and diverse range of individuals found appealing.

Implementing a Diversity Requirement

Once the diversity requirement was passed, its academic credibility remained very much in question. How could UMB faculty teach diversity courses when most of us were in fact the product of graduate training that was anything but multicultural or inclusive in orientation? It seemed clear to me that diversity could never become an *intellectually* defensible feature of academic inquiry at UMB unless faculty were able to acquire the knowledge and experience that equipped them to teach diversity-oriented courses. In this context, CIT's role was crucial. In the 1990s, with enthusiastic administrative support and generous funding from the Ford Foundation, CIT seminars became the venue for collaborative, faculty-led explorations of diversity as a pedagogical and content issue.

My activities as CIT director were frequently concentrated on outreach to faculty across the university. I spent much time telephoning and e-mailing people I knew (and many I did not but whose courses reflected an interest in the CIT focus on students, teaching, and diversity). In 1991, after the first seminar was finished, I attempted to build a sense of community among seminar cohorts by inviting its members to help select the faculty who would participate in the next. On occasion, members of one seminar would meet for lunch or dinner with the next seminar group and share experiences and insights. In this process, many seminarians eventually formed a diverse CIT advisory board. Each year, various members of this group organized an annual, very well-attended potluck dinner for all who had participated in CIT activities—as panelist, workshop facilitator, seminar participant, or seminar leader. In addition, a variety of work-study students worked on a CIT newsletter for all faculty, entitled *Building Connections*. As I see it, these activities contributed to the emergence of a CIT community of faculty linked by friendship as well as common interests.

The seminars remained the core of the CIT project. They were a venue within which individuals—particularly those from historically marginalized groups—might learn to trust in the goodwill of some of their colleagues. According to one African American seminar member, "I never knew before that I had white colleagues who cared so much about students of color. I thought it was just 'talk.'...'Good to know,' he said." A heavy burden lifted.

In Further Pursuit of Academic Excellence:
Students as Researchers

Between 1997 and 1999, a diverse group of UMB undergraduates were invited to join a Ford Foundation–funded Diversity Research Initiative (DRI) that fostered the acquisition of research skills by means of a student/faculty research community that made use of the university as the site of inquiry into issues of diversity. While outsiders like the faculty member cited above were disaffected and alienated from the life of the university, how much more serious was the plight of diverse students who were frequently undervalued, underestimated, and unchallenged in their precollege years? Reluctant to identify with academic values that categorized them as people without significant potential for growth and development, one first-year student observed, "High school was like a penance imposed for some unknown sin. Everything I ever learned that was important to me was learned outside of school. So I never thought to associate schools with learning."

In the DRI project, faculty veterans of the CIT seminars built on efforts by university innovators elsewhere that fostered the acquisition of important academic skills in a challenging and supportive setting.[3] Our challenge was to attract students of diverse backgrounds who ordinarily spent little time on our urban commuter campus to an intellectually demanding project that provided academic credit for engaging in rigorous empirical investigations of their own academic environment.

The Structure and Workings of a Research Community

Over a two-year period, thirteen student/faculty teams engaged in diversity research projects, with each team designing their own survey research projects, developing plans for implementation, and then contributing to the writing of a final research report. Faculty team leaders met together periodically to discuss emerging issues and questions and to set the agenda for cohortwide seminars where student-faculty teams shared research insights, provided supportive feedback to each other, and discussed problems of data and analysis. In this process, it soon became evident that a number of students were becoming "hooked on research." In the words of one student:

> I remember at different times during this research project, I wondered "Why are we taking so many little steps in this gathering of data? It's such a waste of time!" I thought that we could just do the interview and pick out lines or quotes that are important to answering the questions we were asking. But now that we are at the end of the semester, I realize that all those steps were important because we are not the only people working with the data, and that people from other semesters might be looking at the data also. I feel now that I was somewhat selfish before: I didn't think about who else might benefit from the hard work we have done to find out all this information. Now that I realize this, I feel that all the different steps we took to get to this point have not been wasted, and that it was very important to everyone.

Another commented,

> It is so easy to fall into one's own schema of thinking. When we initially analyzed data, we used our own colored lens to view it; after examining our own stereotyping, biases, we saw the data in different ways. We tried to separate our own biases from factual data. That is what I call transformation, because I changed, and I view things differently now, not just in my own little world.

Excited to be researching an aspect of their own learning environment, they nevertheless quickly recognized that "insider research" on such topics as the experience of gay, lesbian, bisexual, and transgendered (GLBT) students on campus or faculty understandings of questions of disability was a risky business. Students raised insightful and academically appropriate questions about the possible repercussions for students interviewed if interview data were widely disseminated. Would there be a danger to students and to untenured faculty researchers if their findings too deeply challenged existing practices and procedures? How were these difficulties to be resolved? In the words of one student, "Are we cowards if we recognize such fears?"

As students and faculty weighed the competing imperatives of bringing potentially explosive issues to light against the need to ensure the safety of researchers and interviewees in a setting where power and status were not equally distributed, they raised questions that lay at the heart of any serious approach to applied research. Aware of the gaps in their institutional knowledge and the obstacles to easy resolution of these issues, students and faculty supported each other's efforts (1) to document carefully, (2) to maintain the strictest possible rules for anonymity, and (3) to emphasize that research findings were intended not as an exposé but as a basis for constructive and positive change. It is difficult to exaggerate the benefits that flowed from the opportunities that the DRI provided for novice researchers who were attempting to consider such questions openly and within the framework of a diverse, student/faculty/staff community. The depth and openness of our discussions also surprised project faculty. According to one Spanish-born faculty member, "I always thought discussions like this were supposed to be typical of the academic world—but this is really my first opportunity to explore these issues in such depth with students!"

Diversity and Difference: The DRI Community Responds

Some 50 percent of the participating DRI faculty were people of color. Students admitted to the project were usually recruited by faculty team leaders; typically, they were juniors and seniors with an interest in diversity but without prior research skills or training. In the project as a whole, 56 percent were people of color. For the most part, they possessed little experience in working with people from racial backgrounds that differed from their own, and few were accustomed to collaborative work either with other students or with faculty. As a consequence, the exploration of common and differing understandings of diversity was a persistent theme in our team and cohortwide deliberations.

Despite the diversity of the DRI participants and our initial shared interest in research on diversity, there were of course no guarantees of internal consensus within and between research teams; we could not take for granted that all would view the seminar or the team as a safe space for risk taking. In one case, a faculty member reported to a DRI faculty meeting that a Haitian and an Italian American student (both female) with strong religious commitments were expressing skepticism about the legitimacy of including gay issues in a diversity project. How to deal responsibly with this issue? We (the faculty and the project director, Esther Kingston-Mann) agreed (1) that the "skeptics" were not ideologues but inexperienced young people who were in the process of clarifying their values and opinions and (2) that in any ensuing seminar discussion, we needed to ensure that participating gay students emerged with a sense of confidence that their presence and contributions were respected.

From a research perspective, the faculty agreed that it was particularly important that students understand that diversity research was not simply a matter of questioning and analyzing diversity issues as they related to "the Other," that is, to their interview subjects. At this point in the DRI cohort's development, it seemed crucial to emphasize that both researchers and their subjects formed part of a larger culture whose messages they interpreted and reinterpreted over time. To engage responsibly in diversity research therefore required that investigators—in this case, students and faculty within the DRI—acknowledge, understand, and clarify their own values and assumptions about diversity and to seriously reflect upon the meaning of inclusion. Eventually, we (the faculty and director) decided to raise the issue of gays and diversity at our next cohortwide seminar and to take responsibility for ensuring that the discussion remained open and respectful. The faculty leader of the research team investigating the experience of GLBT students on campus agreed to consult with her group about how best to frame the discussion.

At the opening of the next cohortwide seminar meeting, the faculty—who foresaw a difficult discussion—exchanged reassuring glances. I (the project director) began by emphasizing the need for empathy and mutual respect in exploring our understandings of diversity and in investigating the views of others. We waited for someone to take the risk of beginning our conversation. A student member of the LGBT research team—her eyes riveted on me in the hope that I could somehow ensure her safety—then proceeded to describe in detail a horrific personal experience of efforts to "deprogram" her by a conservative Christian group to which she belonged. An African American member of her research group commented, "This is reality; this is what happens."

To all present, the issue of whether gay issues belonged in the DRI had become inescapably immediate and personal. In the dismayed silence that followed, seminar members were directly confronted with the impact of anti-gay hostility upon someone they knew. One of the student "skeptics" left the room, and the other was in tears. She crossed the room to where the gay student was sitting and put her hand on her arm. "Real Christians aren't like that, please don't think that." After a moment, the room erupted in applause.

The discussion then continued, with gay students speaking more openly and confidently than ever before in the seminar.

That night, there were many e-mail messages to me, ranging from "Thank you for tonight's discussion" to "Wow!!!!" and "I can't believe we survived that discussion!" to "I was so proud of us tonight."

Although no final resolution was reached, the experience we had shared encouraged us to hope that future exchanges would be equally honest and respectful. We took each other seriously as colleagues and participants. Our cohort was no longer a disparate group of "outsiders" who "disidentified" with the academic goals of the university. In the words of one student,

The DRI was the best thing that I got out of UMB, especially being a senior and not feeling connected to the school. The project made me feel different. I felt a connection from working closely with the professors, playing a part in change and making the school better.

According to another,

In order to do research, I had to find some reason in what this research gives me. Knowledge? Skills? Friendship? Now, I got everything. Taking this class made me comfortable to express myself. It was good practice. I feel that I have found a niche for myself in school. I feel like I belong to the school more.

Equally important, students had begun to view themselves as producers of knowledge—not in the same location but on the same continuum as the faculty who ordinarily teach and advise them. Although many of the research teams were quickly able to enjoy the social and intellectual benefits of collaboration, some students as well as faculty found the process difficult and conflict ridden. Frequently, the most successful teams were those that set aside time for the building of trust before engaging in their research tasks. At the end of each semester, DRI student/faculty teams presented their research to seminar colleagues and produced research reports. Their findings were disseminated in a DRI newsletter and a wider student/faculty/staff conference. Some teams presented their research at off-campus conferences, and others to department chairs and faculty in the unit they were researching; one team's research contributed to the emergence of an Asian American studies program on campus. In the words of one student, "What we came out of it with was the feeling that we can do research. We are researchers" (Kingston-Mann 1999).

Students were not alone in finding the DRI a transformative experience. The DRI inspired a number of project faculty (including me) to engage more seriously with the scholarship of teaching In 1999, I edited and authored the opening chapter of a book that included the contributions of faculty who led DRI research teams. It was entitled *Building a Diversity Research Initiative: How Diverse Undergraduates Become Researchers, Change Agents, and Members of a Research Community* (Kingston-Mann 2000).

Spreading the Academic Word: Successes and Painful Challenges

By the late 1990s, the diversity requirement was well institutionalized; 160 faculty members from across the university were CIT seminar veterans who played a leading role in every campus committee related to teaching, learning, and curriculum change. At the same time, an increasing number of faculty from New England colleges and universities began to attend CIT conferences and expressed interest in learning from our work. At this point, it also became clear to me that if—as I believed—peer-led collaborative strategies should be the hallmark of CIT, then I should not continue indefinitely as CIT director. In 2000, my place was taken by a long-time veteran of CIT activities.

However, even before I withdrew from a position of leadership at CIT, I found myself increasingly intrigued by the possibility of sharing our academic, curricular, and pedagogical strategies more widely and in a more systematic fashion. What if NECIT were to foster regional efforts to work collaboratively and link rigorous and realistic curriculum development to issues of inclusion via CIT-style semester-long, faculty seminars? To test the waters, I convened a series of planning meetings that included a dozen CIT seminar veterans and twenty diverse faculty from fifteen New England colleges and universities in late 1999.

The priorities identified were not unfamiliar: (1) a significant proportion of faculty committed to inclusive teaching and curriculum change reported a sense of isolation (in departments, colleges, and in their college or university communities) and were looking for the support of colleagues on other campuses. This was a concern expressed most frequently by faculty of color; (2) there was a general agreement that all intercampus collaborations should be—as at UMB—faculty owned and directed rather than top-down administrative initiatives; and (3) there was also a consensus that mutual support for teaching innovation was not enough; those present wanted to emphasize as well the intellectual content of the scholarship of teaching, learning, and curriculum change.

These preliminary discussions became the basis for a successful application to the Ford Foundation for an "opportunity grant" that would permit interested campuses to survey the attitudes and priorities of their own faculty and to gauge reactions to the possibility of creating CIT-style seminars on their own campuses. Our initial cohort included self-selected faculty from six New England–area colleges and universities, and most were people of color. In the course of our meetings to develop survey plans, we shared "horror stories" about hostility to diversity initiatives on our campuses, about administrators who viewed interest in diversity as a sign that a faculty member was less academically serious than her or his colleagues, and regrets about the scarcity of collaborative working relationships between faculty from historically marginalized groups and their colleagues. NECIT was the organization that emerged as a result of this process.

Shortly after we received the Ford opportunity grant, I decided to transfer leadership of the initiative to two untenured young faculty members who were CIT veterans and moved into the position of consultant and collaborator rather than project director. To my dismay, the new directors (one from the College of Education and the other from the Psychology Department) came to view me not as a resource but as a threat to their control over the project. In the conflicts that followed, it was particularly painful to discover that I could not count on my other colleagues for support. This came as a great shock to me and made it impossible for me to remain a part of the program I had created. Once I was no longer involved, the Ford Foundation decided not to continue its support for NECIT. The new leaders continued to encourage member campuses to establish CIT-style seminars, but in my absence, they were unable to obtain additional funding to support such activities. By 2010, the organization's activities were more or less confined to annual conferences on teaching and learning.

On a personal level, this extremely painful experience taught me some hard and long-overdue lessons. Although I was often eloquent enough to convince reluctant colleagues to join the collaborative projects that I led, I was too often insensitive to the stresses caused by the effort to balance our valuable work together against the university's more traditional demands for departmental and college service. (These stresses were strikingly diminished whenever UMB was blessed with administrations who viewed inclusive pedagogy and curriculum as one of the university's core values.) Equally important, my untempered and rather naïve delight in the successes that enabled diverse faculty to foster inclusion at UMB and beyond led me to ignore the normal tensions that exist between leaders and even the most collaborative of faculty colleagues. Because I invited project members to lead workshops, form UMB faculty panels to make individual presentations at local and national conferences, and become known as campus-level experts on teaching, it never occurred to me that what I considered to be "our triumphs" would be viewed by some as the *personal* triumph of an all-too-powerful leader. But so, evidently, it was.

Still Crazy after All These Years

Even before these difficult changes and realizations, I found myself increasingly drawn to the research component of NECIT, to the explicitly academic arguments that had long ago helped won acceptance for a university-wide diversity requirement, and to the research focus of the DRI. In 2004, I created a spin-off from NECIT—a Students as Scholars project intended to showcase the achievements of undergraduate students who made significant contributions to diversity/inclusion scholarship.[4] I invited some of the UMB and non-UMB faculty most active in NECIT to join in creating this project. The campuses originally represented in the consortium included Lesley University, University of New Hampshire, University of Massachusetts Dartmouth, Rhode Island College, Massasoit Community College, and Emmanuel College. A majority of the first responders were people of color.

In contrast to the initiatives already described, it was significant that each participant in this new venture was already a leader and activist on her or his own campus. In this respect, they differed from CIT members who became leaders *because* of their CIT experiences. Awards committee members were aware that the success of a New England–area project aimed at fostering the research potential of diverse students was largely dependent on their campus leadership and intercampus collaborations. Committee members also possessed a very real personal stake in encouraging and honoring student submissions from their own campuses.

In our first year, the committee collaboratively created guidelines for student researchers. We grappled with the persistent challenge of developing standards for judging student work produced at different academic institutions with differing missions (from community college to PhD-granting research universities). We agreed that decisions on the prize-winning essays should be reached after a blind reading by all committee members. Because the members of the committee took very seriously the arguments advanced by their colleagues, reaching consensus was often a lengthy but illuminating process. At one meeting, we enthusiastically agreed with the colleague who commented, "I wish that anyone had ever encouraged me to think that way when I was a college student!"

In 2007, in response to my proposal to step back from leadership of the project, committee members volunteered to take on more responsibility for its operation and administration. We subsequently began to share the nitty-gritty task of outreach to students, faculty, and administrators on our campuses and shared the work of preparing for an annual banquet to celebrate and acknowledge student achievements. Immediately afterward, I became codirector with a faculty member from another university. Since 2009, two codirectors from non-UMB campuses have led the awards initiative. The project's future will continue to depend on the continuation and extension of this spirit of collaboration (and a diminishing reliance on my personal contribution).

From the beginning, our annual banquet for award winners included families, faculty advisors, and administrators from each student's home campus. Committee members read aloud from the prizewinning student essays, and a keynote speaker helped our student achievers to situate themselves within a larger context of diverse students who had begun to view themselves as producers rather than consumers of knowledge. Selections from student essays were posted on the project website (www.km-awards.umb.edu). A number of award submissions were published in a scholarly journal, and we are continuing to pursue publication opportunities for the students.

Our funding was initially provided by the Ford Foundation. Before the Ford grant expired, a short-lived provost attempted to appropriate these funds for other projects. But neither Ford nor the Principal Investigator agreed to relinquish them. In recent years, an extremely supportive new administration stabilized funding for the program, and other member campuses contributed funds as well. In 2010, UMB's chancellor decided to institutionalize the student awards project at UMB.

Microcosms: 2007

At our November 2007 student awards banquet, the pride of family, faculty, and campus administrators in their students was palpable. UMB chancellor Keith Motley spoke of his sense of "joyful righteousness" in the room. As keynote speaker and scholar/activist Hubie Jones looked out over the audience, he observed that occasions like this were for all those present "a microcosm of what we want the world to be like—a world in which individuals acknowledged each other's capacity for good works and joined together in appreciation of a younger generation of students." As I see it, we need to consciously create more such occasions. Each one is transformative—in a personal sense, for students who for the first time envision themselves as researchers, and for we others, who are inspired to imagine a world filled with similar achievers. In the words of one student researcher:

> *There may be a particular professor who thinks they are God, but you know they are not. Now that you've worked on a research project, they are much less intimidating. You feel empowered. You are now, potentially, you could be a professor, too, because you did some of what they did.*

In a broader sense, perhaps all of the initiatives described in this chapter could be considered microcosms of a world in which "outsiders" no longer remain outside the imperfect world of academe.

Notes

This essay is dedicated to Hubie Jones.

1. Special thanks are also due to some of the most faithful veterans and supporters of the initiatives on this list: Wornie Reed, the late Ron Schreiber, the late Elsa Orjuela, Tim Sieber, former chancellor Sherry Penney, and Edmund Toomey.
2. Participants were also without exception "white," but since I shared this background and understood less about it then than I do now, this demographic was not oppressive to me at the time.
3. The work of Uri Treisman is one successful example, described in Jerome Dancis, "Alternative Learning Environment Helps Minority Students Excel in Calculus at UC-Berkeley: A Pedagogical Analysis," http://www.math.umd.edu/~jnd/Treisman.txt.
4. Modeled on Paula Rothenberg's New Jersey Project; the awards funding came from the Roy J. Zuckerberg Endowment, from UMB, and from donations contributed by campuses that participated in the initiative. Although I tried to convince them otherwise, faculty participants decided to name the project after me. Each year, I have offered to resign.

CHAPTER 2

A History Lived and Lessons Learned: Collaboration, Change, and Teaching Transformation[1]

Tim Sieber

Talking to colleagues about what we do unravels the shroud of silence in which our practice is wrapped... Checking our reading of problems, responses, assumptions, and justifications against the readings offered by colleagues is crucial if we are to claw a path to critical clarity. Doing this also provides us with a great deal of emotional sustenance. We start to see that what we thought were unique problems and idiosyncratic failures are shared by many others... Just knowing that we're not alone in our struggles is profoundly reassuring. Though critical reflection often begins alone, it is ultimately a collective endeavor.

(Brookfield 1995, 35–36)

Struggles Over Learning How to Teach

It was 1985, and I was feeling frustrated. After all, my thinking went, wasn't I paid to be an expert in my field? To give my students an accurate and current account of the state of thinking in my Ph.D. specialty areas? wasn't that the reason that my department had hired me for the faculty in the first place, a decade earlier? Of course, what the students wanted to know mattered to me, and they had openings in my classes to say something, and were always asked at the end of each presentation, "Does anyone have any questions?"

It was awkward, but there were seldom many forthcoming. Many informal faculty discussions, in the hallways and in the lunchroom, focused on the perennial problem of how to stimulate more "discussion" in the classroom, especially among the seemingly passive, working-class students we had, who supposedly had little experience with active learning in their earlier mediocre or worse high schools. During my classes, in fact, it was obvious that the students looked bored.

Their evaluations of my classes were not the best, either. This was puzzling, because I was so responsible about doing my job correctly and even felt stung because students did not appreciate my hard work on their behalf! Hewing closely to detailed notes, writing out "the lecture" largely in advance, to make sure everything was covered, always kept me working long hours into the night. Some highly motivated students liked the material, of course, and their engagement showed some enthusiasm, reassuring me of this: there are at least a few smart ones academically capable of understanding anthropology. It took me almost a decade of teaching before encountering a major challenge to my very traditional approach in the classroom, one that had been modeled to me earlier by my own professors.

Of course, my struggles were fairly typical among many of us who were faculty in those days, since very few of us ever had any real pedagogical preparation for teaching while in graduate school. In fact, my graduate school had kept me on a research track all the way through my program, with fellowships that were considered more prestigious precisely because they did not require me to be a teaching assistant. Except for a few guest lectures to talk about my research in other people's classes while in graduate school, the university's classrooms were the first ones I ever entered as a teacher. Lacking any pedagogical training, like many others at this time, left little to rely on except replicating the methods that my professors had used. Maybe they were not so bad, I thought—they been effective, after all, in leading me all the way through to the Ph.D.

In 1985, becoming a part of a Center for the Improvement of Teaching (CIT) Faculty Seminar challenged my old assumptions about teaching, suggesting a new way of thinking about my classes. The seminar met weekly to discuss teaching—techniques, challenges, frustrations—and we were a broad mix of professors from different schools and departments. We visited one another's classes and read a thick stack of readings related to the seminar's chosen theme for that term—"Group work and collaborative learning"—neither of which had ever been a part of my teaching repertoire. It was hard to imagine that students had much to teach one another about the material—and that was my job anyway—or that there might be pedagogical roles for me as professor that did not involve my talking, giving information, and being in control of the air time.

The seminar was my first serious exposure to the idea that student learning should be at the center of university teaching, and that techniques to promote it extended far beyond lecturing, beyond "covering the material," to more complex ways of "uncovering the material," including helping the students do more of that critical work themselves. To learn what the students knew, it was necessary to listen to them. To know what to say to them and to know how to promote their learning required, first, knowing who they were and what their questions about the material were—exactly the reverse of the pedagogical process I had been following!

Colleagues teaching in business management, nursing, public service, and education had long used group work and collaborative learning to reach learning objectives. In my own more elite academic area, the liberal arts, faculty tended to employ the most hierarchical and traditional learning models of all, designed in part to ensure that optimal conditions of learning and academic success were not extended to all students but instead validated the educational privilege of the few. This is the kind of teaching that involved what Paulo Freire called the "banking model" of education, where the teacher tries to deposit fixed knowledge into the minds of learners who are thought to be empty vessels and then withdraws it through examinations (Freire 1970). This model is simply not effective with the majority of learners.

After this teaching seminar ended, and even during it, it was exciting to try out the new techniques that we discussed. They yielded good results, and my experiments continued; but, it took me many years longer to shake the feeling that I was being neglectful in my responsibility by not filling the classroom with my own voice. Admitting to departmental colleagues what I was doing did not seem advisable, for fear they would label me as irresponsible. Colleagues in my then-conservative department would not approve of these changes or engage with me in critical pedagogical reflections. Fortunately, a supportive network of Center colleagues from elsewhere in the university helped me find my way,[2] validating for me that these were important and even intellectually stimulating issues to be concerned with.

It is a sad commentary on how thorough my own academic socialization had been that it was so hard for me to accept that what happened in the classroom was not principally about me but instead was about my students and about what promoted *their* learning. What promoted their own learning would also promote my own, it became clear. This was a truly liberating realization in my career as an educator. In the early years of the Center, many young faculty of my generation experienced similar epiphanies as we learned better to understand the challenges of teaching. Teaching could let me see my own disciplinary knowledge from a different vantage point, that of my students, allowing me a fresh, clear, and critical examination of so much that I had come to take for granted in my graduate school training. Seeing our subject through the eyes of our students allows us to relearn the material and reexamine our fundamental understandings about it, again and again, more deeply each time. As Paulo Freire has so insightfully suggested in his writing about the teacher's own learning,

> The learning of those who teach…lies in their seeking to become involved in their students' curiosity and in the paths and streams it takes them through. Some of the paths and streams that students' at times almost virgin curiosity runs through are pregnant with suggestions and questions never before noticed by teachers…Teachers…learn how to teach as they teach something that is relearned as it is being taught (Freire 1998b, 17).

After the seminar, fortunately, this new collegial network of veterans of teaching seminars, all from outside my own department, who understood these more learner-centered pedagogies, and who thoughtfully promoted critical learning in their classes, taught me much and offered their support. The resulting informal faculty conversations, in contrast to earlier ones, did not fixate on why the students were a problem—the problem instead was how to discover the best way to promote their learning. Through these conversations, my own learning about how to teach better also continued, and this process still continues today, almost twenty-five years later. I am grateful for the new stance toward teaching and toward my students learned from participation with colleagues in the Center. It has helped me learn to listen to students, understand them much better, connect my work more effectively with their own hopes and aspirations (Sieber 2001, 2006), and understand and formulate better my own thinking on key issues in my academic field.

The Faculty Seminar: Creating a Climate of Dialogue, Trust, and Innovation among Faculty

These realizations were powerful, gained from collaboration with colleagues, beginning in the faculty seminar. The faculty seminar is, indeed, the keystone of our teaching center's community building among faculty. Forming a seminar means that a group of eight to ten faculty members, coordinated by a senior peer, is granted extra time in their teaching schedule for weekly collaborative meetings to study pedagogy and to reflect critically on their own teaching experience and issues. The university recognizes the value to faculty of a critical reflection on teaching, and the fact this is hard, serious work, by considering seminar participation as part of a faculty member's regular workload, that is, it is "on load," typically replacing one course from which they are released from teaching for that term. It was this kind of seminar in 1985 that first prompted me to reflect in probing ways on my teaching.

Participation in seminars is always voluntary, and faculty must apply to participate, including supplying a narrative of their teaching experience and critical questions they want to work on during the seminar. The Center board makes an effort to select participants who represent all the university's colleges and who come from a broad range of disciplines and a diversity of backgrounds. Some seminars concentrate specifically on issues of untenured faculty, whereas others mixed in faculty seniority are more general in focus. Some have a special agenda within which individuals fit their own issues, related to topics such as "Collaborative Learning," like my own, "Using Technology," or "Grading and Standards," the general topic in the seminar I later coordinated myself in 1995. For the most part, however, in keeping with the democratic and grassroots character of Center activity, seminar members set the day-to-day agenda, which includes grappling with each person's particular teaching issues. This makes the seminars always practical and relevant to participants.

To encourage open communication among seminarians, the only non-negotiable seminar rule is the following: to ensure that the seminars are a safe place for faculty to admit to problems and dilemmas in their teaching, all discussions are confidential, and everyone involved—including seminar coordinators—pledges to insulate the discussion from the university's personnel evaluation process. Nothing that is said or revealed in the seminar can ever be inserted verbally or in writing into any university personnel deliberation. The opportunity for faculty to discuss challenges, doubts, and struggles has been "reassuring," as one participant termed it. Another addresses the resulting and rare sense of "safety" in the seminar setting: "The seminar afforded a 'safe' place to talk about the issues facing the...teacher at UMass Boston...Being given this time for an honest discussion about teaching is invaluable!" Another faculty member said that she was "able to raise somewhat risky issues that I have never discussed before, such as how gender and age might impact teaching."[3]

Being able to compare experiences in this manner has allowed participants, whether they are junior or senior faculty, to understand that learning how to teach more effectively involves a process of ongoing learning for everyone. Faculty continue to be challenged by new types and mixes of students, changing disciplinary content, growth in their own thinking about critical issues, and the results of trial-and-error assessments of their practice. In all of this, one faculty member learned in her seminar that, regardless of their discipline,

> everyone struggles with similar issues and that no one had the "right answer" or "right approach" to any question or situation. Discussing these struggles helped me realize that it is OK to try different things and risk failure since that is the only way to improve one's pedagogical skills.

As another participant suggested, such discussions "provided an opportunity for all to realize that their personal troubles are not just personal but also public issues pertaining to broader aspects of our shared experience" at the university. Another participant found that her "seminar opened up new possibilities for refining or modifying our approaches to teaching so that we might make the most of the particular complexities of each classroom experience, semester by semester."

The seminars help faculty adopt a flexible and nimble pedagogical style more effective with the university's diverse student body. The extensive discussions in the seminars of the challenges of teaching students at different levels of skill and academic preparation in the same classroom fundamentally changed one seminarian's teaching practice. She wrote that

> I used to avoid students in my class by lecturing the entire class and lecturing above their heads. I knew they were bored and disconnected from the class and their exams showed that. Maybe I was afraid of my students because I didn't know who they were. I went to the seminar looking for help and support. I came away being able to take risks, to know students in my class, to let go of my Ivy League notion of higher education—and feel that it was okay to teach differently.

Within the seminars, usually with considerable diversity among participants, the stage is also set for potentially transformative faculty reflections on questions of difference. In the words of one seminarian,

> I never before realized that my white colleagues were really committed to dealing with conflicts and misunderstandings around race issues. I felt differently about my work at the university once I learned that this was the case.

For another faculty member with a complex, ethnically, and nationally mixed biography, the seminar provided an opportunity to reflect on her multiple identities and homes, as she put it, and to find a way to "continue to root myself to this institution, this place, with the sense of community that CIT has planted in me." Yet another expressed gratitude for the way her seminar group helped her work through the difficult issues about under what circumstances, as a lesbian, it might be appropriate for her to come out to her students.

The seminars foster an atmosphere of mutual respect, congeniality, and caring among participants. Virtually all appreciate this feature of collegial relations, especially since this climate is too often absent in the highly evaluative, judgemental culture of regular departmental and collegiate life. In discussing this theme, faculty quickly make the link between the positive collegial atmosphere and the safety they feel for frank and open dialogue. One participant offered this observation: "As the group became closer, members came forward to present problems and situations that confronted them in the classroom and the group respectfully offered support and suggestions in each instance." For many, the implications for their own classrooms and relations with students were obvious; as one observed, "The seminar also set a good example itself, of how highly interactive classrooms can provide a caring as well as learning environment."

This trusting, open climate of dialogue and critical reflection, of course, extends far beyond the faculty seminars to suffuse all the contexts in which, under Center auspices, professors gather to talk and reflect on their teaching—such as one-time forums and panels on different teaching issues (as diverse as "Teaching about Race, Class and Gender," "Plagiarism: Whose Problem Is It?," "Teaching in a Time of War," and "Increasing Student Participation in Large Lecture Classes"), to the annual teaching conference, and countless other informal conversations within faculty social networks.

How and why did faculty at the university create this supportive network of colleagues who have collaborated in constructively helping one another find more effective ways to promote student learning? All of us involved in these conversations knew that we were part of something new and emergent, perhaps even fragile, because few of us had experienced such a climate in graduate school, or, in most cases, as undergraduates. We also knew that openness and trust did not characterize the relations that we had with campus administrators and even with many senior faculty in our own departments. A full answer to this question requires a look into the historical context in which our new university had taken shape in the mid-1960s.

The "Urban Crisis" and 1960s Social Movements
as Historical Factors in the University's 1964 Founding

The Center and its seminars grew out of a strong culture of teaching that characterized the university from its first days. The new university and many of the pedagogical innovations of its mostly young faculty drew inspiration from a wider history of struggles for change that were then omnipresent in the United States. The university's founding itself was a response to the crisis of equity and access in US higher education at that time. Its pioneering faculty were also mostly "children of the 60s," well aware of—if not directly involved in—social movements running through most universities of the time. By the time they became faculty, many of the university's new, young professors were already seasoned activists who believed in collaboration, were not reluctant to question conventional practice, and understood the value of grassroots organizing for change.

There were many compelling models to follow. The contemporary civil rights movement made effective use of decentralized circles of practice and organization that had served well in organizing change. Debates over the democratic, egalitarian politics of Ella Baker and the Student Non-Violent Coordinating Committee were very much in the air in that era, inspiring efforts to promote grassroots engagement by people from all walks of life. Baker contended that inclusive, collaborative types of organization could inspire ordinary people to "assume initiative and act independently" on the basis of "group-centered leadership," rather than "leader-centered groups" (Baker 2009, 399–400; also Grant 1998; Ransby 2003, 245). Baker believed that visionary, dynamic, but distinctly "unheroic" leaders could foster deeply grounded organizations relying on decentralized decision making and the cultivation of grassroots leadership.[4]

Inspired by the African American civil rights movement, related models of participatory democracy and anarchist practice were also evident in general New Left organizing, the antiwar movement, and second-wave feminism—all movements that influenced many early faculty who had come of age in the era. Growing out of these social and cultural transformations of the period, new streams of thinking about pedagogy also emerged and were carried into academia by young faculty entering the professoriate at places like University of Massachusetts Boston (UMB). They included feminist pedagogy, ethnic studies, Freirean methods, critical pedagogy, and discovery- and learning-centered models in science, to name only a few—all of them now largely mainstreamed into higher educational practice as standard varieties within most universities' teaching repertoires. Beyond pedagogy in the classroom, the historical moment lent an air of optimism to those of us who wished to invest energy in promoting change in the wider university. In my own case, it was the reason I joined the first effort to unionize our faculty in the late 1970s and later to accept Esther Kingston-Mann's invitation to join the campus Working Group advocating for curriculum change to address diversity. Esther made it clear to me that this effort was not "just another" university committee with a schedule of meetings, and a narrowly defined bureaucratic charge, that would be another chore to add to my already long list of administrative responsibilities. I knew from my own experience as an activist since childhood that it is quite possible to achieve meaningful change through engaged organizing, that is, through careful, one-on-one, persistent persuasion and encouragement at the grassroots level. To recruit other faculty colleagues to join our wider process of institutional transformation and help convince them to try rethinking their stance toward teaching, of course, was not only a compelling organizing task but also, like most organizing tasks, a pedagogical challenge in its own right. It was clear to me, and to the rest of us involved, that this work could really produce results, that is, genuine change that would benefit both students and faculty.

It helped that the university itself, and its founding, reflected the era's spirit of transformation and social reform. UMB was created during the turbulence and the urban crisis of the 1960s as a grand liberal experiment with a mission to provide quality undergraduate teaching to students previously excluded from higher education opportunities. The need was urgent. According to former university president Robert Wood, before the 1960s, fewer high-school graduates from the city of Boston went to college than in the state of Mississippi (Kingston-Mann and Sieber 2001, 7). As part of the last great wave of university expansion that produced new, urban public universities like the University of Illinois-Chicago, the University of California-San Francisco, and the University of Missouri-St. Louis, UMB emerged in response to a perceived national "urban crisis," evidence of a new political commitment to invest public resources in upgrading urban social infrastructure, including higher education (D'Arrigo 2004, 11).

In Boston, the challenge was to create a university more accessible to lower-income urban students, immigrants, and minorities but comparable in its educational standards and quality to more privileged local institutions. Some even referred to the university as a new "Harvard on the Harbor" for the underserved. As historian (and former dean), Richard Freeland has remarked,

> The idea of creating a campus for urban commuting students that focused on high-quality undergraduate education in the arts and sciences was both idealistic and radical. At its heart was the belief that young people

who were constrained by circumstances to seek education in a public, urban university should have access to programs comparable to those offered by the nation's top residential colleges. (Freeland 1992, 331)

All the elements of the university's educational approach—small class sizes, a liberal arts curriculum, personal attention to the underserved, and strong faculty-student interactions—thus came to be "a hallmark of UMB's commitment to fulfilling its urban mission throughout its history" (D'Arrigo 2004, 43).

Faculty meeting their classes in this unusual university, themselves typically the product of elite research university training, were thus challenged from the outset to understand diverse students who were the first in their families to attend college or worked full-time and raised families while studying. Our students differ widely among themselves in age, ethnicity, social class, educational preparation, learning style, and style of life. About 40 percent are students of color, another 10 percent are international students, and a majority of the white American student body are of working-class origins. Few of them come from families with much experience of higher education, most being the first in their families to attend college. Historically many have been veterans of recent US wars. A strong immigrant presence of first- and second-generation "new immigrants" has been visible, and growing, since the 1980s. The modal student is nontraditional in age, too, the median age being twenty-five years.

Reluctant to view students as a homogeneous group that learned in uniform ways, or to assume that their professorial role was to set all the terms of the educational encounter, most faculty found their students to be quite different from themselves and from their peers at their previous, mostly elite colleges and graduate schools. Thoughtful faculty recognized that it was risky to suppose that they possessed expert knowledge about the lives or expectations of their students. It soon became obvious that to be effective as teachers, faculty needed to learn about them, and in a commuter campus with no dorms, that knowledge had to be mostly generated in the classroom. This also set the stage for pedagogical experimentation, especially toward models of teaching and learning that allow students more voice in the classroom and that permit ongoing assessment and discovery for faculty.

Particular challenges presented themselves, of course, for the 25 percent of our faculty who are newcomers themselves to academia, minorities of all kinds, and many of working-class origins. Strangers to the academy (in Patricia Hill Collins's phrase [1990], "outsiders within"), they may themselves be engaged in uphill struggles to make their way up the career ladder, even as they work as compassionate and constructive mentors toward students with backgrounds resembling their own. Like the rest of their faculty colleagues, however, they learn very quickly that the teaching models used by their own teachers rarely work well in classrooms at their new workplace. They have often been among the sharpest critics of conventional approaches.

Finally, it is important to acknowledge that there has never been consensus about the terms of this "culture of teaching," and pedagogy has always been a contested terrain, between large faculty factions, linked generally to the Center, that promote more critical, learning-centered models and those who hold the torch for more traditional educational approaches. All sides have always defended their approaches as necessary for quality instruction. We have always estimated that about one-third of our colleagues were part of our more collaborative process, with another third potential recruits, and only a third unalterably opposed. These numbers still constituted a critical mass sufficient to make a real difference in the teaching culture of the university and to offer collaboration and encouragement to one another—for us, indeed, to imagine we were part of a "community," as we sometimes called it, even if it did not include everybody.

Developing an Institutional Innovation

This faculty community, however, had taken some time to build. In 1983, English professors Russell Hart and Jim Broderick created the CIT as one of the nation's first teaching centers for university-level faculty. With funding from the Ford Foundation to support faculty training for teaching in a newly revisioned "core curriculum," Hart and Broderick organized the first semester-long, faculty-led pedagogy seminars in the College of Arts and Sciences. A response to the absence of pedagogical training at the graduate schools from which most of the university's faculty members were drawn, the Center provided them with a rare opportunity to reflect collaboratively on effective teaching practice.

In 1991, nearing retirement, they invited historian Esther Kingston-Mann to direct the program. Under Kingston-Mann's leadership, the Center's mission was dramatically expanded to include a particular focus on diversity and inclusion,[5] with all of the university's then five colleges included alongside the College of Arts and Sciences. In addition, Center activities were extended beyond the original seminar focus. Having recently led a successful faculty/student/staff effort to institute a university-wide diversity curriculum requirement at the university, Kingston-Mann viewed the Center as crucial to the academic credibility of this initiative. As she saw it, diversity could only become a standard feature of academic inquiry if faculty were to acquire—through the seminar process—the knowledge and experience that could equip them to teach diversity-oriented courses that were rarely part of their own graduate training.

With enthusiastic support from the chancellor and provost, and generous Ford Foundation funding for a multiyear faculty development project, Center seminars became a venue for faculty explorations of diversity as a pedagogical and content issue.[6] Between 1991 and 1996, the Center coordinated semester-long pedagogy seminars for eight to ten faculty members per semester that focused on issues of diversity and inclusion. In the course of the 1980s and 1990s, faculty gained a new space to share problems, to implement innovations, and—together with colleagues—to reflect on student responses to the changes they proposed. By the mid-1990s, campus administrators were so impressed with the Center's impact on faculty teaching effectiveness that the provost's office and the deans of the five colleges—with the support of the chancellor—decided to institutionalize the initiative and fund the seminars out of their own budgets. The seminars still continue today, a quarter century later.

Administrative support for the Center, however, was not unwavering. The faculty-led entity was a challenge to the traditional "chain of command" notion of leadership within campus settings. As administrators arrived and departed over the years, the faculty's teaching initiative was sometimes the target of opposition by senior officials. Key central administrators in the mid-1990s attempted to sideline the Center and its programs, co-opt the issue of teaching improvement as part of their own leadership agendas, and start a rival, competitive organization for assessment and improvement of teaching, all under central administrative control. In another case, for many years, the response was simply low-intensity hostility from the provost, an educational traditionalist, who resented the Center's independence. Despite administrative attempts to undermine the Center and its leaders, and an enormous investment of resources and the expenditure of much unpaid faculty labor they commanded from allies in their efforts, these attempts to undermine or replace the Center never gained much steam.

In such struggles, the Center was able to persist and survive, thanks to the powerful support generated by the by-now hundreds of its seminar veterans and the continued support of the Ford Foundation. A few especially thoughtful administrators, some highly placed, such as Sherry H. Penney, chancellor of the university between 1991 and 2000, also were consistent and helpful supporters. What was most crucial about their support, as will be explained below, was that such administrators gave encouragement and resources, while continuing to leave ongoing direction of the initiative to the faculty.

Organization and Structure of the CIT:
A Faculty-led Teaching Center

The Center's leadership and inspiration were originally generated by discipline-trained faculty in the liberal arts and sciences, with strong participation from scholar-practitioners from the Graduate College of Education. Long-term adjunct faculty, as well as undergraduate and graduate students, also have been regular parts of the board, and all six colleges are represented. Since the early 1990s, between 40 and 50 percent of the board have been faculty of color, and the majority have been women. The broadly inclusive and participatory nature of the Center is consistent with the manner in which its seminars have always been conducted.

A key feature that has enhanced CIT's integrity and reputation has been that its leadership has operated according to principles consistent with broader pedagogical relations among faculty, that is, according to a nonhierarchical, collaborative model. A study of the Center by a graduate student team from the Harvard Graduate School of Education in 2002 remarked, for example, on the "open, nonhierarchical community" it formed: "The members enjoy the camaraderie, collegiality, friendship, and the overall feeling of community that is missing in so many academic settings today" (Backer et al. 2002, 3, 12). The Harvard group noted that, though Esther Kingston-Mann was the "visionary" for the group, the Center board—composed of a dozen faculty—still accommodated a variety of people exercising shared leadership, who "possess various strengths and leadership styles which has kept the group dynamic and diverse" (Backer et al. 2002, 2). As the study concluded,

> The organizational plan of CIT resembles a web where all members' opinions are valued. Although Esther was the "visionary" behind the organization and the leader for many years, her role was more of a collaborator than an authority figure. Rather than leading the group from the top-down, she efficiently and effectively managed the group from the center.... The members of CIT had professional autonomy and the freedom to explore their own interests (Backer et al. 2002, 5).

At all levels, from the board to individual seminars and forums, the Center has always been committed to acting collaboratively and to sharing and widely extending leadership among faculty, so that leadership is more "group centered." This has always taken the form of involving as many different faculty as possible in typical academic leadership functions—directing seminars on campus, making presentations on the Center's work at national and regional conferences, serving as visiting consultants to other universities, accompanying the director to attend meetings with high-level administrators, doing research on the scholarship of teaching, and writing for publication.

Many of our faculty have come to see teaching at UMB as an intellectually challenging experience—one that fosters a spirit of critical reflection and practical experimentation. Appreciating the unique challenges and rewards of working in a diverse, urban, public institution, many faculty have used our collective reflections on teaching as a crucible for critical scholarship. They have also begun to emerge as significant contributors to the scholarship of teaching, particularly as it relates to questions of diversity and inclusion, and many dozens of books and articles have recently resulted.[7] This is scholarship that furthers the university's most fundamental mission: devising more effective models of teaching for our students, promising people eager to learn who have little other access to higher education.

Interdepartmental Conversations:
A Good Medium for Dialogue about Pedagogy

The Center and its seminars and other activities offer flexible arenas for open discussions of teaching. In most universities, of course, the academic or departmental unit is viewed as the appropriate peer group for work on teaching improvement, and there is surely no better unit for assessing disciplinary or course content, that is, for devising strategies that will help students better understand psycholinguistics, for example, or in deciding which textbook is preferable as an introduction to biological anthropology. Departmentally based considerations tend to be limited, however, precisely because of the priority they usually give to curriculum or disciplinary content. Such forums can easily leave unaddressed broader but important questions of pedagogy that always cut across disciplines. When the focus shifts away from content to pedagogy, on the other hand, faculty set aside more parochial differences in what content they know to address common teaching challenges. Physicists, sociologists, art historians, and nursing faculty, for example, face quite similar problems in teaching critical thinking and problem solving, in using grading and assessment as tools to help discouraged students invest in improving their work, or in managing the numbers of students sitting in large lecture classes.

That the Center offers extradepartmental forums for teaching discussions and considers all conversations off the record are important for another reason. Departments are inevitably the arena in which peer judgments and personnel decision making take place, and they can stifle some types of critical reflection on teaching practice. Not without reason, faculty may fear that open disclosure of teaching problems will be construed as weaknesses for which they will be negatively judged in personnel evaluations or in decisions about reappointment, promotion, or merit pay. Departmental teaching assessments also are typically heavily based on teaching evaluation instruments that survey student satisfaction, often in quantitative terms, but that rarely describe, examine, or reflect on how teaching unfolds in daily practice. Official assessments of this sort seldom give clear indicators for how individual faculty can change or promote their own development as teachers. Center consultations usually pick up where these evaluations leave off, helping faculty understand what to do in response. On the first day of a recent faculty seminar, for example, a second-year professor asked if the group could put this issue on its agenda. As he explained, "Those evaluation questionnaires don't really give me what I need—how can I know, for myself, really, whether I'm really doing a good job or not? How can I tell?"

Another powerful reason for making available a broadly interdepartmental faculty network around teaching is that it can offer a wider range of more specific expertise for colleagues. At a comprehensive university such as ours, faculty teach a great variety of subject matters, at different levels and in different formats (laboratory, lecture, seminar, internship courses, field schools, etc.), and someone with a teaching problem can always find an appropriate person to help. A guiding principle of the Center, in fact, is avoiding any codification of "best practices" that work in all and any situations. Faculty problems are always specific and rarely lend themselves to formulaic solutions. Avoiding the search for "quick fix" packages for those who want to solve their teaching problems once and for all, CIT has instead supported a wide range of solutions that apply to the individual faculty member's particular teaching situation. Individual difficulties are best handled through careful problem-solving with knowledgeable colleagues. This results in a catholic, nonjudgmental approach to what constitutes good teaching and is inclusive of everyone, promotes open dialogue among all kinds of faculty, and steers clear of dogmatism or so-called political correctness.

Solving Professional Problems with Colleagues: Questions of Balance

Seminar support networks are particularly beneficial to junior faculty who may receive little mentoring or support for taking teaching seriously because their departments place such a high priority on the production of scholarship that will aid in progress toward tenure. In their attempts to teach well, diverse student- and community-oriented faculty who are sensitive to the struggles of our students may not receive significant departmental support for efforts to balance their scholarship against their commitment to teaching. Without minimizing the overriding importance of productive scholarship, Center colleagues can validate junior faculty's teaching commitments and can offer critical support for improving their pedagogical craft. Often this enables faculty to teach "smarter," that is, more effectively, and not feel so overwhelmed and drained by early-career teaching challenges, thus resulting in more time for research and publication. Every faculty member—and especially ones early in their careers—require good mentors from within their own department or program, but some types of essential mentoring are best handled by other faculty colleagues *outside* the department.

Getting help is not just an issue for recently hired "junior" faculty. Senior faculty—who are expected to know all the answers—frequently find it as difficult to ask for help, or admit failures, as newer professors. In a seminar I coordinated, a thirty-year veteran faculty member not far from retirement declared, after hearing seminar colleagues report on teaching frustrations and their efforts to work better with students: "These discussions have really raised my respect level for all my colleagues—all this time, I thought I was the only one who was trying!" Meeting the institution's expectations in the areas of scholarship, teaching, and service is crucial to the untenured faculty member's academic survival. Faculty at *every* level of experience and seniority, however, must negotiate seemingly endless, competing campus demands on their time and energy, in order to sustain a balanced, rewarding life as a scholar-teacher and maintain pride in craft. The CIT model suggests that no amount of technical consulting, video instruction, or "workshopping" by outside experts is as effective in meeting these challenges as the sharing of teaching experiences, problems, doubts, and successes by and among teaching faculty.

Administrators and Faculty: Who Should Lead in Teaching Transformation and How?

Faculty initiative needs to be the start of teaching transformation, but it succeeds best with administrative support. Our UMB experience suggests a possible alternative to conventional notions of university leadership and change—one that includes an all-important role for university administrators but that preserves and builds on active faculty engagement. In the course of our work, gifted administrators committed to the academic survival and success of diverse students (and their teachers) have declared faculty development a priority investment for the university's scarce resources. Not surprisingly, they are administrators who themselves value and employ a collaborative model in their managerial style and are more likely to define themselves as change agents, ready to give direct support to grassroots faculty leaders and innovations as a way of nurturing institutional improvement. They give encouragement, without forcing faculty to hew to an often-withering academic hierarchy, requesting support from chairs, then deans, and then provosts, before ever reaching the top, as former chancellor Sherry Penney confided in an interview on February 23, 2007. Most importantly, these administrators are willing to back off, resist temptations to "take charge," and allow for a significant measure of faculty autonomy, even if faculty—like all other imperfect agents of change—can make mistakes in the process.

Faculty development initiatives need administrative support through recognition and material resources. Without this support, faculty may understandably view the investment of time in pedagogical work as a kind of "speedup" that adds to their already heavy teaching, service, and scholarly obligations. Faculty need to know that their professional work in this area is valued. This is one of the important messages of our university's regarding teaching seminars as a short-term part of regular faculty work load. It is cost-effective for colleges and universities to support improvements in teaching practice and student learning through valuing their faculty's collaborative work with this kind of support. Without it, it is obvious to faculty that administrators do not value the serious work required to improve teaching effectiveness.

In our experience in various regional and national interuniversity consortia and collaborations,[8] with public and private institutions, secular and religious colleges, and large and small schools, we have seen that a collaborative model is adaptable to a wide range of institutional contexts. Collaboration is a peer-driven consultative process that helps faculty collectively problem solve about how to be more effective teachers, and this can work in all kinds of colleges and universities. Collaboration lets local faculty find solutions that respect and respond effectively to their own institutional histories and conditions. It promotes locally appropriate, not cookie cutter, solutions. For administrators who care about improving teaching effectiveness and faculty morale at their institutions, it is always a good investment.

Today's increasingly corporate academic culture poses a powerful challenge to collaborative initiatives like ours. As executive decision making more and more privileges activity directed and managed from the top, what opportunities exist for continuing a more grassroots model like the Center's? One chronic dilemma for us, for example, has been the difficulty of gaining a regular stream of resource support from the university. Some administrators have attempted to co-opt our efforts and nakedly sought to extract a price for their support. The Center is, essentially, a unit with a faculty development and training agenda, and resources can be given and withheld in attempts to push our programs toward supporting administratively driven training and personnel agendas, such as making our seminars mandatory as a kind of punishment for faculty who the administration might define as deficient for some reason. Such coercive agendas, in our view, serve neither the interests of faculty collaboration nor student learning. Our fundamental charter of inclusiveness, supportive collaboration, and avoidance of judgementalism toward peers—whose positive results have been proven again and again—has always made it obvious to us what we need to defend and preserve in our activities. Yet sticking to our principles has often left us poor in resources such as budgets, supplies, staff support, and space. We still have no ample, dedicated budget to fund our operations, after all these years.

We face other challenges, as well. As much as we have accomplished over two decades, what we have built cannot be taken for granted and is still fragile. Faculty come and go, they become senior and retire, and important institutional and professional knowledge is lost with them. Grassroots, participatory movements quickly deteriorate without constant, ongoing efforts to engage and mentor newcomers and for participants to continue to support one another through active collaboration in creative experimentation. This is not always easy work for overworked faculty, even if it carries its own rewards. It also needs to be the ongoing commitment of faculty leaders, even in grassroots endeavors, to lead by being collaborative, encouraging collective leadership, and fostering a thousand leaders to bloom, rather than just one. Leaders can sometimes think it is easier to take shortcuts and make decisions alone, without collaborative involvement, supposedly in the interests of being more efficient.

With university governance becoming more and more corporate in its tone and scope, administrators also continue to find it easy to sweep up teaching into their ever-evolving grand institutional plans, thinking it is the mark of their vision and authority to have control over as many facets of university functioning as possible and to try to reform everything in their path. Of course, this seldom works, but in the process toward failure, faculty and their students are often the losers. To put it simply, anything that takes control over what happens in their classrooms out of the hands of faculty damages the ability of professors and students to know one another well, to dialogue over what and how to learn, and to devise effective learning solutions tailored to *those* people in *that* room.

Administrative myopia, the idea that everything is better if it is rationalized from the top, frequently means overlooking and even undermining the more "invisible" and informal networks of consultation and support that faculty can and do build among themselves to solve problems in teaching. Administrators regrettably do not always trust faculty to give good advice to one another, or support faculty's attempts to enlist their students in dialogue over what defines good teaching. Our experience suggests that this type of administrative response is counterproductive to improvement of teaching.

Final Lessons: History, Possibility, and Collaboration

What can be learned from the Center model that could be helpful to higher education faculty more broadly? Our example does not purport to offer one recipe for others to follow, and this presentation has frankly acknowledged the historical particulars that helped define our context for change. Times and circumstances always vary and, of course, continually pose new challenges and opportunities for faculty at each college or university.

Paulo Freire has thoughtfully addressed this issue of how to think about later replications of educational innovations that have grown out of specific historical circumstances. Regarding his groundbreaking 1960s literacy program among Brazilian peasants, outlined for the first time in his *Pedagogy of the Oppressed* (1970), he later observed that each and every example of its implementation would have to be different. As he wrote, "Precisely because the pedagogy is historical, takes place in history, and is being lived by historical beings who, in a way, transform themselves while realizing it, the forms of implementation of this pedagogy...vary in time and space" (Freire 1993, 67).

In Boston, the success of our faculty leaders, more than anything else, was in the way they recognized, responded to, and even helped create the historical opening for institutional change. Our innovation did not spring from imagination alone but also from careful assessment of the possibilities in our situation and from organizing action accordingly.

There are thus two key lessons to draw from the UMB example, and the first of them is certainly that faculty everywhere, in all institutions, have the power to assess historical possibilities in their moment, and in their location, for organizing progressive change. It is always possible to do something, and what we do has an impact. This is especially true in the area of teaching—including pedagogy, as well as curriculum—where faculty have special authority, resting on the wisdom of experience, in defining what works most effectively to promote their students' learning. To organize and coordinate change so that it affects the institution more broadly, and not just a scattering of its individual classrooms, requires numbers, that is, collective faculty effort. Our second lesson is this: to tap faculty's collective commitment, energy, and wisdom, a collaborative model, from top to bottom, in all facets of the change process, is the best way to proceed. It ensures the widest and most productive dialogue over means and goals, promotes coalition building, pools the most wisdom from practical experience, and identifies the most effective strategic directions for change.

Notes

1. Esther Kingston-Mann has been my continual collaborator, interlocutor, and comrade throughout my involvement in the two decades of change described here. As the visionary and principal leader of these developments, Esther has influenced my thinking on my own experience so much that it is difficult any more to separate my own understandings from hers. In addition, she and I have been discussing this history for many years and worked for years on writing together an earlier version of it, upon which this chapter draws heavily. Conversations with Vivian Zamel, Lin Zhan, Emmett Schaeffer, Estelle Disch, and Denise Patmon, including comments from some of them on earlier drafts, have also been important in shaping my understandings of this history. I thank all these colleagues and hope that my reading of our collective history overlaps substantially with their own.

2. Almost a quarter century later, I am happy to report that the climate toward pedagogical reflection has completely changed in my department; many of us are veterans of the teaching seminars and even more are cognizant of the issues they handle.

3. This and all the following quotes are drawn from mostly anonymous written evaluations of the faculty seminars by faculty participants, between 2000 and 2005, in seminars coordinated by Lois Rudnick, Denise Patmon, Peter Kiang, Eleanor Kutz, Emmett Schaeffer, and Raymond Liu. I thank Vivian Zamel and Denise Patmon for making these available. A few of the quotes are from my own personal records of the three seminars I have facilitated and from Esther Kingston-Mann's.

4. Collaborative networks, of course, are now more and more recognized as a crucial feature of almost all kinds of productive work activity in most types of organizations, including those in the business world. A brief comparative glance at the history of social movements as well as commercial enterprise suggests that participatory, collaborative models promote good decision making, productive innovation, quality control, and progressive change. In nineteenth-century England and the United States, for example, Brafman and Beckstrom (2006) have pointed out that both the abolitionist and the women's suffrage movements took root and spread through decentralized circles of practice and organization. Similarly, "participatory management," "quality circles," and "total quality management" are well known to improve product quality, as well as worker satisfaction and productivity, in today's business organizations (Brafman and Beckstrom 2006). It is ironic, however, that within the supposedly most informed and enlightened institutional sector of all—higher education—this broad consensus about collaboration's benefits is not necessarily common knowledge. Perhaps it is another legacy of the hierarchical pedagogies that faculty everywhere have been working to change in recent decades, but in higher education, some administrators still think in the twenty-first century that it is educationally effective for them to act toward faculty in tyrannical and arrogant ways, under the guise of showing "strong leadership."

5. In recent years, the seminars' focus has shifted somewhat from this earlier primary emphasis on diversity, but that issue continues to be relevant today, if for no other reason than the diversity that characterizes the faculty participants themselves.

6. The Ford Foundation was a key actor in philanthropically promoting US higher education's coming to terms with campus diversity, through its "Campus Diversity Initiative" that eventually came to support 300 US colleges and universities in piloting different change initiatives in the area of diversity, including UMB. In a national wave of reorientation of higher education to take account of increasing student, national, and global diversity, more than 200 other colleges and universities were also assisted by the Hewlett Foundation's "Pluralism and Unity Program," the Kellogg Foundation's "Centers of Excellence Program," the Lilly Endowment's "Improving Racial and Ethnic Diversity and Campus Climate" program, and the Irvine Foundation's "Higher Education Diversity Initiative" (García et al. 2002). In addition to the original Ford grant from the early 1980s, in 1993 with Esther Kingston-Mann as principal investigator (PI), the Center received a multiyear grant to fund teaching seminars for faculty, to support the university's new diversity requirement. In 1996, Kingston-Mann obtained further Ford funding for a Diversity Research Initiative that paired students and faculty into research teams investigating campus diversity issues (see Kingston-Mann 1999). Finally in 2003, together with seminar veteran Professor Rajini Srikanth (English), through another Ford grant, Kingston-Mann was PI in the creation of a New England Center for Inclusive Teaching, Learning, Curriculum Change and Scholarship.

7. See, for example, Kingston-Mann and Sieber, (2001); Zamel and Spack (2004); Thompson, Schaefer, and Brod (2002); and articles on such topics as "Encouraging participation in the classroom" (Disch 1999) and "Reconstructing the paradigm: teaching across the disciplines" (Brown and Pollack 2004). A 2005 compilation of representative publications in the scholarship of teaching by Center associates included ninety-seven items.

8. Center faculty have given leadership to a number of regional teaching consortiums or initiatives with other universities in New England or the northeast United States, and these have introduced us to teaching practices and issues of change at other institutions. These include our working in the mid-1990s as a mentor institution with other universities and colleges as part of the "American Commitments" project of the American Association of Colleges and Universities; our initiating and directing of the New England Center for Inclusive Teaching spanning seven institutions from the region; and the creation of the Students as Scholars Program, a multiinstitutional effort that recognizes student diversity scholarship from our region.

CHAPTER 3

Pedagogy for the Professoriate: The Personal Meets the Political

Denise Patmon

In 2005, after decades as an educator in many different settings, I came to reflect more deeply than ever before about the core values that inspire my teaching. This deeper exploration came about when I was invited to lead a seminar for pretenured faculty organized by the University of Massachusetts Boston's (UMB's) Center for the Improvement of Teaching (CIT). This is a responsibility usually entrusted to wise and experienced teachers, and I was delighted to be chosen for this position. At the same time, I was challenged to discover whether I was up to the task and to discover what resources—personal and professional—I could draw on for this important work.

Structuring a semester-long weekly seminar for pretenured faculty, of course, was no easy matter. My effort to unify a diverse and interdisciplinary group of faculty members and to foster collective reflection on their deepest questions and concerns about teaching led me to look more deeply into myself and my own history. I was prompted to examine my almost lifelong odyssey as a teacher, the politics of my pedagogical practice, and to discover what lessons I could draw from my own experiences to facilitate the seminar. The discussion that follows describes the long journey traveled before I became a senior faculty member and seminar leader for younger colleagues in their early years at the university. It will focus on the role of teacher and mentor and describe transformative engagement with pedagogy that the seminar fosters.

I was aware that if my younger colleagues were to share their teaching experience honestly and openly, I would need to lead the way—to reveal my own practice, inquiries, and uncertainties about my own pedagogy. Why is my practice the way it is? What were the most significant transformative moments in my classroom teaching? What impact would the seminar have on the future practice of my younger colleagues? What did I want to carry away from the seminar? I will begin with my own teaching odyssey, from the time when I first became a teacher.

First Beginnings

My teaching career began in a vertical classroom—the deep-blue tweed-carpeted steps of the modest brownstone house where I grew up in Brooklyn, New York (72 Midwood Street). Early on, my younger brother Barry and older cousin Kenneth always humored me by granting me my wish to play the role of teacher during our indoor playtime. I would promote them for correct answers to my many questions, moving them from the basement level of our house all the way up to the fourth floor. I had clear standards about what they needed to accomplish to move them up in my classroom.

My questions were quite easy at the start of our school game. I would begin by showing them my closed fists and asking them in which hand had I placed a pebble. Gradually, my questions became more difficult; most of them were about literature, because I was an avid reader and they were not. As a teacher, I asked questions that I would not myself always answer. The boys would affirm or contest my questions (and oftentimes my answers) and were ever ready to research the correct answers if I showed the least bit of pause. Despite our disagreements, though, I remember that I cared about the three of us as learners. Practicing an ethic of care with clear intentions has become the bedrock of my teaching ever since that time and served as the basis for my work in the CIT faculty seminar.

From the reading and the discussions during the meetings, I learned that teaching is not as simple as transferring knowledge. It involves "intellectual and spiritual growth" (a là b. hooks) that needs passion of teachers, attention to students, and close interaction between teachers and students. Guiding by what I learned in the seminar, I tried to pay more attention to each of the students in my class. I contacted the students who did not perform well in their assignments and/or exams, talked to them, tried to understand their problems, and encouraged them to try their best. I was very pleased to see how the attention and interaction between students and me changed their attitudes and performance in the class. This experience lets me understand the power of caring and how caring can positively affect students' learning. (seminar participant, assistant professor, management science & information systems)

Intentional Teaching and Caring

During my childhood days, teaching was a profession that was greatly respected by the black community in the 1960s and before here in the United States. Teachers were second to God in households like my own. Parents held their children's teachers in high esteem no matter where families lived. They demanded quality materials and a rigorous curriculum. If the teacher raised any questions about my behavior or my work as a learner, my parents agreed (whatever the question might have been). Teachers were honored and respected by families and communities. I still remember the names and faces of each of my elementary school teachers, all of whom were white. In the fifth grade, when I was absent with an illness for more than two weeks, one of them even visited my home to bring homework and to give me a lesson or two. The actions of Mrs. Infante, my wonderful teacher, taught me a vital pedagogical strategy. When I became a public-school teacher, and later, when I managed to fit a similar practice into my life as a professor, I took to visiting colleagues' classrooms at the higher education level.

The teachers whom I met were special people. My mother's former teachers and classmates were all black. They frequently visited our home during the summer. These women were my idols, for they could spend days reading, going to plays, and talking about literature and ways that they could teach certain concepts in their future classrooms. They were fascinating for me to listen to, and I wanted so much to grow up and be like them because I admired them greatly. Conversations about school, class trips, homework review, and learning conditions were common in my home and in many of the homes of the families in my racially mixed, middle-class neighborhood of Flatbush. Teaching and school were constant topics for discussion at church, among friends, neighbors, and even with strangers (for my parents and other adult family members were proud to boast of their children's scholastic prowess, academic success, and future professional goals).

Aunt Doris was a teacher of teacher aides for School District 17 in Brooklyn. I admired her for being a "grand" teacher, because she taught practitioners. I observed and studied her methods when I was in high school. She exuded warmth and understanding, and despite being a teacher of teachers, she made clear to me that she too was always a learner. "*Lifelong learners are the best teachers*," she said. Her example would later inspire me when I became a seminar leader and recognized that despite my rank as a senior faculty member, I had much to learn from pretenured colleagues, and that improving my own teaching would always be an ongoing project for me.

My early teachers in New York City taught me that the best education also links readily with real life outside the classroom. New York City became the resource room that we were taught to use. The City became our text for all sorts of learning. Some experiences were less than idyllic; nevertheless, we were taught to question and then to access all possible answers from a variety of people and sources. I recall taking a trip to the Bowery with Kenneth when we were teens to meet some folks who were not "like us." We came to shake hands, to hear stories, to learn from the mostly men who lived on the streets of our City—this was a time before the term "homeless" was coined in our American lexicon. On a visit there, I was surprised when one of the men spontaneously and eloquently recited Langston Hughes's poem, "Mother to Son" ["Life for me ain't been no crystal stair..."], and he turned out to be someone who had personally known "Brother Langston." That we discover our own humanity in the lives of others is a lesson that I learned early.

I have always been excited to be in a place called school, learning from teachers who—like my family—held high expectations for my academic success. I soared in classroom environments that felt like a network of learners woven together in a tapestry of curious minds—an extended family of caregivers for the intellect. I excelled in classes where independence, interdependence, and self-motivation were fostered. I tried to emulate teachers who helped me locate my voice, my uniqueness, and my academic strengths.

These early childhood memories and adolescent experiences shaped my teaching in a way that the CIT faculty seminar helped me to articulate. Since those early days as a "home" school teacher, I have taught in a variety of institutional contexts—in a large urban middle school in a neighborhood that included housing projects, on a main thoroughfare with brownstone houses on tree-lined side streets, and at a research university with an urban mission. I have taught in different parts of the world (from Boston, Massachusetts, to Hiroshima, Japan, to Villavicencio, Colombia). But the CIT seminar offered the first opportunity I ever had to draw on my experience to create a structure that other, more junior colleagues could use to think about, analyze, and question their core beliefs on teaching as well as their own epistemology, that is to say, how do we understand how we know what we know, and how can we help others to gain this self-awareness?

Mutual strength and inspiration come from a forum like the CIT seminar. Whether through my time as a student, as a PhD researcher..., or on visits home to my family..., or when visiting my college and graduate school friends' family homes around the United States, I know intuitively that I know most of what I know—because of my diverse experiences of sharing knowledge and reflection with diverse others. I have gained this in the...CIT seminar this past semester. I hope to turn these enlightened understandings of what I know into useful pedagogy as I continue to work at UMass Boston. (seminar participant, assistant professor, anthropology)

The Critical Importance of Relationships

I majored in English and teaching at the undergraduate and master's degree levels of my postsecondary formal education. In those settings, I studied many principles of teaching and learning, such as methods to teach reading and analysis of literature. It was my first classroom teaching position in a real school setting that convinced me of a truth that was rooted in my early childhood teaching experience: "Relationships are at the core of teaching and learning."

My first K-12 teaching experience was in a medium-sized city public school in Boston. As a young neophyte teacher, I was given some of the more challenging and "difficult" students to teach. I realized that I had to build trust with and among my students in order for them to trust me enough to learn from me and from each other. I had to form relationships with their parents as well, which lengthened my work time beyond the traditional school day. On occasion, I conducted home visits (thanks in large part to my memory of Mrs. Infante), held meetings at times that were conducive to working parents, and designed authentic learning activities so that students could become engaged in the classroom.

Ketley, an immigrant girl from Haiti, was a newly admitted student to my sixth-grade classroom in the middle of the autumn semester. She was part of the first wave of Haitians who migrated to Boston, so most of my students did not have Haitian American kids among their friends at that time. She entered the curriculum at a point when I had planned humanities lessons that tapped into each child's race, class, and emergent adolescent identity. Each student in the class had to create a presentation about some aspect of their cultural background. Ketley decided to design an in-class presentation that concerned an aspect of *voudon*—the reviving of dead chicken legs. I thought that such a presentation would be a unique opportunity to have Ketley's voice and lived experience valued in a US school while she took English as a second language (ESL) classes in our pull-out ESL program (taught by a non-Haitian-speaking, well-meaning parent volunteer). As in the preceding student presentations, I prepared the class to be respectful and to welcome what Bartolomé calls, "cultural border crossing." Students anxiously waited for the day of Ketley's presentation to arrive. We all wanted to see chicken legs walk!

Though Ketley's experiment did not work—that is, the chicken legs did not walk, but stayed still—she passed an important test for gaining acceptance into the classroom. Even if she "failed" at the experiment, she showed the other students trust and was willing to take an academic risk to reach out to them. Her peers valued her willingness to teach them some of the secrets and processes of voudon, even if she did not yet have the skill to do it. Under Ketley's instruction, we thus shared a special experience together. I had 100 percent attendance and participation during this class period, and students were definitely tuned in and turned on to learning. They were attentive, engaged, and cooperative, and afterward, I felt that I had made an important step forward as a new teacher.

The encouragement I gave to Ketley increased students' trust in me—they became more poised to engage as active participants in the learning process taking place in our classroom. They were also more willing to share aspects of their cultural heritage in a diverse classroom environment—what the education research community would later theorize as a sociocultural approach to teaching particularly meaningful to immigrant children and to children of color. New types of folks entering US classrooms on either side of the desk, especially immigrants from all over the world, at all levels from prekindergarten through the professoriate, need explicit gestures and expressions of welcome and of inclusion. Even for college professors, a welcome could not be taken for granted.

> I am a foreigner to the U.S. and I have lived almost 15 years here. CIT has given me a home…at UMass Boston, a place to make a community. The modules on diversity and immigrant experiences in the classroom were instances within the community of CIT that gave me a chance to become more comfortable with [a] label that includes, and excludes all at once: immigrant. (seminar participant, assistant professor, anthropology)

The word "immigrant" is a powerful label. If a college professor in my seminar feels the sting of this imprint, imagine the inner feelings of Ketley in my sixth-grade class. I was so proud to have provided the welcome mat to Ketley by inviting her to participate in our class. Yet, the morning after Ketley's presentation, I was reprimanded by my principal. She was very upset that I was practicing a nontraditional method of teaching English. She said that I excited the students about "voodoo," that my class was too noisy with student talk, and there was not enough lecturing from me. I was stunned to find out that the school did not value peer exchange and building authentic classroom relationships.

The message was clear, "Shut your door, manage the students, keep them quiet, and use didactic strategies!" Building relationships, a more participatory student engagement in class activities, and responsiveness to the cultures students brought with them were not a part of this equation. I was devastated. I had no one with whom I could discuss what was really happening with and to my teaching. Going to the principal was like announcing to the staff that I had problems in my classroom and could not control my learning environment. Many teachers had already complained that my room was quite noisy and disruptive to their teacher-centered practice. I had so many questions but could not trust anyone due to the discord of ideologies and teaching methodologies that created a gulf between my colleagues and me.

Unfortunately, my relationships with other teachers at this public school never jelled. They did not agree with my approach to teaching. So I shut my door, shushed my students, and in the privacy of my classroom quietly kept on using methods I knew would turn on learning. I began journaling in order to capture my observations, questions, and feelings. I needed a place to unload, a safe place to reflect and to discuss pedagogy without there being the threat of evaluation. In retrospect, I think that I needed a CIT seminar at the public middle-school level. Even then, I knew that good teaching gained much from collegial support for reflection and dialogue over means and ends.

I soon left the K-12 public-school system, armed with more questions about what makes good teaching and a thirst to join a teaching community where I could discuss them with others. Such a professional community based on trusting relationships was the faculty ingredient that I yearned to find at a school. Pancho Savery, a previous CIT seminar participant, noted that "a course only works when there is a shared sense of community that includes teacher and students." My experiences told me that Pancho's insight held much truth. My K-12 teaching experiences up to this point in my career demonstrated that I could not recognize and analyze the power (or the lack thereof) of my pedagogy without being a member of a professional community of teachers who were willing to share and give deep thought about practice. I was desperate to find a space to talk with peers about my experiences that I had captured in my journal.

Cross-Cultural Currents

I accepted a tenure-track faculty position at a small private college in the Greater Boston area, with high hopes that it would be different from the

K-12 arena. My hiring was one of several designed to bring diversity to this otherwise homogeneous, mostly white institution. My goals at the college-teaching level were, nonetheless, the same as they had been in my public middle-school classroom: to form relationships with and among students, to build a collaborative community of learners and teachers, to provide a safe place for each individual to establish membership in our shared humanity, and to elicit ways that facilitate authentic voice—all for the purpose of knowledge dissemination and knowledge creation. High-minded goals? Yes. Was my energy diverted? Yes. Could I go it alone? No.

I remember bursting into a colleague's office on one afternoon because I was deeply disturbed about my teaching that day. I had encountered a student who challenged my authority and knowledge concerning Japanese literary theory, in a course I was teaching on Japanese literature in translation. My dissertation research was conducted in Japan and involved the matter being discussed in my classroom, which was the purpose and place of literature in Japanese culture. The white female student was not of Japanese ethnicity, but her uncle had served in the US military in Japan after World War II, and she tried to contradict my observations by advancing a different and fairly stereotypical understanding of the issue. I handled this classroom disagreement in a clumsy way, became race conscious and defensive, and was utterly relieved when the class was finally over.

I went directly to a colleague from my department right after class, looking for help, needing someone who might redirect my energy—someone who might help me solve my problem. Instead, the colleague gave me a lecture about the type of "sheltered upper-middle-class white student" who attended that institution and how he (white male that he is) didn't try to teach about "foreign" places because he was well aware of the overall narrow life experiences of the students at that school. His message undermined my expectation of finding a place in the academy for talk about cross-cultural discord in the college classroom. But it didn't end my search for the right kind of support from colleagues.

Course evaluations suggested that most of my students were excited about learning in my class, but teaching at the college level continued to be a lonely journey. In faculty meetings, others appeared to be so self-assured about teaching content and confident in their teaching. But I was desperate to find the safe place to share with others my observations and experiences about cross-cultural interactions with students and instructional insights. I wanted to talk about the power dynamics in my classroom as a brown-skinned professor teaching all-white students of privilege. Having learned the "close your door and lecture lessons" from earlier teaching experience, I was skeptical about finding a place for such discussion. And of course, I also wanted tenure. The politics of the school hierarchies, and the dangers of openness toward administrators or superiors who disapproved of my methods, outweighed my desire to enter into an honest dialogue about practice with folks whom I thought that I simply could not trust. I continued to write in my journal.

My pedagogical practice changed after I began to analyze my journal entries. Instead of starting my courses with research- and textbook-based knowledge, the first item on the agenda was sharing my personal experiences and ways of knowing the word and the world (Freire and Macedo 1987). My interest in multiple frames for knowing the world, reading the word, and making sense of the times in which we teach and learn stem from those early experiences growing up in New York City. I began to realize how much my approaches as an educator were shaped by my entire life, educational and professional experiences, and by my own ethnic identity, and this helped me be aware of the need to question and attempt to see through the lens of others. Whether riding the No. 3 train underground for 1½ hours from my home in Brooklyn to Harlem with Bach and Chopin in my arms en route to piano lessons or stopping for a good book at the library on 42nd Street, I was reared in an environment that caused me to constantly move in and out of cultures, depending upon the situation at the moment. I became confident and competent at this cross-cultural shifting while maintaining my core identity, recognizing that as a professor, I bring into my classroom my cultural lens, personality, individual ideology, and vision of the world. My lens shapes what I see but does not limit it, and I have always worked to support my students and colleagues in reaching this recognition for themselves.

Bleich (1995, 44) has identified a pedagogy of disclosure, defined as "sharing, confiding, and exchanging parts of [one's] inner and unapparent [life] with others," and this approach came to shape much of my educational practice. After the Japanese literature fiasco, I decided to share with my students my hopes, my dreams, my fears, and my points of view concerning a variety of familial, local, state, national, and global issues concerning teaching, particularly the teaching of literacy in today's urban schools. For me, such practice sets the tone for building collaboration and community in the classroom and demystifies the role of instructor, which is especially crucial because for much of my career as a university professor I have taught future teachers for the K-12 classroom. I know my model will affect what my students will carry with them into their own classrooms and shape the educational experiences of another generation of learners. Teachers are mediators, and sometimes gatekeepers, where issues of culture arise in today's diverse classrooms; so, it is crucial as part of teacher preparation programs to have them examine their own cultural lens and learn about "others" who might be different from themselves.

From Soliloquy to Dialogue

Capturing my thoughts about teaching in my journal slowly gave way to dialogue when I joined the faculty at UMB in 1995. Trusted colleagues who helped to recruit me to the Graduate College of Education talked about their pedagogical strengths and challenges at our then-small department meetings, over lunch, tea, or just in passing. The university's urban mission contributed to such exchanges because it was clearly so important to be aware of the particular needs of our diverse student body—and because so many saw faculty diversity as an asset rather than a deficit. Diversity and the urban mission are what attracted me most to UMB, and among faculty and staff I am not alone. I was beginning to feel nourished at this university, a place where my long-standing values seemed congruent with the mission.

> My teaching here is a combination of life experience and the opportunity to work among such varied student body immensely satisfying [which] often produces rich dialogue that can't be replicated simply through colleges that have a student body that is privileged. What I really appreciate most about UMass Boston is how incredibly varied student experiences are. (assistant professor, counseling and school psychology)

My application to be part of a Center seminar during my fourth year of UMB teaching was followed by a welcome acceptance. It was exhilarating to be in a room with faculty from a broad range of discipline areas representing different colleges as well as life experience. Peter Nien-Chu Kiang, the seminar facilitator, did a marvelous job of having us form a community of peers, regardless of rank and/or full-time versus part-time status. He had us meet as a group for a few hours prior to the beginning of the semester-long seminar. We put faces with names, shared schedules, and began getting acquainted, so that our seminar focus on student evaluation could be launched at the onset of the semester.

As my seminar project, I conducted a small self-reflective, student-centered research study concerning my methods of student evaluation. Although I had designed a variety of learning assessment tools for students in this course, I had never before asked students how they viewed these instruments. The anonymous data collected over the course of the semester turned out to be invaluable to my teaching and to my future students' learning and grades. Being able to collect, analyze, and interpret data from my students in my class and then be able to discuss these findings with a diverse group of scholars truly altered my teaching for the better. My colleagues helped me define the right questions to ask about my own teaching, so that I could learn to be more effective.

That semester's seminar experience indicated to me that my earlier teaching experiences from middle school through two private colleges, one in Boston and one in Japan, were necessary components of my journey to find a safe place to engage in interdisciplinary conversations about the scholarship of pedagogy. Unfortunately, my journal writing stopped. However, connection to other people across campus had begun. At last, I felt safe and supported in the domain of teaching.

After this seminar, the CIT advisory board invited me to join—and a few years later, I was myself invited to facilitate a CIT seminar. Understanding how important it was for me to learn to trust myself as a teacher, to trust my students as active participants in the classroom, and finally, to trust my colleagues, I gladly accepted, affirming my earliest belief in the fundamental value of relationships in the teaching and learning transaction.

Preseminar Preparation

Poring over the individual applications to the seminar and searching for some way to unite the group in a relatively quick period of time during the first week was my first task. The mix of faculty represented many colleges and disciplines, in the liberal arts, business, education, and the sciences. Being a member of the Center advisory board had already involved me in recruiting faculty participants and actively discussing and choosing a group. Given the diverse representation of colleges and departments, at least one person on the board is sure to know at least one of the applicants, which will provide me with some insight into the individual. In addition to this knowledge, I read again and study each application, which includes requests that the applicant describe her or his teaching history, and to identify teaching and learning issues that most interest and/or challenge them.

My analysis of three sets of seminar applications indicates in response to the second prompt, as one might imagine, most people identify "safe contemporary issues" in teaching. On the other hand, some colleagues do identify specific challenges they face in their classrooms. Here are some examples of issues that seminar participants put on the agenda for our work together:

How can I create discussion environments that encourage students to think critically about hot-button issues (e.g., immigration, racism, class inequality, etc.) and to come to terms with the beliefs and experiences that both connect and distinguish their world view from others?

In some ways, I am scared of and for our students—scared they are not learning, reading and writing; scared that they are bored and that they will not learn from my courses; but I am also scared for them. A graduate student who is having many difficulties at home and school came to my graduate class late. She appeared to be under the influence of some kind of drugs. When I spoke to her after class, she informed me she was taking two kinds of anti-anxiety drugs and vicodin.

I was approached by a student in an undergraduate course and asked if I had a "beef" with her. When I admitted I was frustrated by her disruptions in the classrooms—coming late, leaving early, not turning assignments in on time. She said, "You don't know me and you are judging me!"

If time allows, I search out these colleagues and meet them on an individual basis to introduce myself, welcome them to the upcoming seminar, and find out if we need to talk about any burning issue prior to the seminar meeting. As was done in my own first seminar earlier, we all meet together as a group prior to the start of the semester for two or three hours for a general orientation to put names together with faces to get a general feel of one another, to establish agenda items for our syllabus, and to talk about what participation entails.

The Semester and the Seminar Begin

Leading a pretenured faculty seminar is much more than getting a courseload reduction to sit and chat with colleagues once a week (which alone would be a delightful professional development experience). It involves a commitment to inquiry, a deep level of comfort with silence among peers, and the confidence to decentralize the seminar to make it participant based and not facilitator focused. These, of course, are essentially the same challenges involved in all teaching efforts, wherever they occur.

As faculty, in the seminar, we are forced to acknowledge that our roles are complex, and there are multiple faces of our practice. There is the face that my students see—the expert on the subject matter, the visionary who can excite them about a new field, the person whom they have paid to impart knowledge and skills. There is the face that I see—the self-reflective/ teacher-reflective one, with my thoughts about what I hope to achieve in class. Finally, there is the face that looks to my colleagues, and that they see in me. This is the face that helps me grow as a pedagogue. This is the space where the Center seminar has become a professional home for me on my campus, a place I have searched to find for many years past. In order for this third face of one's teaching to become manifest in a seminar, trust and respect must occur among faculty who come from different disciplines and life experiences. The exercise of what I have come to call the Cross-Cultural Teaching Odyssey serves this purpose quite well.

Everyone's racial/cultural/socioeconomic/religious/gender-awareness odyssey is constantly being tapped as a resource by each of them as a source of personal power, a source of inspiration, and as such influences one's personal way of knowing the world. This has implications for all facets of professional life, including work with students in and out of the classroom. All of one's early learning and life experiences deeply impact one's frame for seeing the world and the work of the classroom. Locating these early messages that are deep within one's being has been essential to me in helping to identify self with others.

My plan for our weekly meetings envisioned colleagues from across the university sharing our odysseys with one another, practicing Bleich's "pedagogy of disclosure," defined as "sharing, confiding, and exchanging parts of [one's] inner and unapparent [life] with others" (Bleich 1995, 44). We could tell our individual stories based on the following focus questions:

1. Who are you? Describe yourself. Where did you grow up? Who were your family members/friends? What impact did they have on you as a learner/future teacher/scholar?
2. Where did you attend school (K–higher education)? Who was a mentor/model teacher for you at any period of your education? What characteristics were outstanding to you? How are these characteristics manifested in your teaching today?
3. Whose scholarship/teaching most influenced you? Explain.
4. How have these experiences prepared you to teach at this institution? In your particular college/department? What are your successes? Where does service fit into your scholarship/teaching paradigm?
5. What teaching/scholarship/service challenges do you face today?
6. Other comments about your humanity, you as a cultural being.

Fatima is a Latina who confided that she had experienced a life-threatening illness shortly before the start of the semester. Her cross-cultural odyssey was lyrical, metaphorical, almost poetic, as she described her life adventures, struggles, and epiphanies to our rapt seminar. About four weeks into the seminar she was absent. It was an unexpected absence that caused a sharp pang in each of our hearts. At the onset of the meeting, a couple of people asked if I had heard from Fatima. "Is she coming? Is she OK?" I replied that I did not know. Silence filled the room as we each looked at her empty seat. When any of us saw her the following days prior to the next seminar meeting, she received reassuring hugs and a welcome back to our pedagogical home space.

This cross-cultural protocol has helped to form caring, supportive, respectful relationships among seminar participants and has served as a catalyst for cross-disciplinary, cross-cultural/global exchange among and between seminar participants in a proactive fashion. It is incumbent on me to disclose first in order to model the process, taking my time and sharing honestly my responses and musings about my scholarship and teaching development. I have learned that it is critical for each person to take as much time as needed to present their self to the group (sometimes we need three full seminar sessions to complete this odyssey). Time is not a factor. The rich exchange is empowering and assists in cementing a close community early on in the seminar.

> It was important that the members of the group got to know one another given the amount of sharing and open discussion which was to take place. During the opening session we went around the table and talked a little about ourselves, where we came from, people who were influential in our lives and a little about our pedagogy. The diversity of the group led to very interesting reflections and an appreciation for the fact that there was more than one way of looking at a situation. (assistant professor, sociology)

> I plan to follow Denise's lead and to begin my class with the 'Cross-Cultural Teaching/Scholarship Odyssey' questionnaire, which all of the members of our CIT seminar completed and then discussed in class during our first meeting. I learned so much about my colleagues that first day and I was able throughout the semester to reflect on where each of us had come from, who our teachers were, and what we most valued from our educational experiences. It will be a fascinating exercise I think to see where the students in my class are coming from as they prepare to teach Shakespeare's poetry and plays. (assistant professor, English)

As the "chicken leg experiment" had served to bond Ketley, my middle-school students, and me when I was a public-school teacher long ago, the Cross-Cultural Teaching/Scholarship Odyssey becomes the first experience that securely joins the seminar faculty as a community of scholars focused on pedagogy.

After the completion of the odyssey exercise, we then return to the pro-posed draft syllabus for our work together and make any additional shifts or changes. Never has my syllabus been 100 percent on point after my first draft. I have always needed to revise it at least once more and resubmit for approval by the group because after the odyssey, we truly open up and think progressively about the work we want to cover over the course of the semester. These early sessions are the only times during the seminar that may feel like a class. After the odyssey (and sometimes during the odyssey sharing), the atmosphere is one of give and take.

Expert practitioners constantly battle against "knowingness" by questioning and raising perplexities. How this manifests itself in our different contexts is unique to each of us; so, early on in the seminar after the cross-cultural sharing, we distribute our syllabi and talk in detail about the type of teacher we think we are. Here Peter Filene's protocol (Filene 2005) has been very useful as a framework for presentation:

I bring to teaching a belief that_____
In the classroom I see myself as_____
I believe students are_____
I seek to foster in students_____
I think learning is_____

These two major exercises, the cross-cultural odyssey and the examination of syllabi, create an atmosphere of participation and collaboration, so that when issues arise, we have a shared framework, and knowledge of one another, to serve as a foundation for problem solving as well as problem posing.

In this, we always allowed interruptions in routine and gained much from them. These are the moments when crises and problems in our classes intervene and capture our collective attention. In a seminar meeting shortly after the group has completed the first two exercises, while we do our initial "check-in" with each other, a colleague is obviously upset about a classroom experience. She is a junior faculty member who grew up in a country in Asia and has had zero contact with black men. Her only exposure to black people prior to coming to UMB had been in her native country, through carica-tures on television and news stories (which were mostly violence-filled/law-breaking images). She revealed that the source of her angst on this particular day was that she simply could not understand the "cool pose" posturing of two black men in her class who she felt challenged her authority on a regu-lar basis. As we seminar participants help her unpack some of the hidden and taboo mind-sets in which we all operate with this particular student population, I realized that such a breakthrough was not only a beneficial to her but to us all. Many US-born faculty, of all ethnicities, reveal their perplexities about teaching and learning transactions with this population as well. A large part of the CIT learning experience is to find a place to process the diversity issues that arise in our own classes and to examine our own assumptions about difference.

Encountering Pedagogy—the CIT Seminar

Dialogues in the seminar that I facilitated were rich in collective problem solving and reflection on the everyday challenges of university teaching, as in the following example from my seminar.

John: Last semester I had a true problem student, the worst I've ever had. I had a student from Russia who would continually make odd, off the mark, sometimes shocking statements in class. She had an inability to recognize inappropriate social cues in this society. The situation culminated when a guest presenter to my class discussed rape and the dynamics involved and this student blurted, 'What about women who liked to be raped?' I was taken aback as was everyone in the class including the visitor. I sent her an e-mail to say that I was disturbed by what she said, but she refused to come in and talk to me. I also sought the advice of other faculty in my department and tried to get her to go to counseling.

Rachel: I'm happy to note that you stayed on the issue and didn't let her increasingly disturbing remarks silence the entire class.

Clara: Perhaps you can limit the number of questions she is allowed to ask in class.

John: I communicated my point to the woman, and it helped for a short while. Then she went back to the same behavior. I struggled with not losing my patience. Once I remarked, "Oh so and so, I don't want to hear more of your crazy theories." The class found my comment amusing, but I felt bad after saying this.

Morris: Yeah, it's so hard when you have well-prepared students who dominate the class too. That can be a problem.

Tiago: I have a practice to subvert the conversation and manage the flow away from the dominant student by simply asking, "Anyone else?"

Washington: You have to address the issue, however thorny, rather than backing off. I also share qualifiers with students like, "I'm still wrestling with this; society is wrestling with it too."

John thus was able to process this difficult and challenging classroom moment, gain support for engaging with the problem student, get suggestions for how to respond, and learn something valuable from sharing the experience with colleagues. This kind of scenario involving faculty conversation is a glimpse of the type of thoughtfulness and authentic sharing that goes on in a seminar. The CIT seminar has many levels of complexity, and it takes time to build the atmosphere of trust, and community, that makes this kind of conversation possible.

What may be the most important component of the seminar is precisely the weekly "check-in" time. These are the moments during the seminar when members bring hot-button issues about their classrooms into our inquiry-based thinking space. This is a crucial aspect of the seminar because oftentimes this is the only place where colleagues feel safe sharing classroom experiences that may not be going so well. The safety and confidential nature of the seminar allows for people to show vulnerability as teachers and to seek help without conditions. This, unfortunately, is a rare opportunity in the academic context for faculty, especially if they are junior.

Food and breaking bread together is important. Each seminar member signs up to prepare lunch or a snack for the group at least twice over the course of the semester. Serving ourselves buffet style, passing around the apple cider, or just standing in line waiting to get utensils allows the "down time" needed to transition from the pressures of the institutional universe to a quiet, trusting place where reflection and not action is the constant focus. One colleague stated in his final reflection,

> The idea of having food on hand to munch while we discussed and shared took on an important role in the seminar. During the course of the semester the group got to sample some very interesting delicacies and old favorites brought in each week by a member of the group. Through it all it was another way in which the group was able to bond and to share.

Readings are always helpful as one of many tools to help highlight particular issues, strategies, and/or resources. Works by Peter Filene (1995), Estelle Disch (1999), and bell hooks (1994) have been especially insightful in provoking probing conversations. I have been careful to not overwhelm the syllabus with texts or readings as sometimes these become foils that block authentic conversation—which is exactly what I do not want to happen. Typically, I assign readings authored by those members of our community (tenured and pretenured; administrators and professional staff) whom I have invited to present during a portion of our weekly seminar time together.

Final Thoughts

In 2009, who I am as a teacher is a product of all of the places where I have taught from the steps at 72 Midwood Street in Brooklyn, New York, to rediscovering pedagogy with peers at an institution of higher education in Boston. I have learned that teaching is not simply the transference of knowledge but so much more. The cultural context and conditions for exchange are critical variables. How can my Asian colleague teach brown-skinned men if she fears them at an unconscious level? How can Ketley learn from me if she thinks that I see her as an empty silo with nothing to offer in the classroom, especially if she cannot speak English well? How can I teach a white female the lessons that my Japanese oba-san taught me if we don't share the same level of respect for all cultures from an indigenous point of view?

Almost two-thirds of my teaching career has involved searching for the safe space to talk with peers about my work, the faces of my classroom, and the dimensions of my questions. It is fortunate to be at a university that supports the investigation of inclusive pedagogy. Colleges and universities everywhere should shoulder such financial support for faculty to reflect about pedagogical practice, especially for faculty working toward tenure. There was no doubt about the university's interest and its urban mission being at the core of all the seminar discussions. This meant knowing that we were always willing to think, and think again and again, about how we could best teach and meet the needs of a vast diversity of learners. This benefits the institution, the faculty, the community, and most importantly the students, especially because our students learn more effectively and authentically. The Center seminar has been a win-win situation for all.

A major current challenge is to transfer this collaborative process that I have learned and refined in my work in the Center seminars into the K-12 educational structure outside our university, through my work teaching schoolteachers. Hopefully, they will find its lessons useful and be supported in using them, as I myself was not when I was a school teacher. Another arena for using the model is in my current work with teacher-training faculty at universities in other countries of the world, such as Colombia and Japan, two countries where I have long been consulting and teaching. My sense is that our discoveries about the power of collaboration have wider applicability outside North America. It is a privilege to continue to evolve professionally and be part of a process of ongoing faculty renewal that collaborative, critical reflection brings to colleagues who are committed to working together to improve their practice.

PART II

Faculty Identity as a Resource for Effective Teaching

CHAPTER 4

Imaging the Spaces between Art and Inclusive Pedagogy

Vivian Poey

Diversity: Experienced and Perceived

> Do you work around here?
> Yes, at the university.
> Oh, do you clean?
> No, I teach.
> Conversation with a stranger on the bus, 9 A.M. on a weekday

This is one of many personal encounters with strangers, including students on the first day of class, that have inspired a deep recognition of the assumptions many people in the United States bring when confronted with people who look or sound like me. The repeated response from strangers to how I look and the position I hold as a university professor reflects a set of expectations about who I am that place me firmly outside the dominant culture in this particular context. Whatever it is I am, two things are evident: first I am perceived as a member of a minority. And second this minority status carries implications for where I am perceived to belong in the context of American society.

I was born an American citizen in Mexico from Cuban parents. I lived in three different countries throughout Latin America before arriving in the United States just in time to start high school in Miami, Florida. In the context in which I grew up, I was white. It was not until I went to college in Tampa that it became apparent to me that in this new context, I was a person of color. I have since experienced a wide number of interactions that are both enriching and disturbing. But the most salient of these in recent years have been with my students.

Based on my appearance alone, my identity is ambiguous, but there is clearly a visible difference that sets me apart from the dominant culture. A student in South Carolina once asked, "You are not really white, are you?" Another student in Washington State wrote in her reflection on the course that when she saw me walk in she could not imagine having anything to learn from me. She also mentioned that she could hardly understand my accent even though my Spanish accent is slight enough that many people think I do not have one.

Many of these experiences have left me temporarily speechless, but they have also inspired productive rage that has resulted in a great deal of work both in the studio and in the classroom. I teach in a graduate program for K-12 teachers focused on integrating the arts into the school curriculum. Many of the faculty of color who teach in this program have also expressed frustration with the preconceived notions and expectations many students have of them and the challenges these assumptions present in teaching the values-charged content of arts and education. But as adults and as professors, we are in a position of power. Our students, however, teach kids who have far less power than we do and who understand that their culture is often not highly valued in this country.

> I can't think of anything in Spanish because I am American. (bilingual third grader in a Boston public school)

It is the thought of these expectations superimposed on children's lives and their potential effect on how children perceive their own identities that drive my work in this chapter. I will discuss how I use artists' works to challenge stereotypical images of the other and to *complexify* student's ideas about the relationships between racial and ethnic groups and the historical and cultural context of the communities we live in. Through this process, I hope to complicate our understanding of how people are represented and to model a pedagogy that listens to and values all voices no matter how marginal. By complicating the ideas of who we are and what we expect others to be, I hope to interrupt the cycle of assumptions that assigns students diminished expectations simply because of the ethnic or racial and closely related socioeconomic communities they belong to.

As a young female faculty of color, I am aware that students often question my authority and expertise. Many faculty of color echo this sense of deficit expectation, and some studies have documented the student resistance that results from these assumptions (Ludlow, Rodgers, and Wrighten 2005). In this paper, I elaborate on what I do in the course to shift students' attitudes, particularly the attitudes of the most resistant, mostly white middle-class women who teach in public schools and attend our program. I discuss how I select, present, and use artwork as a basis for pedagogy. I also consider evidence of students' questioning and re-evaluation.

Why Art?

Although I also have a background in education, in the Integrated Arts program where I teach, I come primarily as an artist. My students are experienced teachers but generally have limited knowledge about art. My role is to introduce art as a new model for thinking, teaching, and learning. In the Art and Culture in Community course, I engage students in investigating the role of the arts in multiple communities beyond the school setting. Because a lot of contemporary art deals with issues of voice, identity, community, and culture, and because most of my students know little to nothing of contemporary art, I focus my examples for the course on work made by a diverse range of living artists. I provide multiple examples of artists working through their process of research, reflection, and production, so that we can discern possibilities and make connections between art, our communities (including our students), and our daily lives.

Art in this context serves as a primary source of information (Cahan and Kocur 1996). It invites students to consider other people's stories; stories that are often left out of official historical accounts and provide alternative historical truths (Greene 1993). The arts also allow students to be hopeful as they engage students' imaginations and invite them to consider possibilities of what else could be, or as Maxine Greene would elegantly put it, they "awaken us to alternative possibilities" (Greene 1993, 215).

My intent in the course is twofold, as it addresses both pedagogy and art content. First I hope to model an arts-based pedagogical practice that is inclusive and democratic. This is a practice that invites student voices and does not devalue students' personal experiences regardless of who the students are. It values personal and alternative narratives as well as research and challenges students to consider the intersections. It engages students in methods of inquiry that will challenge them to take into consideration multiple viewpoints and to consider their own subjective experience as related to these alternative perspectives.

In terms of content, my expectations for the teachers I work with are that they acquire a body of knowledge about art's relationship to society and people's lives that takes into account how art challenges and interacts with cultural values and life experience. I want them to apply their new knowledge toward developing an attitude about art that involves intellectual curiosity, questioning assumptions, valuing diverse perspectives, and imagining new possibilities of thinking and perceiving. I want them to apply this knowledge in an open-ended pedagogy that recognizes and encourages student questions and curiosity and allows for making these connections to students' lives in their classrooms. For this pedagogy to be effective, it is important that teachers suspend their assumptions about their students and invite their students to define themselves and their own complexity.

Art, Inquiry, and Telling Stories: Narratives in the Spaces Between

At the beginning of the Art, Culture and Community class, I ask students to mention the names of artists they know about. Students, with few exceptions, name exclusively nonliving European artists. It is extremely rare, even when asked specifically to consider more contemporary work, for students to come up with the name of a single living artist, especially an artist of color. Although contemporary art is directly connected to the current cultural context and reflects current issues and communities, it seems to lie completely outside educational practice, even for many art teachers.

So as a vital part of the course, I share the work of diverse artists who deal with complex contemporary issues in their work. I focus on resources that allow students to not only see the work itself but most importantly to see the complex and indirect process of developing the work in the artists' own voices. To this end, I use videos that show artists developing a body of work from start to finish. I choose formats that show artists' research process and influences. And I assign readings that provide artwork along with artists' statements about their lives and influences (Cahan and Kocur 1996, Corrin 1994). I share the work of many artists working in a wide range of media from painting and sculpture to installation and performance, and coming from diverse communities including African American, Native American, Latino, Asian, Jewish, and white artists from various regions of the country and from varied socioeconomic backgrounds.

In a most immediate sense, these artists' works provide additional ideas and inspiration for the process, form, and content of student work. Once students gain an understanding of the subjective search process that art requires, they are more willing to follow their own processes in unexpected directions and to notice how their own experiences diverge and intersect with potential viewers of their work, including their students. The process of art-making engages us in telling our own stories from our own vantage points even, and perhaps especially, when they are in conflict with official versions. This makes multiple narratives and perspectives not only possible but also visible and accessible. So in a larger sense, the work of these artists also provides a window into the lives and motivations of artists from diverse racial, cultural, and socioeconomic backgrounds.

To this end, I often choose artists who make work about marginal histories such as Judy Baca, a Chicana muralist who has collaborated with multiple communities around Los Angeles including women farm workers and urban gang members on developing murals. She strives to "represent the voice of people who lacked representation in public life," a population of primarily Mexican and indigenous people, that had "been disappeared in textbooks, in the media, in cultural markers of place" (Baca 2004). We also look at the work of Fred Wilson, who addresses the treatment, and often exclusion, of African and Native Americans in historical museums (Berger 2001), and Beverly Buchanan, who investigates shacks and the lives of their inhabitants in the rural south.

These are only a few examples of the range of artists I focus on. As we view the work we discuss the context, compile a list of the artists' multiple and unusual sources of information including their own lives, interviews, photographs, buildings, and so on, and discuss the various roles that particular works play in the community in which they exist. These artists' works and processes exemplify the complexity inherent in the experience of each individual artist and present stories that are generally absent in official histories and in the mainstream curriculum. They illuminate the spaces between.

As a Latina artist with a particular set of experiences, I also share my own work with students and walk them through the thought process, the research, and the connections I made as the work developed. To what degree should I make my own beliefs an explicit part of my teaching? Bérubé (2006) says he considers this "every time I walk into the classroom," and he mentions that the range of subjects included in literature allows him great latitude in this regard. Art, like literature, encompasses an enormous range of human experience and invariably brings to the classroom key questions about culture, politics, and personal experience. When I share my work, these issues are especially visible. I share my beliefs and biases, insofar as they are part of my artwork and intertwined with my experience.

I share my work at the beginning of the class because it provides an introduction to who I am as an artist and a teacher and provides an important window to the course content. By sharing my work, I model how an artist's work is intimately intertwined with the artist's life. I also begin to introduce an alternative narrative to nationality, identity, and history, and how art may engage us in investigating, processing, and communicating difficult subject matter both on a personal level and as social commentary.

In addition to what students learn about my work in particular and about art in general, sharing the work also addresses the need to establish both my identity and my own authority as an artist. From the moment I walk into the classroom, students have so many questions about who I am and where I come from. Based on some of their writing, I also know that at least some of them have initially questioned my authority in any field. When I share my work, I provide a complex image of my cultural background and I establish myself as an artist in their minds. In addition, many students have mentioned that the fact that I share so much of myself in my work has allowed them to feel safe to question and share their own identities, struggles, and doubts about their work in class.

My Artwork

I show various bodies of work including work I did investigating ideas of authenticity, work about particular current events, and work about cancer in my family. This work is full of stories of rage, pain, recovery, hope, and strength. For the sake of conciseness, I will focus on only two pieces that are part of my older work but also the most relevant to the topic of this paper.

Little Havana (1994)

This piece consists of three major parts: a small hanging box, sound, and text. The box may represent various things ranging from a memory chest or a jewelry box to a fictional raft or a floating island. On each panel appears a different image of a Cuban pre-revolutionary postcard representing an idyllic state such as a palm-tree landscape. Combined with the images are short texts extracted from August 1994 editions of the *Miami Herald* relating to the Cuban exodus crisis. An old clock sits hidden within the box, and although it remains hidden, its audible ticking suggests both the passing of time and the anticipated explosion of a time bomb. The suspended box is supplemented by a backdrop of golden handwritten text on two corner walls that begins "1959 Next year in Havana" and continues as the years progress "1960 Next year in Havana," "1961 Next year in Havana," and so on until it finally reaches 1994, where the blank space that follows awaits the new year to be filled in, predictably with the same worn phrase. The text not only frames the box within a specific time and place but also accentuates the endless monotony of the wait, the persistence of hope, and the undying faith in the existence of that idyllic homeland to which Cuban exiles often refer to as *La Cuba de Ayer* (the Cuba of yesterday).

I made this piece in 1994 when thousands of Cubans were risking their lives in homemade rafts to leave the island and get to Florida. My family emigrated from Cuba in the early sixties (after the visas for the United States had been closed) and moved to Mexico City where I was born. I grew up with Cuban food, Cuban music, and fantastic stories of *La Cuba de Ayer* as well as stories of oppression by the Communist regime. I share with students my ambivalence about Cuban politics. The stories I grew up with are emotional and one-sided, but they are personal and resounding. My family was torn apart by the revolution, with half leaving and half staying. I share my inability to be objective about the situation and my need to make art as a way to process and give meaning to my ideological struggle. This piece wrestles with the idea that there are two sides, pro- and anti-Castro, each perceived by the opposite group as evil and oppressive. I belong to communities on both sides, and this informs my own divergent perspective. This is an emotional piece. It intersects politics, but at its core is the personal struggle to come to terms with a painful reality affecting the lives not only of the thousands of human beings risking their lives to cross but also with what that might mean to the rest of us both in the United States and in Cuba not only as citizens with national and political interests but also as empathetic human beings.

I proceed with the assumption, real or not, that all my students are concerned and reflective members of a teaching community, and I establish an expectation that these histories are important to all of us for our understanding of the world and of each other, particularly in the context of diverse schools. Of this piece one student wrote,

> My thoughts drifted back to my beginning ESL students and their lives as new immigrants in this country. I have listened to them recount the hope of the older folks to return to their home country to die someday. They have unique perspectives on why they are here and their future relationship with their homeland and with this "new land." (Student, Tri-Cities, Washington)

This student went on to do in-depth personal research into her own family stories of migration during the Depression era. She used photographs and family objects to mine her stories eliciting stories from her parents and grandparents. She shared these stories with her ESL (English as a Second Language) students and developed a unit where students used personal objects, photography, and storytelling to document and share their own stories of migration while using language, both written and oral, extensively in the development of the work. This work not only supported the students' language learning and helped students investigate their relationship to this country and to the English language, but it also provided the teacher with new insights into her student's lives and the wealth of information they bring with them. It helped to forge a bridge between the experience of the teacher and the students, and it *complexified* their understanding of each other.

On Fictional Grounds (1995)

This work came about when I entered graduate school. During a studio visit, a prominent black female photographer questioned why I chose a format that she perceived to be very "white male" (small, pristine black-and-white prints). Later that semester, a well-known white photojournalist told me that my work was "too clean to be Mexican." I was offended and puzzled by both of these critiques, and I set out to investigate what it means to be culturally authentic.

Perplexed about the issue of authenticity, which I had been grappling with all my life (am I American or Mexican or Cuban?) as I pledged allegiance to various flags along the way, I was driven to make sense of the issue through my work. I recalled being taken aback in a restaurant in Tampa when I was served a Cuban sandwich with lettuce and tomatoes (the Cuban sandwich does not have lettuce and tomatoes). Considering that the Cuban sandwich is made with bread that is similar to French bread and Swiss cheese along with other ingredients, none of which are native to the island, I caught the irony and used the sandwich as the center of my investigation into this emotional, cultural, and historical notion of authenticity.

I began to research the origins of different foods and connected the interweaving of the history of food and human migration. Looking for ideas about cultural authenticity, I did some research into white supremacy movements in the United States. I also looked into the history and culture of the Caribbean in terms of language, music, and, of course, food. I searched for models of cultural hybridity and found plenty of literature about Cuba's hybrid identity.

My research was not limited to books. I spent plenty of time in the library, but I also engaged in both formal and informal conversations with other students who had complicated cultural backgrounds, with family, with recent Cuban immigrants, and with anyone interested in these kinds of issues. I had dinners where diverse guests brought food and discussed their relationship to food and to their cultural identity. I traced my cultural roots as far back as possible, making connections to the Middle East, France, Spain, Cuba, and eventually in my own lifetime to Mexico, Guatemala, Colombia, and Miami, Florida. I gathered stories. I read poetry by Cuban writers, looked for art by artists of mixed heritage, and listened to a lot of music. I recorded conversations, photographed food and events, collected maps, wrote in my journal, and processed information through ongoing transformations into visual work.

This work culminated in a photographic installation consisting of large photographic murals (3 × 5 feet each) documenting my meals (including food that originated in faraway places all over the world) hanging in the space as flags, the backing sewn with blue fabric and white stars (Poey 2003). A table with multiple place settings was set among the photographs and was brought to life with a performance based on stories about the Cuban sandwich with its range of ingredients, accompanied by American patriotic music modified by a pair of congas. The performance culminated in a dinner party complete with Cuban food, Chilean wine, diet Coke, and salsa music. The dinner was designed to encourage conversations about the issues raised during the performance, which included some humor but also some potentially difficult material about what it means to be American. The dinner conversations ranged from questions about the real Cuban sandwich to ethnic cleansing in Yugoslavia and potential legal issues arising from the use and transformation of the Star-Spangled Banner (figure 4.1). (For a detailed description of the work and to view a short video/documentation of the performance, go to http://www.lesley.edu/journals/jppp/7/poey1.html.)

This work was based on my personal experience as well as on ideas that I was invested in. I could have never imagined what the final outcome would be. It required trial and error and a lot of feedback from students and faculty. It also forced me to collaborate with other members of the community, as I needed help with sewing, cooking, and playing the congas. I learned not only about my complicated background but also about the American context in which my identity plays out. I also learned about multiple communities and made particular connections to local communities of people both similar and different than me. This process requires the artist to make personal connections and can potentially motivate and empower students to make sense of their world and use their voice.

This work in particular draws the attention of teachers. They are unfamiliar with installation work and with performance art (outside of theater). As I walk them through the journey of developing the research and making artistic decisions, they begin to grasp the notion of questioning histories and assumptions, and they also begin to understand that art is about making meaning of experience and developing new narratives. Because the work explicitly challenges the notion of cultural authenticity (as neither the Cuban sandwich nor I fit into a single cultural history), and because it is

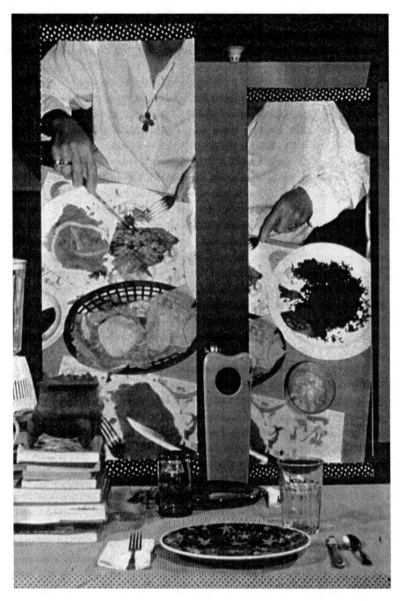

Figure 4.1 From "On Fictional Grounds and Culinary Maps"—Vivian Poey (2003).

grounded in a series of specific historical facts intertwined with an individual's complex life, it directly challenges many assumptions about culture and ethnicity. In addition to the important cultural content, the work introduces students to ideas about how to make meaning of the world and create narratives without necessarily being able to draw (the limited perception of art many students have). This piece opens up the possibilities of the work they can do not only in my course but also with their students in their classrooms. It provides an entry point for students as they begin their own investigations into their social issue project.

Art and Pedagogy: The Social Issue Project

Through the social issue project, students experience a compressed version of the art process in a guided investigation of an issue that is significant to them. As part of the process, they work both individually and collaboratively through a variety of art forms and eventually develop a collaborative piece using art media of their choice. The process is designed to get them to think expansively at first, making connections with unexpected bits of information and later moving on to more focused research and consensus leading to the development of the final work.

To get them started thinking expansively, I give students a slide frame and ask them to find and frame a little piece of the world. They record that fragment in some way (writing, sketch, digital camera) and consider how many thoughts and ideas they can derive from that little piece. I encourage them to make as many connections as possible. The goal is to get them to see that every image around us carries multiple possibilities for meaning. Some students write extensive lists of words and phrases going in multiple directions and others make poems or focus on specific issues, but they all make associations based on their interests and experiences. A high-school ESOL (English for Speakers of Other Languages) teacher looking at the lines of a barcode through her frame thought about the hidden messages within barcodes, which "are a mystery for most of us to read, although we know that they contain meaning." She was reminded of "the student with no literacy skills who needs help decoding the mystery of the black squiggles and lines." Then the students in small groups share their thoughts, which inevitably leads to conversations about issues in their schools.

We follow this exercise with a brainstorm of possible topics for investigation, many of which come from their associations and conversations. This ensures that the work focuses on their own interests and encourages students to be personally invested in the process. These lists often include all kinds of issues from illness, war, and death to spirituality, sexuality, urban sprawl, and globalization. Students get in small groups based on the issue they want to examine, and the investigation through various art forms begins.

The work is interdisciplinary and extends well beyond visual art. Students start working to define the issue as expansively as possible through a visual brainstorm. They work individually to find articles related to their social issue and write poems using only words taken from the article that distill, question, or transform the content of the original piece. They share the poems and move on to recount personal stories with their group about instances when the issue has played itself in their own lives. They develop a visual essay using visual images from the media and create an accordion book that presents in each panel a different perspective on the issue at hand. Outside class, each student collects their own data by conducting interviews, taking photographs, and finding other sources of images and information. This process constantly takes students back and forth from their own introspective ideas to those of the group while constantly introducing new information from other sources.

Through these exercises, students research various perspectives including those informed by their personal experience, as well as those they may not understand or may even inspire hostility in them (such as my own research into white supremacy movements). Armed with their new insights based on their work through various media and the conversations these fueled in their groups, and with inspiring ideas gained from looking at a variety of works by contemporary artists, students set out to generate a final collaborative piece in a medium of their choice.

One group, following the thoughts of a student who in the initial exercise had framed an eye of George Bush next to a fragment of the American flag from a magazine picture, developed an investigation of vision. Through their poetry, their stories, and visual essays, they investigated lack of vision in both personal and societal contexts such as issues in family dynamics, in their schools, and in the war with Iraq.

For their final piece, they built a maze with walls of paper and text about potential causes for this lack of vision, such as ignorance, racism, and so on. Some of the text was severely jumbled, misspelled, or otherwise obscured. We each entered the maze wearing the glasses they provided. Each pair of lenses obstructed our vision in different ways; some made it more difficult than others to get through the maze and read the text. The passage began to resemble a bad traffic jam, as some viewers were slow to move through and others, with better vision, grew increasingly impatient. Some of us walked out of the maze with headaches after struggling to see through narrow uneven slits or tiny holes and nearly everyone walked out frustrated and even angry.

On the surface, this work was simple but the outcome as evidenced in the discussion that followed was completely unexpected. We realized that we each assumed that our visual handicap was the same as everyone else's, and this greatly exacerbated the irritation of those who got stuck behind students who were nearly blind with their glasses. In the discussion, students made all kinds of analogies to their classrooms and their impatience with kids who do not understand the class work as readily as others. They talked about blaming victims and about their own ignorance and intolerance in various contexts and of the need to be more generous and compassionate even when the actions of others seem difficult to understand. In this context, issues of diversity entered the conversation as languages, values, and assumptions vary widely among their students. In the microcosm of the maze, we experienced the effects of our own erroneous assumptions and applied this experience to our understanding of the diverse classroom.

With this guided investigation, I hope to get students to think about the process as both unpredictable and productive. In an artistic investigation, you do not know where you will end up, and teachers have little tolerance for such uncertainty. They struggle through the process and at the end are invariably surprised at the results. One student wrote in her reflection paper weeks later:

> When I heard and saw other people's artistic presentations I didn't really understand why each one was so effective. I thought it was solely the result of each group's creativity. Only now I am realizing that the powerful message of the social issue evolved as different perspectives were developed or voiced.

For their final projects, students design an art-based inquiry project that involves a community of their choice. Some students develop work with their classroom and school communities and others develop more personal work that focuses on their family or other more personal contexts.

Toward Inclusive Teaching

Many students go on to develop work in their classrooms that includes sharing their own artwork and the work of other artists, while engaging them in art-based inquiry methods. Other students do work that turns out to be intensely personal.

Molly set out to investigate the aesthetics of food and unexpectedly made a beautiful handmade book that intertwined images and text about food in her household and in different countries with a deep reflection of her struggle with the course content and with difficult issues in her life. The artwork shared throughout the course along with the discussions had sparked some interesting and uncomfortable emotions. Her work in turn provided a window into ideas that challenged me to apply my own notion about a "pedagogy that values every student's voice" in the opposite direction.

She conceded that during my course she felt left out. It was clear that she was uncomfortable and at times angry. The range of artists that I show in class made her feel marginal. She experienced an emotional dislocation similar to what young students who are underrepresented in the curriculum experience on a daily basis. She wrote, "I am feeling that as a white middle class person, that my voice is not welcomed...that unless you are ethnic, you aren't important and that your experiences are not equal to the experiences of minorities."

These are the kinds of statements that make me and many of my colleagues cringe as we consider the hegemony of the white middle class in American education. I also cringe at the idea that only others are "ethnic," as if the American white middle class did not have its own ethnic and cultural traits. But for this student, this was an earnest statement. We can argue and present research about whose voice is most often represented and heard in most school curricula, but we cannot deny what she feels. Moreover, she is not alone. This is not an uncommon reaction to courses that purposefully bring in diverse voices or to schools' efforts to honor diversity. And some researchers argue that it is a direct inversion of the model of resistance presented by critical pedagogy in which subordinate groups resist institutionalized knowledge because it is inconsistent with their own experience (Ludlow, Rodgers, and Wrighten 2005).

This is an important element in inclusion: if everyone's voice counts, we cannot silence *any* student. The key question is, how do we deal with statements that we find problematic and even reprehensible? How do we address the discrepancy between our own ideas and understandings (as well informed as we may believe them to be) and students' deeply held emotions and beliefs?

There are many reasons why it is a bad idea to shut out or even discourage these voices. For one, silencing them does not make these ideas go away. When students/teachers go back to work with their diverse students, they will continue to bring these ideas with them into their classrooms. Second, when we hear these voices, we have a chance to understand where students are coming from and to capitalize on what they bring. This makes us better equipped to address their issues through the content of the course in ways that invite them to question their ideas rather than push them into a mode of resistance. Furthermore, listening to students should also challenge us to continually revisit our own ideas. We cannot ask students to be open-minded if we are not willing to accept that there might be some blind spots and even intolerance in our own understandings. In another section, the student continues this train of thought:

> Throughout this class I have cringed at having to hear about human suffering and ideas that challenge convention. I am realizing the comfort I have received from listening to conservatives who tell me that there is no racism; that the war is just; that poverty is a choice; and that any change opens the floodgates for destruction of moral values.

This paragraph surprised me. There are things we know but that do not always sink in (does anyone really believe that there is no racism and that poverty is a choice?). I was also surprised about her comment regarding "human suffering." I do not make direct references to human suffering (unless students' projects themselves explicitly bring it up). But the course led her to rethink her understanding of these issues. In her reflection, she conceded that maybe I just wanted to

> introduce us [them] to a few author/artists that are sharing their life experience through art. But where I think my understanding of this class became most useful was in the realization that my conversion to conservatism may need to be reconsidered. Not to be abandoned but tempered with wisdom...I want to thank you for your subtle nature, for had you been more overt in the delivery, I might not have heard you.

This student's comments indicate that the artists' works and stories played a significant role in this shift. She mentions my "subtle nature," which I attribute to my respect for students and my intention to provide them with the space to struggle with their own ideas, which might in turn feed their classrooms. Her work challenged me to see that I too have preconceptions about the students that I work with and their relationship to the curriculum I teach. It pushed me to consider a perspective that is foreign to me and enriched not only my teaching but also my understandings about marginalization.

Conclusions, Challenges, and Possibilities

The strong sense of feeling marginal in the curriculum and the powerful dislocation this engenders in these adults further accentuates for me the absolute need for a wider cultural, racial, and ethnic representation in K-12 curricula. I think of what this exclusion from the curricular frame means to five-, ten-, and fifteen-year-olds who are in the process of finding their place in the world. Early in my teaching career, a black student pulled me aside and asked, "Do you expect *them* to teach black kids about black culture?" This question still hounds me as I consider the challenge of encouraging teachers to be inclusive in their curriculum without further colonizing the experiences of others.

I do not expect anyone to teach anyone else's culture but rather to follow a model that provides resources of information (in this case artists' individual works and voices) and allows the students/viewers to investigate their own relationships to the material and its context through additional research into issues in their own communities. As students design and reflect on their final projects, I also expect them to consider how *their* students can investigate alternate sources of information that invite multiple perspectives into their classrooms beyond official texts.

But an inclusive curriculum is only part of the picture. Reflecting back on my opening statement and that revealing question "Do you clean?" takes me back to when I taught a class in a heavily Mexican district. I asked teachers why it is important for their students to learn to read and write. The response was that these skills would make it possible for the kids to fill out job applications (presumably for jobs that do not require a high level of literacy). As a former teacher of young children, I am aware of how goals shape teaching and can only imagine what kind of curriculum this diminished expectation translates into. At the root of a truly inclusive pedagogy, there must be more than diverse representation in content and a superficially democratic teaching practice. There must be a genuine willingness to see students as complex human beings with individual drives and aspirations who bring valuable experience, knowledge, and a sense of agency to the classroom and to their communities.

Throughout the course, students view the work and listen to the voices of diverse artists. These works and voices speak for themselves and defy easy classification or even the loosest generalizations. They define their identities, biases, experiences, and histories in vastly different terms. It becomes impossible to construe even those belonging to similar racial or ethnic groups as a unified whole as they each present complex identities, internal struggles, and aspirations that not just defy stereotypes but that also challenge mainstream perceptions of American life and culture. While this might not outright transform the curriculum, it has a potential effect on the teacher's perceptions of others, including their students, as they can provide students the space to define themselves and their own individual complexity through their own art-based inquiries.

By developing their own artwork based on their own research, students gain further understanding of the complexity of the issue and of their complicated and biased relationships to the social contexts in which the issue plays out. My expectation is that students translate this into a larger frame, that this points them in a direction to question their attitudes not only toward any ethnic, cultural, or racial groups but also in relation to issues that arise in the multiple communities they participate in.

I hope that through the insights into the lives and works of diverse artists, through their own investigations, and through the work they develop in their schools, teachers learn to see their students anew, full of unimaginable potential, free of fixed assumptions about their past, present, or future. I want them to consider not just supplementing their textbooks with additional resources that allow their students new opportunities to investigate their place in the curriculum but also to acknowledge their own assumptions about curricular content and to invite their students to bring their own voices and stories into the classroom. And perhaps in the process, the teachers will learn something about themselves and their own place in a complicated world.

CHAPTER 5

Inexplicable Desire, Pedagogical Compulsion: Teaching the Literatures of the Middle East

Rajini Srikanth

E very few years, I feel compelled to venture into territory that all logic dictates I should shy away from. It is a form of penance, if you will, a form of supplication to the great God of pedagogy, a reminder to be humble and to make oneself vulnerable and admit cluelessness (I take the word from Gerald Graff's book *Clueless in Academe: How Schooling Obscures the Life of the Mind*, though Graff focuses on the students' cluelessness in the face of instructors' opaque presentations). About ten years ago, I entered apprehensively into such territory when I developed and taught a course on postapartheid South Africa, not a region I had any formal expertise on, but for which I had an unshakeable fascination—one that was personal, geopolitical, and humanistic. In the process of developing and teaching the course, I like to think I made the journey from cluelessness to "partial knowing" and, I would hope, enticed the students to make a similar journey and to hunger for more such ventures.

As I explain in my essay "Overwhelmed by the World: Teaching Literature and the Difference of Nations" (Srikanth 2007), my complete unfamiliarity with the lived experience of South Africa provided me a supremely teachable opportunity to demonstrate to my students how knowledge gets constructed. I used my syllabus as the first text we interrogated in the course—subjecting it to the kind of rigorous analysis that we would use for the texts that followed. My students learned why I had included the material I had, and what texts I had left out and why.[1]

That same kind of inexplicable desire that impelled me to develop and teach the course on South Africa gripped me about four years ago in relation to the Middle East. I use the word "desire" very deliberately—with its associations of consumption, fulfillment, and ownership, calling to mind Trinh Minh-ha's (1989) critique of the colonialist discipline of anthropology and its desire for the Other, as well as Edward Said's (1979) groundbreaking observations in *Orientalism* on the European project of surveying and knowing, and thereby establishing superiority over, the Middle East. But my desire for the Middle East is, I would hope, a desire not solely for *comprehension* of a certain cultural and geographical region of the world but also a desire for *reconnection*, a desire to engage the Middle East not just as the focal point of today's European and United States' preoccupation but to see it also as an ancient, contemporary, and future participant in a thriving network of Asian and African nations. The project is intensely personal, I will admit, but it is also, I would argue, a way to take students beyond the borders of the United States and Europe to imagine additional complexities in the vastness of a world out there and to take them back to periods in history in which transnationalism, though not an articulated idea, was an active and robust practice.

At the University of Massachusetts Boston (UMB), where I teach, I offered the course for the first time in the Spring 2007 semester. Titled "Literatures of the Middle East," it was an upper-level undergraduate English department seminar, and it served as a capstone, or culminating experience, for the English major. At UMB, the English major is the second most popular undergraduate major on campus (psychology has the largest number of majors). Our campus is a nonresidential public institution that was initially founded to address the higher-education aspirations of working-class and inner-city residents, many of whom are the first in their families to seek a college degree. Though our campus is ethnically and racially diverse (42 percent students of color in 2006), the English department is far more homogeneous. English majors are by and large white, but their class status is diverse. The capstone course in "Literatures of the Middle East" was a small class of ten students. There was one student of color (a Haitian woman who had a superb understanding of power structures, particularly as they applied to representation, economic asymmetry, colonialism, and political enfranchisement), and the rest were white. There were two Jewish male students, one woman who asserted her lesbian identity, and two women who revealed that they had been brought up in fundamentalist Christian households but had distanced themselves from their parents' extreme religiosity. The rest of the white students did not reveal particulars of their background. With the exception of the one lesbian woman, who had spent several months in Turkey, the other students had not visited any country in the Middle East.

I entered the task of teaching this course with more than a little trepidation, because there were many "landmarks" to visit and make sense of, both to myself and to the students; by showing the landmarks—that is, the historical occurrences, memories, mythologies, and legends—that carry significance to me, I hoped to encourage students to call up the landmarks of their own significance within the context of their engagement with this region we call the Middle East. The inspirational source for me is Amitav Ghosh's hard-to-classify work, *In an Antique Land: History in the Guise of a Traveler's Tale*.[2] An amalgam of genres—memoir, anthropological treatise, and history—this work is an extraordinary portrait of an twelfth-century Indian slave, whose only record of existence lies in two brief entries in letters written by a Muslim merchant in Aden (in Yemen), Khalaf ibn Ishaq, to his Jewish trading partner and friend Abraham Ben Yiju, who at the time was living in Mangalore, a port in southwestern India. The two letters are dated 1139 and 1148, and Ghosh discovered them in a library in Oxford in a collection by the Princeton scholar S. D. Goitein titled *Letters of Medieval Jewish Traders*. In these letters, in the midst of a host of other communications regarding family members and trade commodities, Khalaf ibn Ishaq inquires about the Indian slave, who, we learn from Goitein's footnote, was in Ben Yiju's household and a respected member of it; Khalaf ibn Ishaq requests Abraham Ben Yiju to give the slave "plentiful greetings." Ben Yiju, Goitein's scholarly notes informs us, was

> a Jewish merchant, originally of Tunisia, who had gone to India by way of Egypt, as a trader, and had spent seventeen years there. A man of many accomplishments, a distinguished calligrapher, scholar and poet, Ben Yiju had returned to Egypt having amassed great wealth in India. The last years of his life were spent in Egypt, and his papers found their way into the synagogue in Cairo: they were eventually discovered in a chamber known as the Geniza. (quoted in Ghosh 1992, 19)

That encounter with the slave, through the two translated letters, in a library in Oxford, sets Ghosh on a quest: he writes that in Oxford, toward the end of 1978,

> I was a student, twenty-two years old, and I had recently won a scholarship awarded by a foundation established by a family of expatriate Indians. It was only a few months since I had left India and so I was

perhaps a little more befuddled by my situation than students usually are. At that moment the only thing I knew about my future was that I was expected to do research leading towards a doctorate in social anthropology. (Ghosh 1992, 19)

Within a few months of his reading the letters, he was in Tunisia learning Arabic. At about the same time next year, in 1980, he was in Egypt,

installed in a village called Lataifa, a couple of hours journey to the south-east of Alexandria. I knew nothing then about the Slave of MS H. 6 except that he had given me the right to be there, a sense of entitlement. (Ghosh 1992, 19)

What unfolds in Ghosh's book *In an Antique Land* are two rich narratives: (i) a complex reconstruction of the possible movements of the two merchants and the slave in the active Indian ocean trade of the twelfth century AD and (ii) the deeply personal immersion of Ghosh in the lives of his host families in 1980s Egypt.

The spirit of inquiry, the sense of intellectual adventure, and the joy of discovering connections and of experiencing epiphanies of understanding—these are the treasures of Ghosh's book that have sustained me and that I hoped to communicate to my students through this entry into teaching about the literatures of the Middle East. I came to this subject matter with tools of the trade (of literary and cultural studies) but not with the cloth (deep academic knowledge of Middle East history and politics). This cloth I fashioned out of my own fragments and scraps (wide reading and engagement with scholarship and literary texts of the Middle East) and then displayed it as a backdrop in the very visible arena of the classroom.

Because this is a course of literatures in translation and because it engages texts from a part of the world that neither I, at the time of my teaching, nor the majority of my students had visited, it was important for me to cultivate in the classroom an atmosphere of "adventurous humility."[3] Paradoxical as that phrase may sound, I wanted my students to be willing to enter cultural territory that was dauntingly "unfamiliar" and, at the same time, not to despair at the difficulty of interpreting the landscape. I hoped they would welcome the anxiety attending cross-cultural interchange and recognize that the disequilibrium and disorientation they might feel was salutary rather than a sign of deficiency. It was important for me to frustrate any objective on their part that they would "know" the Middle East through the texts we discussed. Yet it was my deepest hope that at the end of the semester they would leave with a sense of humble confidence in their ability to enter the

material and cultural worlds of the Middle East and enjoy meaningful connections with individuals who live or are from there. Saeeda Shah (2004,
567) notes, albeit cautiously, that a cultural outsider can be "an opponent; a
stranger; a tourist; a learner; a guest; a friend." (Her caution to us is that we
not see these positions as exhaustive or as fixed points on a scale.) It was my
hope that whatever posture my students entered with, they would leave the
course as "learners." I wished as well that they would resist the easy seduc-
tion of literary texts as windows into unfamiliar cultures. I have written
elsewhere that the

> textual experience of unfamiliar cultures and peoples is alluring, because
> it gives pleasure—of the encounter with well-crafted language, complex
> narrative, rich characters, and urgent questions requiring our intellectual
> and emotional commitment. This pleasure can become fulfilling in and
> of itself and take the place of the hard work, the labor, of interrogating
> the self and restructuring frameworks of perception that must accom-
> pany any truly meaningful interaction with those unlike us. (Srikanth
> 2010, 129)

Thus, as I have argued,

> while it is essential to bring translations of texts to the English-speaking
> reader, it is also critical to cultivate in the reader the interrogative stance:
> What does this text reveal? What does it not reveal? Why does it reveal
> what it does in the manner that it does? What intellectual journeys does
> this text suggest might be valuable? (Srikanth 2010, 130)

Gayatri Chakravorty Spivak (1998, 104) has cautioned against a posture
of wishing to know all, to explain that which eludes explanation, and of
"desir[ing]" to imagine "a world that can be known." Her admonition was
helpful to me in selecting primary and secondary readings and in charting
the intellectual journey I wished for my students. My objective was to create
in them a comfort with indefiniteness and to help them realize that a need
for quick understanding of the unfamiliar is likely to result in irresponsible
knowledge.

With these guiding pedagogical principles in mind, I foreground the
indeterminacy of meaning and highlight the fluidity of our interpretive terrain in the course description that opens the syllabus. (I taught the course
again in Spring 2008, but this second offering was at the graduate level.)
The language of the course description underscores complexity, multiplicity,
and diversity. At the outset, I want to shatter assumptions of a monolithic

"Middle East." Even the identifier "Middle East" is contested, I alert my students, with some scholars resisting the European and American construct of a region that they feel ought more accurately to be called "West Asia." Thus, I promise the students,

> We will examine the very contours of how we perceive this area of the world. We will engage a selection of literary and cinematic texts from several nations, including Egypt, Iran, Israel, Lebanon, Morocco, Palestine, and Turkey; our authors and filmmakers include men and women of varying religious faiths (Christianity, Islam, and Judaism) and political opinions.

The syllabus includes a long list of secondary readings, the majority of which are historical and grounded in the interdisciplinary fields of women's studies and cultural studies. The literary and cinematic texts are an entry into the material realities of lives in the Middle East; they are not isolated objects, delighted though we may be to revel in their narrative or poetic construction. Against a backdrop of relevant historical detail, we read poems, novels, short stories, plays, and essays from these areas and explore their treatment of such themes as identity, nationalism, religiosity, gender, feminisms, memory, conflict, and home.

As with the initial careful examination of the syllabus for my course on South Africa, my students and I attend to the syllabus for this course. One student asks whether all the literature we will read is contemporary—twentieth century based. He had hoped we would read some traditional narratives (e.g., *The Arabian Nights: Tales from a Thousand and One Nights* and the Babylonian epic of *Gilgamesh*), but he is not disappointed, he assures me. I acknowledge that I had not really considered any pre-twentieth-century text, because I am principally interested in creative expression within the context of the rise of nationalisms and the sociocultural and political landscapes of the Middle East following the dismantling of the Ottoman Empire at the end of World War I.

This student's question supplies a perfect segue to my invitation to the class to critique and engage the forces that form the backdrop of my syllabus. This backdrop that I now explain is a field of influence made up of fragments that I have collected from different types of experience: lived experience, communicated experience, studied experience, desired experience, and imagined experience. I call these fragments landmarks, the buoys that guide me through these turbulent waters, reminding me both of the roughness of passage and, at the same time, promising help. When I began teaching the course on January 29, 2007, I made clear to my students that I had no claim to insider knowledge. But rather than viewing the lack of lived experience as a handicap, I presented it as an opportunity that would make it incumbent on me to demonstrate to them how I had selected the readings and why I considered them important.

Landmark 1

Having grown up in Bombay (now Mumbai) in India, I had many school-mates from the Parsi community. The Parsis, also called Zoroastrians (because they follow the teachings of the prophet Zoroaster), trace their ancestry to Persia (now Iran), from where they fled to escape the proselytizing force of Islam in the eighth century A.D. The story of their arrival in Gujarat, on the west coast of India, and the legend of their acceptance by the ruler Jadhav Rana is a narrative that resonates with me for what it reveals both about the cleverness of the Parsi supplicants and the inclusiveness, I like to believe, of an eclectic Hinduism.[4] The legend goes that when the Parsis arrived on the shores of Jadhav Rana's kingdom, they had to convince a reluctant ruler that they would be valuable subjects. His kingdom was already full, he declared, and he had no room for them. They sent an emissary with a bowl of milk filled to the brim and the message that they would dissolve as unobtrusively into his kingdom as sugar in milk, sweetening his kingdom without placing a strain on its resources. Jadhav Rana was impressed by their wit and accepted them on the condition that they would learn the local language, wear the local dress, and not impose their religious views on others. They agreed.[5] The largest number of Parsis anywhere in the world is in Mumbai.

The Parsis of my childhood are my connection to ancient Persia. I claim their history as my own not the least because, like them, I too consider Mumbai my spiritual home. They give me "permission" to dwell on Iran, as do the Iranian students of my late adolescence, who form my second land-mark. The texts in the syllabus through which we study Iran are the graphic novel *Persepolis* (2004) and the film *Baran* (2002). Along with these primary texts, we read secondary material that introduces relevant issues to deepen our discussions: these include the significance of the genre of the graphic novel and whether it constitutes an appropriate medium for the issues raised in *Persepolis* (the betrayal of the Iranian people by the Islamic revolution, which had promised an economically and culturally balanced society following the overthrow of the Westernized Shah and his elitist economic policies); the reasons for the eager participation by working-class women in the revolution against the Shah; the various kinds of feminist activism in contemporary Iran (and the weight Westerners place on the hijab as a marker of a woman's apparent submission to religious authority); the upper-class perspective of *Persepolis*; the richness of the post revolutionary Iranian film industry; and the presence of large numbers Afghani "undocumented workers" in Iran (among the many pedagogical surprises of *Baran* was that it allowed us to talk about the similarities between the United States and Iran as countries of affluence relative to their neighbors).

Landmark 2

In the early to mid-1970s, the last decade of my residence in India, I lived in the southern town of Bangalore. At the time, the engineering colleges there had many Iranian students, young men and women who were fleeing the Shah's oppressive regime. A group of them lived on the same street as I, and we became good friends. They would visit me and my family and stop over for tea; through them I learned about the politics of Iran. One evening, they invited me to an exhibit they were attending at the British Council library, an exhibition of photographs from Palestinian refugee camps. Though India was one of the first nations to recognize the Palestinian Liberation Organization, I was blissfully unaware of the conditions of the Palestinian refugees because before coming to Bangalore I had attended a school started by and for expatriate Americans and had found in its library the compelling novels of populist Zionist authors—Leon Uris, for one. Therefore, I knew quite a bit about the founding of Israel but nothing about the accompanying displacement of Palestinians. Becoming aware of my ignorance was a powerful lesson in humility, one that I will never forget. I remember the incredulity in my Iranian friends' voices when they learned how little I knew. So, one could say that the Middle East was my first encounter with the phenomenon of selective knowledge—it was how I realized that we can only know what we are encouraged to know. But even then, I didn't fully comprehend the extent to which my consciousness had been shaped both by the legacy of British rule and by the new cultural and economic imperialism of the United States.

That awakening would come a few years later. This dual influence of British colonialist sentiments and American emphasis on liberal individual-ism is not a shaping that I reject—on the contrary, I welcome and revel in the richness of the Western cultural and political influences in my life. What I do regret, however, is the delay in my understanding of power and how it operates. Perhaps I can trace my deep interest in power—both in *what* I teach and *how* I teach it—to a desire to compensate for the many years in which I had no awareness of the pervasiveness of power and its many mani-festations on my consciousness, the years in which I judged my worth by the standards of British and American ideals.[6] For instance, it was not until the publication of Salman Rushdie's novel *Midnight's Children* in 1981 that I felt authorized to claim the English language as my own property; Rushdie's novel uses a breathtaking Indian English that is robust and vibrant in its unabashed flouting of the strictures of British English. Reading that novel was akin to finding and reveling in my postcolonial voice (an experience certainly not unique to me. Most postcolonial scholars consider *Midnight's Children* the fictional standard bearer of postcolonial literature as Said's *Orientalism* is the ideological standard bearer of postcolonial studies).

Thus, the texts I select for the course by Palestinian and Israeli writers engage head on the deeply entangled histories of these two peoples and the structures of asymmetrical power embedded in their relationship. Mahmoud Darwish and Ghassan Kanafani supply the Palestinian perspective of displacement, longing for home, and the conflicted emotions of resilience and despair; David Grossman and Syed Kashua provide the Israeli Jewish and Israeli Arab perspectives, respectively. In selecting Grossman to speak for Israeli Jews, I was turning to a voice that has not shied away from addressing the deeply problematic Israeli occupation of the West Bank and Gaza. I wanted my students to see how thoughtfully and painfully Grossman negotiates his privileged position as an Israeli. Because I knew that the Israeli-Palestinian issue would be the most volatile topic of the course, I invited as guest speakers three faculty members—two Israeli and one Palestinian—to help students understand the personal dimension of the fraught politics of the ongoing situation.

Landmark 3

Like Ghosh, who began a journey into the distant past spurred by the two twelfth-century letters he read, I began a journey into the blank spaces of my own global perspective. Knowing about the Middle East, understanding its connection to South Asia and the world—not just its role in the European and American imagination—became a measure of my development as a global citizen. Ghosh's memoir and his retracing of the trading routes of the Indian Ocean in the medieval world revealed to me the shared dependencies of Asia, North Africa, and the Arabian Peninsula. Sugata Bose turns a historian's eye in *A Hundred Horizons: The Indian Ocean in the Age of Global Empire* (2006) on these vibrant linkages and argues that the Indian Ocean is an "interregional area," a body of water that has from ancient times brought together disparate peoples and facilitated networks of robust cultural and economic exchange. He and Ghosh resurrect the lived connections among the Middle East and South Asia, encouraging me through their writings in my project of teaching the literatures of the Middle East.

Landmark 4

The old trading routes survive in new ways that have their unsavory aspects. Jon Goss and Bruce Lindquist (2000, 393) observe, "The migration of workers to the [Persian] Gulf is the largest of the contemporary international labor migrations, with an average of over one million workers deployed annually from the mid-1970s to the present." Their analysis situates the current flow of labor from Asia and the Pacific regions to the Middle East within the broad historical framework of indentured servitude, guest labor, and contract labor, extending from the nineteenth century into the twenty-first. In this regard, Karen Leonard writes about the links between India and the Gulf during the British domination of the Indian Ocean region: "The Indian rupee was the principal currency in the Gulf, Indian stamps were used...and Urdu (Hindustani) words infiltrated the Arabic coastal dialect" (Leonard 2005, 678). She notes as well that currently "India and Pakistan are major suppliers of labor to the Gulf," with remittances from the Middle East "constitut[ing] the single largest source of export earnings for Pakistan" (Leonard 2005, 679). The economies of many Middle Eastern countries—Saudi Arabia, Kuwait, and the United Arab Emirates—are sustained by the labor of men and women from South Asia—Indians, Pakistanis, and Sri Lankans—and Filipina women. There are entire villages in India whose livelihood depends on the money sent back from "the Gulf" by family members working there. The employment and living conditions of these individuals—who range from professionals such as accountants, nurses, doctors, and engineers to artisans such as carpenters and plumbers, and to unskilled laborers—can be severely restrictive. Nearly twenty years ago, Cynthia Enloe wrote, "At one hospital in Pakistan psychiatrists have treated so many women whose husbands work in the Middle East for symptoms of mental stress that they talk now of women suffering from 'the Dubai syndrome'" (Enloe 1989, 186). Ghassan Kanafani's story "Men in the Sun" (1999) enabled me to make the connection between migrant Palestinian laborers who journey to other Arab nations and the South Asian men and women who do the same.

Landmark 5

No South Asian can ignore the influence of the Mughal rulers on the Indian subcontinent, their generations-long sway in the region (beginning in 1526 and ending in 1707, but continuing in depleted form until 1857) and the gradual anchoring of Islam into the subcontinental landscape. There are more Muslims in South and Southeast Asia today than in the Middle East, a fact that many in the West do not know. India itself has 110 million Muslims, a greater number than in many countries that are exclusive Islamic states. The juxtaposition of several religious symbols and structures in active public space is something that I have grown up with; mosques, temples, and churches standing side by side in Mumbai and Bangalore. Lebanon, with its multiplicity of religious and ethnic groups and individuals' complex intersecting loyalties and allegiances, provides a similarly complex terrain, though it is perhaps less pluralistic than the India I remember. My students are, not surprisingly, bewildered by the sectarian politics of Lebanon (one of them cannot hide his frustration and says, "I just don't get it! Why can't they see themselves as Lebanese?") But they grapple with it, because they realize that unless they familiarize themselves with the fracturing of the civic landscape that resulted in the fifteen-year Lebanese civil war (1975–1990), they will miss the emotional force of Etel Adnan's novel *Sitt Marie Rose* (on the brutal slaying early in the war of a Maronite Christian woman because she casts her sympathy for the dispossessed Palestinian refugees), first published in French in 1977 and translated into Arabic in 1977 and English in 1982, or Darwish's anguished cry at the bombing of Beirut in *Memory for Forgetfulness* (1995).

Landmark 6

But where I feel the most "authority" of voice, where I feel the strongest linkages with the peoples of the Middle East, is in knowing myself and feeling myself to be a postcolonial subject. Let me make a disclaimer: my academic field of expertise is not postcolonial theory or postcolonial literature (rather, it is American literature); so when I speak of authority on the postcolonial condition, I don't mean the authority that comes from years of careful study. But I also do not mean the specious and suspect authority of lived experience; simply because I am from India does not confer on me a postcolonial consciousness. My claim to postcolonial understanding comes from my many years' study of power, an exploration that began with the knowledge of my own ignorance at the British Council library in 1975. In his book *The Darker Nations: A People's History of the Third World* (2007), Vijay Prashad recalls the powerful shared vision of Jawaharlal Nehru and Gamel Abdul Nasser (leaders of postcolonial India and Egypt, respectively) and the promise of the Bandung Conference of April 1955, that brief moment of intoxication of newly decolonized nations that they could be the authors of their own futures, free from the meddling of Western powers with imperialist designs. It is this hope for an *independent* future that I wish to convey to my students, just as I wish them to realize the immense disappointment

of its unfulfilled condition. The retreating powers left behind turmoil—
the India-Pakistan conflict, the Israel-Palestinian impasse—problems
of an intractable nature, challenges that would drain, erode, weaken the
capacity of decolonized nations to direct their own economies and political structures and display good judgment in their decisions. Our study of
Naguib Mahfouz's taut novel *Miramar* raises questions about the promise of
Egyptian nationalism (and the corresponding decline of cosmopolitanism)
and Nasser's focus on the peasant class. This text allows us to study literary
craft and national politics in almost effortless harmony, so skillfully does
Mahfouz use the devices of characterization and symbolism.

Landmark 7

The day, December 30, 2006, that Saddam Hussein was hanged, riots broke
out in Bangalore in one predominantly Muslim neighborhood. Cars and
buses were burned, shops were looted. The situation was fragile and could
have erupted into communal violence—the hanging of Saddam leading to
a confrontation of Muslims and Hindus hundreds of miles away. The irony
is that the protests in India had nothing to do with the people's dissatisfac-
tion with the Indian government; instead, they were venting frustration that
Saddam's hanging, though ordered by a government of Muslim individuals,
nonetheless was master minded by the United States.

There is a similar discontent in South Asia with the United States' involvement in the politics of Pakistan. The Pakistani public (across class lines)
resents the United States' use of Pakistan as a base from which to conduct a
campaign against Al-Qaeda; meanwhile, India sees US support of the erst-
while military dictator of Pakistan, General Pervez Musharaff, as intensely
hypocritical, given the United States' declaration of desire for democracy in
the Middle East and its citing this desire as one reason for invading Iraq. In
a related vein, the United States' encouraging of the late Benazir Bhutto's
return to Pakistan caused deep suspicion among diverse constituencies (the
prodemocracy factions, Musharaff supporters, and Islamic militants) in
Pakistan, who saw the US backing of her as an unwanted intrusion into the
affairs of their state. One could read into this project for the Middle East
and South Asia, as articulated by the Untied States, the long shadow of orientalism: the entitlement of Western powers to affect the politics of nations
in Africa and Asia.

On the first day of class, I present these landmarks to my students. I
disclose to them that in choosing to design and teach this course it is less my
intention to impart knowledge (for I am no expert, as they see) and more
my hope to engage them in uncovering their own individual reasons for

wanting to learn about the Middle East and to become aware of how they absorb and make sense of information. Their willingness to embark on this venture with me—the self-declared novice—is profoundly reassuring. One student says that he really appreciates my "confession" because he, too, is anxious about this course. He has been asking himself, he says, "What was I thinking that I felt I could learn about the Middle East! What foolishness led me to believe that this was something I could do?" Now he can do the readings without feeling stupid, he says with relief. I want to tell him, but I reserve the comment for a later, more teachable moment, that to admit cluelessness is not weakness; it is self-righteous certainty that he should fear, both in himself and me.

The texts we read come to my aid over and over again, providing fertile terrain for rich discussion, contradictions, ambiguities, and frustrations. Through the secondary readings, we immerse ourselves in context, context, context, coming close to feeling overwhelmed but recognizing that this surfeit of secondary reading is essential, critical, to complicating our encounter with the novels and memoirs we are studying. And so we are learning about the breakup of the Ottoman Empire, the emergence of nationalisms, the heterogeneity of ethnic groups, and the meaning of Islamic feminisms.[7] I reiterate for students the implicit message of landmark 3, the importance of heeding history and of paying attention to the links among nations. The Middle East is what it is today because of historical forces—the Ottoman Empire's diminished power at the end of the nineteenth century, the role of European nations, particularly Britain and France. I remind them, too, of the force of colonialism and its impact on the rise of nationalisms in the Middle East (the thrust of landmark 6). Through the fullness of this dense foliage of historical and political context, there flow the literary and cinematic texts.

(a) The students, as always, astonish me with their wisdom, their disarming pronouncements. In a first response paper, one student quotes from Moroccan writer Fatima Mernissi's *Dreams of Trespass* (the first primary text we read) to say that she understands how she should engage the material of the course: like the narrator of Mernissi's memoir, she realizes that "you don't necessarily ask questions to get answers. You ask questions just to understand what is happening to you" (Mernissi 1994, 22). I feel triumphant, because I am confirmed in my belief that *Dreams of Trespass* is a deceptively simple entry into the many complexities of Middle Eastern cultures. Mernissi's language is fluid, accessible, conversational, and lightly humorous. Her tone is familiar and charms the students. She complicates the notion of the "harem" and destabilizes their sense of it as a restricting boundary imposed on women by men. She upturns the urban-rural relationship, showing that it is the upper-class urban woman who is confined, while the rural peasant woman enjoys an unfettered movement. She introduces them to ninteenth-century Egyptian feminists, and she shows them that women like her mother find autonomy and assert their creativity through their home-concocted beauty products.

(b) Of course, I know that the journey cannot always be so intoxicating; I expect that the students will find some texts impenetrable or displeasing, and they do. Most of them reject Hanan Al-Shaykh's novel *Women of Sand and Myrrh*, faulting its awkward prose, its rough transitions of plot, and its exoticized portrayal of helpless women in an unnamed desert nation of the Middle East. They are becoming discerning readers, I can tell, when they critique Egyptian physician and feminist Nawal El Saadawi for her self-congratulatory memoir *Walking through Fire*. They do a close reading of the text to show how El Saadawi uses the unlettered women among whom she practices her medicine as a foil to her own defiance and aggressiveness. They are perhaps too judgmental about what they perceive as El Saadawi's exceptionalism, but the ebullience of their debate delights me. They are learning how to question the narrator's reliability and learning to interrogate her representations of her own country women.

(c) For their final assignment, the students are required to "become editors" and create their own edited version of a literary text from the Middle East. Early in the semester, they identify a "text"—novel, collection of short stories, memoir, or film—that is not on the syllabus and immerse themselves in its "world"—the cultural, historical, and political contexts in which it is set and/or written. At the end of the semester, they write an editor's "Introduction" and carefully select at least five accompanying documents—which could be a mix of primary and secondary material or exclusively secondary material—that illuminate the social, political, and historical contexts in which this work emerged. For every document selected, they include a 250-word rationale for its value. My objective for this assignment is that students see how they use their particular text as **one** window into the vast world of the Middle East and how they actively shape their hypothetical readers' understanding of the Middle East just as I, too, have shaped theirs.

I am gratified that they find this final assignment valuable, as their course evaluations reveal. One student presented a thoughtfully constructed edition of Turkish novelist Elif Shafak's novel *The Bastard of Istanbul*. Another student resurrected for me the beauty of Darwish's poetry and reminds me that I should include his poems in the next offering. Like the course I taught on South Africa, this pedagogical experiment was deeply fulfilling. My students have shed their anxiety at encountering these translated texts and have succeeded in becoming learners. They appear to have acquired an eclectic outlook and the ability to combine "incompatible ideologies and critical viewpoints" (quoted in Huggan 2002, 265). They are the worthy heirs of Edward Said's remarkable intellectual legacy to scholars and readers of the Middle East: a body of writing whose call to see the Middle East with one's eyes, and mind, and heart wide open is too urgent not to heed.

Notes

1. I have written elsewhere (Srikanth 2007) of how a Zimbabwean playwright castigated me for being presumptuous enough to teach a course about a place that I hadn't (when I first taught the course) visited. My initial reaction was to get defensive and to wonder whether he might have a valid point. But more considered reflection revealed to me that I could use my disadvantage to good pedagogical purpose.
2. Ghosh's acceptance in May 2010 of Israel's Dan David Prize for his literary accomplishments has disappointed many of his admirers. Both he and Margaret Atwood (who shared the prize with Ghosh) received letters of appeal asking them to decline the award and to lend support to the campaign to boycott, divest from, and enforce sanctions against Israel for its illegal occupation of the West Bank and its violation of Palestinian human rights. Ghosh's acceptance of the Dan David Prize is particularly surprising, given his rejection in 2001 of the Commonwealth Writers Prize for his book *The Glass Palace*. In a letter to the Commonwealth Foundation, Ghosh wrote,

   So far as I can determine, *The Glass Palace* is eligible for the Commonwealth Prize partly because it was written in English and partly because I happen to belong to a region that was once conquered and ruled by Imperial Britain. Of the many reasons why a book's merits may be recognized these seem to me to be the least persuasive.... The issue of how the past is to be remembered lies at the heart of *The Glass Palace* and I feel that I would be betraying the spirit of my book if I were to allow it to be incorporated within that particular memorialization of Empire that passes under the rubric of "the Commonwealth." I therefore ask that I be permitted to withdraw *The Glass Palace* from your competition.

   The full letter can be accessed at http://www.doononline.net/pages/info_features/features_spotlights/spotlights/aghosh/letter.htm (last accessed on September 6, 2010).

3. In March, 2008, I visited the West Bank for a week. It was my first trip to the Middle East.

4. Beginning in the late 1970s, there has been an unfortunate increase in public expressions of a fundamentalist Hinduism in India, which reached its horrific pinnacle in the 2002 genocide of Muslims in the state of Gujarat, the very region that welcomed the Parsis in the eighth century C.E.

5. Sooni Taraporevala observes,

> There are only 100,000 Parsis in the world today, mostly in India, particularly in Bombay. Demographically, we are a dying community—our deaths outweigh our births. Parsis like to quote a remark that Mahatma Gandhi once reportedly made, "In numbers Parsis are beneath contempt, but in contribution, beyond compare." Out of an Indian population of more than one billion, Parsis number a mere 76,000 [most of whom are located in Mumbai]. (2004, 9)

6. I write about my gradual awakening to the reality of Palestinian dispossession in "Why the Solidarity?: South Asian Activism for Palestine" (2009).

7. Specific secondary readings on the Ottoman Empire include Rob Johnson's "The Decline of the Ottoman Empire"; Maya Jasanoff's "Cosmopolitan: A Tale of Identity from Ottoman Alexandria"; and appropriate selections from Akram Fouad Khater's *The Modern Middle East*.

CHAPTER 6

Teaching Women's Lives: Feminist Pedagogy and the Sociological Imagination

Arlene Dallalfar

Twenty-one years ago we struggled with the recognition of difference within the context of commonality. Today we grapple with the recognition of commonality within the context of difference...Activism is the courage to act consciously on our ideas, to exert power in resistance to ideological pressure—to risk leaving home. Empowerment comes from ideas—our revolution is fought with concepts not guns, and it is fueled by vision. By focusing on what we want to happen, we change the present.

(Anzaldúa 2002, 5)

Beginnings

It is 8 A.M. on a cold January morning. I sit in my freezing car waiting for it to warm up. Excited and nervous, I anticipate the dynamics of my first class of the semester, a weekly three-hour junior/senior-level seminar course titled "Women's Lives: Global Perspectives." Having previously visited the assigned classroom, I know that it will take some time before the students arrive to transform it from a traditional lecture style setting (instructor desk in front of the blackboard and rows of tables and chairs facing the desk) into a formation that allows all participants in the seminar to see and engage in discussion with any other classmate or with me.[1]

My designated classroom is empty, so there are still a few minutes to rearrange the room. As I move and realign tables, desks, and chairs to a rectangular formation, some students enter the room and help me with the task. After over two decades of teaching, I know that these rearrangements are the first essential step toward re-creating the classroom setting consistent with my particular approach to teaching and learning. It will be necessary to engage in this exercise every week for the rest of the semester because the chairs and tables will inevitably be shifted back to their original formation at some point before our next class. This welcome window of preclass time also provides a more spontaneous opportunity for students to approach me. They see that I appreciate their help in moving the heavier tables around. Because the majority of our students work long hours off and on campus, they often do not have time to meet me during office hours—for some, this is the only time we meet outside class.

By 9 A.M., students begin to arrive in larger numbers. I recognize a few from previous sociology courses that I have taught in the Global Studies and Child and Family Studies major. For many, this is a first encounter, and we are strangers. I am also acutely aware that the students know more about me at this moment than I know about them. They have the privilege of access to the "campus street" and have heard about me from courses that their friends have taken. This class is an upper-level elective that satisfies the global perspective requirement in the general education curriculum. It is not a required course; many students are still "shopping" and will decide later if they want to enroll. The stakes are high, and I feel as if I only have this three-hour session to engage, challenge, and entice them to join me in this journey.

To illustrate my pedagogical approach, I use three classroom practices that make use of both sociology and feminist theorizing as an aid to framing, teaching, and engaging in learning as a social process alongside my students. In keeping with the theories of liberatory education set out in the works of Antonio Gramsci, Paulo Freire, Dorothy Smith, C. Wright Mills, Patricia Hill Collins, Henry Giroux, and bell hooks, my goal is to engage students in the act of critical thinking by reducing power imbalances in the teacher-student relationship and arriving at what Gramsci (1992) has termed "the organic intellectual."

Even in my graduate student days, many attempts were made to convince me to accept a hierarchical "banking model" in education and teaching (with the professor as sole authority). But I was drawn instead to a pedagogical perspective grounded in dialogue, reflection, critique, and experience. As Freire eloquently writes,

In the banking concept of education, knowledge is a gift bestowed by those who consider themselves knowledgeable upon those whom they consider to know nothing. Projecting an absolute ignorance onto others, a characteristic of the ideology of oppression, negates education and knowledge as processes of inquiry. The teacher presents himself to the students as their necessary opposite; by considering their ignorance absolute, he justifies his own existence. The students, alienated like the slave in the Hegelian dialectic, accept their ignorance as justifying the teacher's existence—but, unlike the slave, they never discover that they educate the teacher. The *raison d'etre* of libertarian education, on the other hand, lies in its drive towards...reconciling the poles of contradiction so that both are simultaneously teachers and students. (1998a, 53)

As a progressive educator, I am committed to using the dialogical process of addressing both theory and action to cocreate a classroom environment that fosters communication and a more democratic experience. My intention is that students simultaneously negotiate multiple subjectivities in the learning process.

While waiting for the remaining students to trickle in, I ask them to briefly review the syllabus and course requirements. With the exception of one student, all of the students are women (unsurprising, since Lesley College only became coed in 2005). About ten minutes after class has officially begun, I introduce myself, narrating my own story and positioning myself within the larger dominant cultural landscape in the United States. I start with the solo journey in 1973 that took me from my parents and home in Tehran to Boston, where I became an international student. After describing my Jewish Iranian background, I ask if anyone has met any Middle Eastern Jews or Mizrahi Jews before. No one raises her or his hand.

Using this first encounter, I model what each of them will be expected to do after I finish my comments. I begin to describe how one of my primary identifications as a first-generation Middle Eastern immigrant is as grounded in my Jewishness as it is in my being Iranian. It is not hard to explain to them that in both my scholarship and my daily interactions, I challenge the Eurocentric, static, and homogeneous category of a Jewish identity that marginalizes or renders invisible the non-European Jewish experience. My Jewish Iranian experience embodies cultural, culinary, and linguistic rituals that differ greatly from the dominant American Jewish experience.

Now it no longer brings me frustration or annoyance when people express surprise on hearing that I am a Mizrahi Jew. Instead, I use such interactions as an opportunity to explain the rich history of Jews who have lived for more than 2,500 years and continue to live in Iran. Students learn that my husband is a Muslim Iranian man, an anthropologist, and an ethnographic filmmaker, and that we are a secular family. We have two sons born in the United States who identify as Iranian American and are bilingual. The story moves next to my Iranian identity and the discriminatory experiences I encountered as a graduate student at University of California Los Angeles (UCLA) after the Iranian hostage crisis in 1979, and even more so now post-9/11, in my role as a mother with two sons who have been "racially profiled."

Photographs also tell part of my story. I often bring a picture of myself as a little girl and also a more recent one of myself as an adult wearing a head scarf brought back from a recent trip to Iran. These autobiographical remarks always evoke many questions and expressions of interest. Student responses provide me with opportunities to describe this course's focus on understanding the complex intersections of social identity not only by studying and reading about the "other" but also by reflecting on our own identities. This personal introduction is a pedagogical strategy, a moment to model and address the importance of considering one's own epistemology and subjectivity before we set to work on the course content and complex cross-cultural issues about gender and representations of otherness. My next step is to ask each student to self-identify and to similarly focus on a particular aspect of their identity that is important to them, to indicate what topics in the syllabus they are most interested in, and to point out topics they would like more attention focused on in our seminar. I tell them of my academic training and doctoral studies in sociology at UCLA and my areas of specialization in diaspora and immigration studies, sociology of family and work, and ethnography and film, as well as in the now-established interdisciplinary domains of women's studies and feminist theorizing (Felman 2001).

Then I ask students to introduce themselves, to mention what their major is and what courses they have taken to fulfill the prerequisites for this class, to provide a bit of information about their family background, how they self-identify, and what topics they are most interested in studying. This exercise represents a critical step toward transitioning us from a group of strangers to a community of learners. It often takes up more than an hour of the first class. Student introductions vary; some provide in-depth identity disclosure, others do not. This is our first exercise in listening and hearing each student's voice; it introduces the notion that each student's active participation is necessary if we are to engage in meaningful exchange of ideas in the weeks ahead.

On the surface, the majority of the women in the class seem rather homogeneous in age (20–22 years), ethnically Euro-American, Christian or Jewish, and middle class. It is only after the salient individual introductions that the complexity of social identity becomes more apparent as students mention the often-invisible aspects of their individual membership in particular group identities such as being gay or lesbian, growing up in a rural community, growing up poor, being raised in an orthodox religious family, having never traveled internationally, being Muslim or Buddhist, coming from a first-generation immigrant family, or being the first in the family to go to college (Smith 1987).

After this exercise, what was formerly invisible becomes noticeable, and we acknowledge that there is much more "diversity" in our group than had originally appeared to be the case. We link these individual introductions to conceptual categories of group identity and status relative to power and one's differential access to privilege in the social structure. We explore how access to power is based on sexual orientation, class, religion, ethnicity, color, national identity, and one's physical attributes. I refer back to Anzaldua's recognition of commonality within the context of difference and how the focus of this course will be to use the acquired knowledge from this class to challenge assumptions and normative expectations about their own lives and to find points of commonality with women's lives in other countries.

This multicultural exercise is linked to my own commitment to critical pedagogy and to the creation of authentic and meaningful classroom learning experiences. A variety of thinkers in this field have given me inspiration, including Nieto (2000), Giroux (2000), Gallavan (2002), and Patti DeRosa and Ulric Johnson (2002). Using examples from my own as well as student statements, I attempt to illustrate the interconnection and involvement of students as well as myself as teacher in the construction of new knowledge. In this way, we begin the complicated process of becoming a community of learners and developing skills in negotiating intergroup power dynamics within the particular sociocultural context of our classroom.

A student looks at the clock, and as I glance at the time, I notice that an hour and a half has already passed! I stop and ask the students to take a ten-minute break and stretch. Afterward, I refer back to our initial exercise in critical pedagogy and to our active process of creating an intergroup identity—one that encompasses the recognition of individual identity as well as difference and respect for other students' life experiences.

Next, we review the syllabus and discuss in detail the use of inclusive scholarship to study women's lives, specifically women in non-Western cultures, in Africa, Asia, Middle East, Europe, and the Americas. I draw their attention to particular sections of the syllabus that indicate how we will examine the intersection of gender relations with other systems of social categorization in exploring the ways that this interaction impacts women's lives. By referencing particular readings and concepts, this introduction helps them see how this course links with the multicultural scholarship that they should have been introduced to in earlier courses. We discuss the presence or absence of diversity within their previous coursework and the importance of adding a global perspective in seeking and asking different questions about women's lives. Our discussion of the syllabus in this first class is intended to serve a very specific purpose. It helps students to understand that reading alternative texts, watching ethnographic films, and hearing guest presentations provide an interdisciplinary framework that draws on sociology and feminist theorizing to reframe and critique traditional androcentric scholarship on gender, the family, the economy, and the state.

As an Iranian American, I also reflect on how teaching about women's lives in other parts of the world—especially the Middle East—has become increasingly complicated since 9/11, as the US government became involved in the wars in Iraq and Afghanistan, and associated Islam with the ongoing "war on terror." Referring to particular sections of the syllabus, I discuss these controversial issues as well as the stereotypical views of "Middle Eastern" and "third-world" women—the "others" whose lives are seen as so different from theirs. We reflect together on why this is so. We discuss popular images of women, especially Middle Eastern women and portrayal of the body and veiling as representation of otherness in popular culture and media.

I then initiate a dialogue on how feminist scholars have critically examined and offered new theoretical understandings of gendered relations of patriarchy in a number of important domains, including politics and power, economics and globalization, environment, sexuality, and culture. I indicate that we as a group will begin our theoretical orientation or reorientation by reading chapters in Spike Peterson and Anne Runyan's *Global Gender Issues* (1999). Students are required to come to the seminar with their weekly reading and response logs and be prepared to reflect critically and discuss specific questions posed and/or developed for each chapter of the book. In addition, each week, four students will be responsible for initiating the discussion using their personal responses to the questions raised. In this way, we reinforce the importance of student voice and engagement, validating the ever-present dialectic between teaching and learning that occurs for all participants in the seminar.

Feminism and the Sociological Imagination

My teaching as a feminist sociologist has been profoundly influenced by C. Wright Mills's concept of the sociological imagination and the distinction he draws "between history and biography, between private individual troubles and public issues" (2000).This pedagogical approach emphasizes the link between social forces and historical cultural phenomena as an aid to understanding one's private, individual, everyday experiences. The interplay between "history and biography and the relations between the two within society" has also been a core principle in feminist theorizing and the coining of the famous phrase "the personal is political."

Among the theorists, most influential for my work as a teacher is Patricia Hill Collins, who addresses the marginal status of black women in the academic profession and coined the valuable concept of the "outsider-within" to reframe mainstream conceptual categories in sociological discourse. In Collins's (1986, 14) words: "I argue that many Black female intellectuals have made creative use of their marginality—their 'outsider-within' status—to produce Black feminist thought that reflects a special standpoint on self, family, and society." My own academic focus on Iranian immigrant women in Los Angeles emerged out of an outsider within status that (1) helped me to identify my particular interest in gender resources and women's work in the ethnic economy and (2) moved me to examine differences in the acculturation experience and host society discrimination based on ethnoreligious identification as a Jewish or Muslim Iranian.

In addressing outsider within status among sociologists, Patricia Hill Collins suggests a third alternative, that is,

> to conserve the creative tension of outsider within status by encouraging and institutionalizing outsider within ways of seeing. This option is valuable not only for actual outsiders within, but for other sociologists as well. The approach suggested by the experiences of outsiders within is one in which intellectuals learn to trust their own personal and cultural biographies as significant sources of knowledge. (1986, 29)

Addressing these issues stimulates the students' inquiry into their own experiences of being an outsider within. I encourage them to create a section in each weekly log to begin the process of linking readings to personal experiences.

Feminist International Relations

A few weeks later, we are discussing another dimension of the feminist view that "the personal is political," and relating it to Cynthia Enloe's (1990) feminist approach to international relations and her statement that "the personal is also international." Students are required to answer specific questions that relate to these readings in their writing log and to draw connections to their own lived experiences in examining the conceptual issues raised. Typically, each week, three or four students have the responsibility of a five- to ten-minute presentation to initiate the discussion around concepts and applications from the weekly readings. At this point, I don't even have to remind students to bring their reading logs to class; they are ready to contribute to an open discussion that elucidates other meaningful issues and questions raised by the readings. The following student response illustrates the power of using a lived experience and a sociological feminist imagination: Lina responds to the readings and lectures on women's work and devaluation of their labor when privatized (as reproductive labor or use value) as compared to labor that is commodified (as productive labor or exchange value) in the labor market with the following statement:

> When thinking of Enloe's statement that the "personal is international" and the feminist slogan "the personal is political," in relation to my own experiences with the use/exchange value I think of a barter system my friend Molly and I once had. My friend Molly had set up a barter system with her friends where she would exchange her services as a hair dresser for whatever service one of her friends could provide. Molly would agree to cut or color my hair in exchange for me babysitting her daughter. In order for my hair to be done I would have to watch her daughter for several nights for around three or four hours a night. On the other hand, a male friend of ours who was a handyman once fixed her door, and that same day he got a haircut and color. When we went over use/exchange value in class the barter system that Molly and I once had came to mind . . . My friend Molly had assigned higher value to my male friend's work than to my work. His work was seen as exchange value; his service of fixing her door was part of the public sphere and therefore held greater value. This greater value meant that I would receive Molly's services later than he would and had to also work longer for the exchange in services.

This methodological approach to creating voice and encouraging students to engage in a participatory educational experience is primarily focused on students' active participation in their own knowledge creation and premised on the critical examination of their lived experiences. Alice McIntyre (1977, 10) has used "Participatory Action Research" in her book *Making Meaning of Whiteness: Exploring Racial Identity with White Teachers* as a means of "breaking the silence about what it means to be white in our society." Similarly, students are urged to reflect back and recall memories that can be reframed and viewed from a feminist international relations lens by using readings from Cynthia Enloe's *"Bananas, Beaches and Bases: Making Feminist Sense of International Politics* (1990)—in order to discover a different point of entry in the critical reexamination of a particular memory and experience. Erin, in response to the chapter on "Base Women and Military Wives, Rest and Recreation or (R&R) and Prostitution,' wrote,

> When living in Germany, during the Gulf War...it just so happened that one Saturday night as we were leaving the base the van pulled up and about 15 women stepped out of the van. I asked my mother how come all these women were coming onto the base...My mother replied that they were just visiting friends. The following weekend I saw the same van pull up and the same 15 women get out of the van. Again I asked my mother what they were doing and again she said that they were just visiting friends. The van appeared at least once a week until the end of the war. [When] I was reading the chapter about R&R...I again approached my mother about the van on the base. Her response was much different this time as you can imagine. At the time I was too young to understand that these women would be paid to come onto the base in order to entertain our troops.

Alongside the weekly required readings and class discussions, students are also working on a two-part research project. Having selected a specific country/region on which to gather sociodemographic data, they investigate some of the historical, cultural, economic, and political contexts that have impacted women's, men's, and children's lives. This research paper offers a unique opportunity for each student to apply many of the theoretical concepts we have read and to become something of a specialist on a particular country. Students are empowered to take a leadership role both in their individual work on a particular country and in their group work by preparing a presentation on the regional context of the issues they have chosen to focus on. This process allows me to decenter some of my authority in the classroom and reposition myself as both learner and teacher. This engagement with different groups also leads to a better understanding of processes of learning that take more time than I originally anticipated. I am now more flexible and open to student requests to change due dates or decrease certain required readings for a particular week. This process of dialogue and negotiation is an illustration of cocreating a curriculum and moving beyond the banking model of teaching and learning. In addition, students maintain a log in their weekly reflections on their group project, identify tasks and responsibilities carried out by different members of the group, and individually engage in evaluation and assessment of cooperative group work assignments (Fobes and Kaufman 2008).

Students are also encouraged to apply concepts from Esther Ngan-ling Chow and Catherine Berheide's book *Women, the Family and Policy: A Global Perspective* (1994) in their examination of issues of gender inequality and social demographic data. Jennifer's country paper was on Viet Nam and entitled "Street Vending: A Significant Economic Activity in Viet Nam."

> I was startled to realize that in my own experience in Viet Nam every day I had purchased the goods of street vendors. I remember frequently buying the goods from women street vendors in both the cities and the rural villages where I traveled. The fact that this economic activity escaped my radar when I first embarked upon my research in this area is humbling and signaling that indeed women's work often goes unrecognized.

Jennifer's comments clearly link a theoretical concept to her lived experience and contextualize it outside the classroom experience. They reflect a new awareness that reflects active learning and an epistemological and relational application to her learning experience.

Curriculum as a Political Choice

Following Giroux (2000), I recognize how curriculum and the political choices I have made are a way for me to turn theory into action. As a sociologist and feminist in the academy, it has always been clear to me that the classroom is a politicized site where paradigmatic structures of power and privilege regarding class, cultural differences, gender identity, and white/colonial privilege are deconstructed and placed at the center of the learning process. To illustrate the dynamic debates in international feminist theorizing students read both Chandra Talpade Mohanty's original 1984 article "Under Western Eyes: Feminist Scholarship and Colonial Discourses" (1991) and her 2002 essay "Under Western Eyes' Revisited: Feminist Solidarity through Anticapitalist Struggles." In these two publications, Mohanty revisits and historicizes her own theoretical framework after sixteen years and assesses how her work has been read and misread. According to Mohanty,

> It is time for me to move explicitly from critique to reconstruction, to identify the urgent issues facing feminists at the beginning of the twenty-first century, to ask the question: How would "Under Western Eyes"—the Third World inside and outside the West—be explored and analyzed decades later? What do I consider to be the urgent theoretical and methodological questions facing a comparative feminist politics at this moment in history? (2002, 500)

These two publications offer an opportunity to understand the importance of subjectivity in historicizing feminist theories and transnational feminist practices and to demonstrate how Mohanty's thinking has changed as she reflexively considers her past identifications and present role as an educator and scholar in the United States. In class, we discuss the complex cross-cultural issues that Mohanty examines, but more importantly, students address their increased awareness not only about otherness but also about their own subjectivity in that dialogue.

Along similar lines, students read Lila Abu-Lughod's (2002) anthropological examination of "liberating or saving Afghan women"—one of the rationales given for US military intervention in Afghanistan. Abu-Lughod examines the politics and meanings of veiling from the local point of view in Afghanistan, Iran, Algeria, and Egypt and counterposes it with the Western desire and obsession (even among some feminists) to liberate and emancipate Muslim women from the veil.

To expose this fracture even further, I utilize an ethnographic film such as *Under One Sky* (reflections by four women on issues of veiling, Islam, sexuality, and activism) in order to access the first-person perspective into the classroom (Kawaja 1999). We break down many myths, prejudices, and stereotypes through using concrete examples from lived experience to deconstruct the theoretical issues presented in the readings and provide place for the authentic voice of the "other." Orientalist, Eurocentric, and ethnocentric assumptions inevitably enter the public space of the classroom and need to be addressed to arrive at "learning" as a social process. Students consider how to "unlearn" certain assumptions, to reexamine our own beliefs and to make adjustments in order to "relearn" and to take ownership of the process (Wink 1997). A comment by Claire reflects on the impact of the film *Under One Sky*:

> This documentary shows a balanced view of Muslim women who were asking questions of themselves, the world, and their religion that pretty much anyone can relate to regardless of their religion, or background. Viewing this made me ashamed at how I have neglected to realize how far the U.S. process of profiling and "othering" has gone.

In our current post-9/11 global climate, documentary and ethnographic films provide an entry point for students to engage in a cultural analysis of media and text representations of the Middle East and Arabs, the Israeli/Palestinian conflict, Islam, and the veiled women who often become the ultimate symbol of the "other." For some, this perspective is challenging and creates moments of discomfort. Exposing ourselves to these alternative images, embodied in both real or imaginary differences, allows us to

discuss how value is assigned to these images in a way that fosters essential-
ization and justifications of cultural xenophobia (Said 2002; Roffman 2005;
Memmi 2006). The class discussion also allows us further entry into frag-
menting the discourse in media coverage and "news" and into how political
elites and public opinion influence and frame the "other."

For educators, an important site for enhancing cross-cultural and multicultural understanding in this era of rapid globalization is the arena of media
(both informational and entertainment) in communicating and framing
international affairs. As an ethnographic filmmaker, I am interested in exploring how global mass media impacts cultural identity, and how visual literacy
combined with cultural analysis can be used as a pedagogical tool in teaching. Students are asked to bring two distinct images of the "other" to class.
As a group, we discuss the images, what is being framed, and what is being
illustrated, that is, context and misrepresentation in the media, films, and
TV at that particular historical conjecture. Exploring ways to understand the
persistent and powerful negative images and notions of different groups and
cultures within our society and worldwide is an important component of the
interdisciplinary pedagogical approach used in my teaching and scholarship.

In addition to using visual documents to address the importance of
media representations and global politics, guest speakers are invited to offer
a feminist international perspective on diverse issues such as veiling, mili-
tarization of civil society, and the feminist press in Iran. This engagement
serves as another medium for bringing voice and lived experience to the
classroom. These individual narratives serve as a counterpoint to the hege-
monic narratives of gender loyalty and patriotism in times of war and conflict, particularly in relation to Israel/Palestine. Student reflections on one of
the presentations by an Israeli peace activist, Irit Halprin, make it clear how
valuable guest speakers can be to student learning. According to Dianne,

> It is a rare opportunity for me (a feminist from small-town New
> Hampshire) to come in contact with a feminist from another country...I
> think any time you can attach a face to an issue, it's extremely helpful. Irit
> shed new light on the Israel-Palestine conflict, giving me a face, a name,
> and a real life story to attach to my previous knowledge.

Ronnie states,

> I grew up in Israel and I was amazed to learn about her perspective...I
> felt that Irit gave us one point. I was glad to be in class and give my
> point...I learned that it is OK to have many points of view and that it
> benefits and not harms the discussion.

In my teaching, I try to make visible the clear connection between the theoretical and the experiential in order to encourage intellectual development and holistic growth. In my teaching, I am committed not only to broadening students' intellectual horizons but to providing them as well with the analytical tools that permit them to independently pursue their specific interests and professional goals with more confidence. One morning toward the end of the semester as we were discussing the feminist backlash, Lauren, a quiet yet engaged student, described herself as a "closet feminist." Many other students in the class nodded in agreement. By the end of the semester, Lauren was critically examining her own work history in the light of the course material. In her words,

> Before taking this course, I was not aware of the many inequalities I face just because I am a woman...I have always had to financially provide for myself, and waitressing is a profession that allows potential for a large money flow. This summer I worked at a restaurant back home in Gloucester, which was highly patriarchal... Typically, a waitress's duties replicate the many domestic labor duties that are considered part of a woman's gender role... The gender hierarchy in this particular restaurant was never revealed until this class provided the awareness... Now, I realize that... this profession is highly gendered and perpetuates the stereotypical gender roles of women within the public sphere. I wish I had taken this course a while ago, so that I would not have allowed myself to continue the oppressive nature of this business just because of my gender.

In one of my last writing assignments for the class, I hand out the following question for students to respond to in their log and to share with the class:

> *This short answer question is going to be used to help me reflect on the pedagogy I used in teaching this course. Based on readings, writing logs, class discussions, film and presentations, please discuss some new questions or ways of thinking that have come about in how you approach the study of women's lives from a feminist and international perspective. What do you consider most important and discuss the reason for your choice. Please be as specific as you can. Thank you for your feedback.*

Kat's response is particularly revealing:

> The most important part of this class was to embrace the notion that feminism is not just a fight against sexism but rather a lens with which to combat all forms of inequity worldwide... To fight sexism you must also

address racial/ethnic barriers to access, classism, and all the binaries that work to separate and categorize.

Wenjun rethought the entire history of her parents' marriage and divorce in the light of our discussions of the feminist sociological imagination and the quotation with which we began the course:

> Before their divorce, my mother took on the "triple shift" of full-time mother, doing almost all of the use value work, cooking cleaning, caring for me in addition to working full time, waitressing, and being a full-time student, taking three courses at a time for her MBA. Despite her hard work,...my father wanted to be the head of the household and make all the decisions, but he was unable to sustain a job for longer than a couple of weeks, months at most.... The situation can be considered comparable to Rhacel Salazar Parrenas's "Care Crisis in the Philippines" piece from *Global Woman*, by which the men who were left at home while the women went overseas to send back remittances felt their masculinity being threatened because they were not fulfilling the male-provider role. Because my father was not able to economically rule the family, he used brute physical strength to "take charge," throwing his relationship with my mother into the cycle of domestic violence. It took my mother a couple of years to finally divorce my father, breaking free of his tyranny...Again, the "personal is international" as we see my mother move from a woman of Second World country status, oppressed by limited economic freedom and consequently private patriarchy, to First World status, having the financial means to hire other women to do the reproductive work.

The Local Here and There:
Constructing a Feminist Global Sociological Imagination

Using weekly writing logs that link the personal to the international encourages a critical awareness of one's own embeddedness in a particular historical, economic, sociocultural, and political milieu. It also fosters student understanding of other cultures in their own terms. As I attempt to make the students' encounter with feminist theorizing and epistemology rigorous, creative, challenging, and invigorating, I have become more attentive to student backgrounds. Based on the particular projects and interests expressed in the class, I have become more open to revising my original syllabus to incorporate their academic interests as well. It has also been important for me to acknowledge that sometimes this course

represents an initial (and difficult) encounter of students with the aforementioned topics and that there will be other opportunities to continue
refilling the learning cup.

Epistemologically, my multicultural and interdisciplinary approach is
reflexive and relies on principles that emphasize multiple, differing subjectivities through the articulation and critique of the lived experience. As an
educator, I am committed to this vision of change. Fortunately, the classroom is a site where I can bring this vision forward in the courses I teach,
the students I mentor and in scholarship deeply influenced by feminist
transnational paradigms. My lectures, ethnographies, theoretical readings
and weekly writing logs, films, and in-depth class discussions are designed
to engage students. Concepts of family, state, culture, stratification, political economy, and gender are examined cross-culturally to provide students
with an appreciation of the interrelation of different domains of social life,
as well as the range of variability in human social and cultural formations.
Attention is given as well to the historical dynamic of social change among
different peoples and societies.

I focus on the global but allow students to connect their own biographies
and local context to the material being studied. By the end of the semester,
most students—and not just those who are transmigrants or "others"—have
begun to recognize their part in the global system. They can use the skills
they have developed from analyzing it in order to examine their own realities. The readings, writing exercises, presentations, and discussions illustrate
how important the global is for understanding not just the local "over there,"
but the local "here," linking the personal with the intellectual and theoretical. The openness of students to reading out loud from their weekly logs in
our discussions solidifies our classroom environment as a safe space to take
risks, to take ownership of learning, to engage in both dialogue and reflection, and to listen to and appreciate the vast differences in experiences.

As the weeks progress, classroom dynamics become a powerful example
of how to de-essentialize gender identity within our own community as well
as in relation to women's lives around the globe. We discuss the intersection
of daily private/individual negotiation with patriarchy and power (regardless
of region or country or gender) and clarify the feminist sociological imagination. We consider how one's private experiences with patriarchy are contextualized within the public sphere and embedded within a specific historical,
sociopolitical, and economic dynamic. The personal and private is no longer
separate from the public sphere and broader collective institutional group
experiences. The public-private boundary has been destabilized, and in a
period of four months, a fresh perspective is evident. Personal experiences
that were seen as marginal, invalid, separate, and external to economics,

politics, and international relations are now central to the methodology of feminist analysis and the sociological imagination. This process allows other binaries to also break down and dissolve: us/them, here/there, local/global, self/society, civilized/uncivilized, modern/traditional, liberated/oppressed, and freedom fighter/terrorist. The imaginary of difference is contested and the realization that despite the rhetoric, we are more alike than different. It is only through recognizing our differences, our particularity, that we can understand what unifies us as human beings.

This approach defines my approach to pedagogy. Using both the feminist sociological imagination and the concept of the "outsider within," I have learned to trust my own biography as a source of knowledge and a critical lever for examining my pedagogical practice. By using spontaneous examples from my lived experiences in the United States and abroad, I have been able to illustrate how the personal (private) and professional (public) are embedded in one another. Engaging in critical pedagogy brings forward the complexity and ambiguity of social identity—not just as a theoretical exercise but rather as a way to think through experiences to challenge stereotypes, binaries, and labels one is often boxed into. I am reminded of Anzaldúa (2002) and her statement "by focusing on what we want to happen, we change the present." My students have also been collaborators in this choreography and process. Through our engaged and intentional inquiry, we have created a special space for learning that we all are going to carry away from the course after its formal end. Many of them, in fact, will continue to pursue their often new-found interests in feminist and global studies.

Note

1. I would like to thank all my students who thoughtfully participated in the Women's Lives Seminars at Lesley College from 2003 to 2006 and, in particular, Katherine Dunn, who contributed both as a student and as a research assistant. Their voices and contributions are reflected in this article.

CHAPTER 7

Teaching Art History at an Art School: Making Sense from the Margin

Sunanda K. Sanyal

What made me decide to contribute to this volume of essays was a feeling of exclusion, so to speak. Although the literature on the scholarship of pedagogy and the New England Center for Inclusive Teaching (NECIT) seminars indeed resonate with many of my concerns as a person of foreign origin in American academe, none of the speakers at the local NECIT events or the authors of the literature I surveyed represents my discipline. They come overwhelmingly from English departments, followed by a few historians, sociologists, psychologists, and, more rarely, a scientist. So it seems to me that if exploring difference to recognize common grounds is one of the primary concerns of my teaching and scholarship, then it would only be logical to use my apparent otherness among my colleagues in this enterprise as a productive springboard to locate allies. So drawing on the issues of diversity, multiculturalism, and racism in the classroom and in the institutional setting, in this chapter, I examine my discipline's idiosyncrasies that determine its position within academe, its role in an art school setting, its effectiveness as a tool to engage in discussions of social inequities, and my position in the classroom as a male teacher of color representing this discipline. I see this exercise as a form of self-reflection, even as a self-critique at times.

The literature on the politics of pedagogy frequently addresses the question of difference, especially the problem of student hostility that professors—those of color, in particular—face when approaching the issue of race and diversity in predominantly white institutions.[1] Some of those encounters echo my own early experience in the American classroom. My first-hand acquaintance with American academe and culture began in the late 1980s, when I came to the United States as a graduate student. During my early years as a teaching assistant, not too infrequently did I face one or more defiant students who clearly had an I-don't-have-to-take-you-seriously attitude. It didn't take me long to understand that my alien origin, evident in my demeanor, body language, and accent, was responsible for such a defiant gesture. As a countermeasure, I eventually developed a two-sided classroom persona. One was the polite, humorous I-am-here-to-assist-you side, whereas the other issued a silent warning: "Don't try to be smart with me!" I cannot explain how exactly this strategy evolved, but I definitely built "an armor," one that Karen Leong mentions when recalling her ordeals in the classroom (Leong 2002, 193). What Leong sees as a necessary protection for a female instructor of color against student resistance, I needed no less as a male teaching assistant of color. This gradually made my interactions with my students much smoother. It was merely a question of my survival with dignity—a task of moving from my marginalized "third-world status" to the center, where I could return their gaze to assert my presence. To this end, I had to appear abrasive at times to specific individuals, who most often got the message.

The occasional difficulty I had in that early phase, however, had entirely to do with cultural difference—my South Asian male presence in the American classroom. But I hardly ever had to face the problem of classroom controversies over course content, a recurrent issue critically discussed in the literature. This, I believe, is due primarily to the peculiarities of my discipline. It seems, therefore, that a quick look at the character and status of my discipline is important, in the context of which I can then discuss aspects of my teaching.

Art History: A Marginalized Discipline

I believe that the dynamics of an art history course involving such static visual media as painting, sculpture, photography, and architecture fundamentally differ from that of a course in most other humanistic disciplines on at least two counts. First, despite the undeniable immediacy and concreteness of visual images, the referential function of language, notwithstanding all possible contingencies of textual meaning, is capable of triggering much more sustainable emotional links to reality (never mind the cliché, "a picture is worth a thousand words"). The visual arts, on the other hand, have a much stronger legacy of self-referential abstraction, emblematized by slogans such as "art for art's sake"; not to mention a very different kind of market by virtue of the tangible, rather than temporal, character of the end product. Second, although all the arts have their own histories, the history of the visual arts is the only one that functions as an independent academic discipline. At least in American institutions, art history most often stands alone as a department, with no obligatory relation with the art department, the historical reasons for which are too complex to explore here. But the fact of the matter is, with almost two centuries of institutional presence, the discipline has an extremely influential discourse of its own, the mediating role of which is simply indispensable in any systematic understanding of art.

Thus, a visual representation, I argue, is relatively more embedded in its own discourse and that of its history than, say, literature. In other words, if one is willing to restate the generic observation "art reflects life" (a specific referent for each signifier) as something such as "art *refracts* life" (signifiers with ambiguous referents), then the reception of the visual arts in an art history class is less likely to generate controversies. Social and cultural contexts are indeed instrumental in determining the production and consumption of art. But the peculiar trait of art history is that once that art is historicized, social concerns cannot be addressed independently of that history. They can only be approached through issues that are more immediately representational than social. Phrased another way, if representations are refracted images of life, then a discipline that studies those images is at least twice removed from life, because it looks at reality not only *through images* but also *through texts about those images*. This is what I mean by the refracted presence of life in an art history course. Let me illustrate with an example.

I offer an advanced-level course called "African American Artists: Harlem Renaissance through the Civil Rights Movement." I begin with examples of the grotesque visual stereotypes of African Americans pervasive in American mass culture in the nineteenth and early twentieth centuries, such as the little black sambo, the zip coon, the picaninny, the mammy, and the black-faced minstrels. During this segment of the course, especially when I show the incisive documentary "Ethnic Notions," I watch a noticeable combination of discomfort, disbelief, and disgust among both my white and African American students. They ask questions and make observations, the white students speaking with caution. But never have I encountered any uncomfortable debates or critiques.

Later, as I show them sculptures by Augusta Savage and paintings by Aaron Douglas or Archibald Motley, Jr., from the 1920s and 1930s to explain the significance of the dignified images of the "New Negro" in light of the previous stereotypes and place them in the history of American art, the discussion underscores the role of visual representations in a racial discourse without foregrounding race as such. Or, when I talk about the influence of Diego Rivera and other Mexican muralists on the work of Hale Woodruff, Dox Thrash, or James Lesesne Wells, the fact that Rivera and his cohorts were committed communists hardly ever becomes a point of contention. Politics, while always relevant, remains rather off-center.

Fondly recalling his literature classes at the University of Massachusetts Boston, Pancho Savery remarks that they were "always an extension of one's experiences of the real world" (Savery 2001, 210). This, in my view, is not quite the case in a course in art history. The question is, am I using art in this class as an illustration of a racial discourse, or am I regarding art as a sign system codified, among other things, by discourses of power and politics of otherness? The former approach will inevitably trivialize the role of visual representations, not to mention that it would force me to wander into uncharted waters in terms of expertise. It is entirely possible that a presentation of Jerusalem's Dome of the Rock sparks anti-Arab or anti-Semitic sentiments in the classroom, or a discussion of the Danish cartoon controversy in a history of design class offends a Muslim student. But although such an outcome will contradict the claims I am making here, they will also definitely undermine the rationale and purpose of a class in art history.

How do these peculiar traits affect art history's position in academe, especially among practicing artists? The discipline has undergone a major shift beginning in the 1970s, though it was probably the last discipline in the humanistic arena to open itself to that revisionist trend. Its narrow focus on questions of connoisseurship and authenticity (closely tied to museum practice) gave way to the recognition of art as a polyvocal marker of historically specific discourses. Despite this recasting, however, it is still largely marginalized as being especially elitist. Historians consider art historians an ill fit in the larger field of history, and because the majority of art historians and critics are not practicing artists, they are often regarded in American art institutions as a species of pedantic parasites divorced from real-life creative struggles, making a living out of other people's creativities (this resentment ironically stems from the fact that the art critic/historian is one of the agents of the art milieu on whom artists have to depend for their own publicity). Simply put, many artists think that it is an enterprise they can do without (a resentment that ironically stems from the uncomfortable reality that they have to depend on this breed for their own exposure). In summary, it seems that an average art school student has more respect for a historian or anthropologist than for an art historian.

Teaching primarily art history majors at an art history department is obviously far less problematic, because one begins by implicitly acknowledging—or at least eventually learning to recognize—that real-life issues, as they surface in various courses, are a mediated presence. But serving art majors, many of whom literally accept the notion that life can be transformed by art, is a different matter altogether. How, then, can I use such a marginalized discipline indicted of pedantry and elitism to make students aware of social issues, especially when most of them are artists in the making? Rather than be confined by art history's peripheral status within academe, I have always attempted to push boundaries in my teaching and exploit the idiosyncrasies of the discipline to make it meaningful to students. Let me address that more elaborately, after quickly locating my position within the current trends of the politics of education.

The Politics of Knowledge Brokerage

The new awareness of marginalized voices signaled by the revisionist trends of the 1970s challenged the West's hegemony over the right to speak on behalf of the formerly colonized. It has produced a generation of scholars from the third world writing their own histories and telling their own stories, a shift that has eventually been reflected in the altered demographics of faculty and students in previously all-white institutions. This new scenario has acknowledged the birthright of an art historian of Chinese origin to specialize in Chinese or Asian art, that of a Nigerian to study African art, and so on.

Although no one can doubt the tremendous benefits of this shift, one cannot ignore its flip side. An academic culture has gradually emerged in the last few decades, especially in the humanities and social sciences, that presupposes expertise on the basis of race, culture, or other such identities. There is a tacit assumption in seminar rooms, for instance, that a black individual is the most authentic speaker on Africa or the black diaspora. What is more, this trend has created a culture of tokenism in the name of diversity. Instead of any serious revaluation of curriculum on a fundamental level with critical attention to diversity, a few faces of different colors are introduced into a still predominantly white faculty and student body, and an occasional course about "other cultures" is offered, as if diversity is a politically correct task to be accomplished before one can go back to one's primary duty of imparting a sort of value-free, color-blind knowledge.

Not only have such feel-good endeavors given political correctness a bad name, but they are also responsible for engendering a new breed of stereotypes. If an art history department has one historian of Chinese art who is also of Chinese or at least Pacific Asian origin, and a black individual specializing in African art, they are often referred to as those who do "their stuff," as if their areas of interest have special agendas. The specializations of their white colleagues in the various subfields of Western art, in contrast, appear to be all about that value-free knowledge. I find this trend deeply troubling because despite the revisionist sweep, a white scholar's right to specialize in any subject was never really given up; only the right of the Other to self-represent was recognized. The obvious result of this is an unseemly integration without equity.

I was uncomfortable at the outset of my career trying to picture myself teaching South Asian art and being neatly categorized as the Other who, understandably, is an "expert in his own stuff." If postmodern cultural politics has opened up new channels for marginalized voices and encouraged them to transgress borders and celebrate hybridity, then why should a student of African origin studying Renaissance art *by choice*, or a Chinese scholar researching African cultures be considered the odd person out? I felt that the only way I could empower and legitimize my position in the American classroom was by teaching topics that students and colleagues "normally"—that is, in light of my brown body—*wouldn't* expect of me. Discussing the problematic question of an instructor's legitimacy in teaching certain courses, Bonnie TuSmith and Maureen Reddy (2002, 6) observe, "The unspoken understanding that ethnically identified courses are best served by a proper race/ethnic match (although whites are often exempt from this requirement)—while non-ethnic courses are best served by white faculty—is itself a statement of institutional racism."

I precisely wanted to subvert that assumption. Any frustration at the receiving end for failing to overdetermine me was exactly the outcome I desired. So I specialized in modern and contemporary art in the global arena, primarily that of former colonies. I was particularly interested in contemporary artists from those countries who frequently transgress national, cultural, and aesthetic boundaries, offering themselves as hybrids. This not only prepared me to teach and research modern and contemporary Western art because of these artists' obvious connections with it, but it also helped me to expand my knowledge base of various other cultures. As a generalist at the Art Institute of Boston (AIB), I was expected to teach a medley of courses, except Asian art.

Teaching Art History at an Art School

It wouldn't be unfair to say that my institution is currently in its infancy in addressing difference. Students are overwhelmingly from white middle-class and lower-middle-class families, with a handful of Asian Americans and fewer African Americans. There used to be a modest international enrollment, mostly consisting of European and Pacific Asian students, but that has dwindled since 9/11, at least partly owing to stringent visa regulations. To my knowledge, I am the first full-time faculty of color hired at AIB since the merger, and only a couple more have been hired since. Simply put, the institution usually acts as if it is "unraced," meaning that it is often oblivious to its own subject position (Elias and Jones 2002, 10, 12).

Although usually confident about their artistic potential, students seeking admission to art schools are often significantly insecure about their academic abilities. For all the postmodern awareness of the discursive relationship between the practice and theory of art, this is the disappointing reality in most American art schools. When I joined AIB in 1999, it was suffering from growing pains in the initial phase of its merger with Lesley. It had a confused curricular and administrative system in transition. Art history courses were offered mainly by adjunct instructors to satisfy credit requirements for studio majors (now it is a major), without any effective institutional directives or curricular planning. The academic standard was simply appalling, and most students considered the subject expendable. Most of the existing courses were severely lacking in breadth, depth, and variety. Most importantly, they demonstrated very little effort to introduce students to cross-cultural perspectives and the discourse of difference. I therefore decided to design special-topic courses for advanced-level students, as I believed that a course based on a specific theme, rather than a movement or an era, would not only be more enlightening but would also generate more interest in the subject. Two such new courses are "The Nude" and "Art and War." I have offered the former three times and the latter twice until now.

Because the tradition of studying the human form from unclothed live models has come down through the centuries as an essential part of art school training, it seems to me one of the most effective themes for introducing students to issues of gender and racial otherness and the politics of gaze, topics they otherwise would find too esoteric. The course examines cases from different periods of Western art history to investigate the image of the naked human body as an idea playing a crucial role in the politics of representation. The basic objective is to demonstrate that the pictured naked body is a cultural sign laden with contradictory meanings, contingent upon its presentation and context, and that there are multiple voices—some of them silenced by others—behind its production and consumption. Students read selected sources covering a variety of topics, ranging from the nineteenth-century views of nude images, objectification of the body of the colonized, to the contemporary artist's nude self-representation. Like most of my classes, the student population in this one was not even close to being diverse.

The usual format of art history teaching is hardly conducive to interactive pedagogy. Everything from a twenty-foot-long mural to a twenty-inch-tall portrait is standardized by reproduction. Such a role of technological mediation in driving a wedge between the classroom audience and the actual artwork is nowhere as forceful as in an art history class. Furthermore, although students in a literature class can sit in a circle in a well-lit room to discuss texts, the celebrated genre of slide lecture in art history, with its inaccessible lecturer at the podium and the audience facing the projection on the wall in a dimly lit room, automatically imposes a sense of hierarchy and makes free exchanges difficult. To circumvent these obvious pitfalls, I do not lecture from the podium but speak, answer questions, and provoke discussions while walking around the class. This is not too difficult, because none of my advanced classes has more than twenty-five students.

Perhaps because the course deals with the sensitive issue of the human body in its most vulnerable state (at least in a society where clothing the body is the norm), discussions spurred by images often seem to challenge art history's disciplinary mandates. For instance, female nudity in modern art or contemporary photography can ignite debates, even irate exchanges between certain male and female students when a male student, claiming to "speak his mind," dismisses the critique of objectification of the female body in a male-dominated society as a "feminist fuss." The discussion of pornography as a tentative cultural construct also occasionally slips into equally charged—if art historically irrelevant—gendered debates over moral questions concerning pornography. The only time there aren't any disagreements is when I show photographs of naked African or South Pacific women displayed in nineteenth-century trade fairs. Because hardly any of my students have had even the slightest exposure to such racially charged historic material, the discourse of power and colonial racism that frames those images unequivocally shocks them, leaving little room for conflicts of opinions.

Needless to say, the occasional "digressions" from art-historical inquiries present me with interesting challenges. Although most of the debates and controversies my students engage in are intriguing and instructive, they frequently overlook the discourse of the *image* of the naked body as a codified sign and veer off into questions of social consequences of nudity. I agree with Peter Powers (2002, 32) that having an "anything-goes" approach in student discussions never really serves the purpose of inclusive teaching. So whenever I find the basic premise of the course overlooked, I step in to bring the point back home. I am committed to making my students aware of the idea that artists are neither social isolates nor are they social moralists or ethicists who merely use images to make their case. If, for instance, they are to comprehend the historical significance of Edouard Manet's celebrated paintings "Olympia" or "Luncheon on the Grass" from the 1860s, it is not enough—or even a priority, for that matter—to understand the social outrage those paintings caused in the 1860s or the double standards of the male chauvinistic Parisian society of that era. It is more important to learn how previous pictures of the nude inform Manet's work, and how, through radical changes in style, technique, and iconography, the two controversial paintings play a pioneering role in presenting the question of the female nude in art as a complete construct, a product of overlapping power discourses of gender, institution, and class. This will then help students examine the social outrage at those images from an art-historical perspective. Therefore, I have to moderate those debates to make them view social and political concerns obliquely, through the representational lens. My intervention mitigates irate debates and prevents them from regarding the images as incidental to social discourses.

In addition to assigning some writing tasks, I also introduced a week-long class exhibition as the final assignment for this course. The exhibits are not meant to be straightforward academic exercises of nude images but are interpretations of the different ideas and discourses of the nude that the course material covers. Many of them turn out to be innovative appropriations of existing images. Each student has to submit an artist's statement explaining the rationale for her or his project, which is printed and displayed next to the exhibit. Although this is quite an unusual strategy for an art history course, I have always argued in its favor because I believe it offers a particularly valuable learning experience for practicing artists and makes art history more meaningful to them. The show has indeed been responsible for making the course popular.

The other course, "Art and War," had previously been designed and taught by a colleague. After I completely remodeled it, however, it resembles the earlier version only in its title. Because the subject of warfare is no less charged than that of the naked human body, making this theme relevant as an art history course is equally challenging, especially with the United States currently involved in two major conflicts. So I make two points very clear to my students at the outset. First, like the "Nude," this course deals with *images* of war and considers the politics and controversies surrounding those conflicts only insofar as they are relevant to those images. Second, the class is not simply about images *of* war but about images *and* war, meaning that many images may not actually represent war but are tied to it indirectly.

Like the other course, this one also examines selected case studies, with an emphasis on the twentieth century through the current era. Students are first introduced to the power of images in propaganda efforts through such iconic eighteenth-century paintings as Benjamin West's "Death of General

Wolfe" and Fredrick Church's "The Banner of Dawn," so that they can apply some of that logic to critically evaluate the infinitely more complex visual culture of twentieth-century warfare. Unlike "The Nude," this course makes use of a number of documentary films, such as Leni Reifenstahl's controversial "Triumph of the Will," which at the same time has been highly rated as a film and harshly criticized for its alleged valorization of the Nazi convention of 1934. It presents the interesting dilemma of the historical notoriety of a specific subject injecting a discomfort into one's appreciation of a work of art.

On the other hand, a film such as "Resisting Paradise" by Barbara Hammer shows Henri Matisse painting flowers, nudes, and landscapes during the Nazi occupation of France, when his own daughter was arrested for being involved in the underground Resistance efforts. It raises the thorny question of the artist's role during war. Students speak their minds in the journal they keep throughout the semester and engage in debates in online discussions. One of the other provocative topics is the war memorial and the changes in its philosophy, structure, and impact through centuries of warfare. A documentary on Maya Lin's Vietnam Veteran's Memorial demonstrates to them the intensely politicized character of such monuments. I also take advantage of the history of Boston. One assignment is to research one of the many local war memorials.

In this course, I try to equip my students with the awareness and critical tools necessary to deconstruct the visual culture of war. There is perhaps no other democracy where the notion of the "war hero" or that of "serving the country" permeates the mass psyche as much as in American culture. It has an almost religious status in this society. But although I understand the historical reasons behind it, I don't raise the question directly or preach my political views in this class. Instead, I discuss the demise of the myth of the war hero through images related to World War I and obliquely address the issue when showing photographs of the My Lai massacre in Vietnam.

As the course progresses into more and more current conflicts, more and more images that are not generally labeled as "art" and are controversial for political, rather than representational issues, become crucial. Media coverage of current conflicts and informal photos, such as those leaking out of Iraq's Abu Ghraib prison, are notable examples. I maintain an especially dispassionate tone in such contexts, emphasizing instead the psychologies behind the making of such images and their impacts on public perspectives and tastes. The last time I offered this course, I had a male student in the class who had just returned from his service in Iraq. What is more, he had been stationed at Abu Ghraib a few months before the controversial incidents. I consciously avoided putting him under the spotlight, not only because I didn't know how he would feel about that, but more importantly, I didn't think his combat expertise or any other experience from there had much relevance for the course. Though he occasionally volunteered information about Iraq and the army in general, it was quite clear that he, too, was cautious not to draw attention to himself.

Through the years, my two-sided classroom persona that I discuss at the beginning of this chapter has distilled down to a moderate image of authority and a strong classroom presence. Without silencing reasonable voices, I do let my classes know that I am in charge and reserve the right to intervene in debates, but that I am also eager to maintain respectful relationships. As a woman of color facing the question of power in the classroom, Rajini Srikanth (2002, 147) astutely notes, "The teacher's willingness to negotiate must never be seen as a gesture of capitulation; rather, it must be seen to proceed from a position of strength and security." This is precisely my message to my students. Teaching is indeed, as Karen Leong (2002, 194) remarks, "a performance on multiple levels."

I think my "performance" subverts and confuses any monolithic assumptions my students might have about me. It displaces my brownness with a chameleon-like appearance or perhaps a collage, in which the South Asian "I" remains, at best, a part of a whole. The fact that I teach topics that my students probably don't expect me to offer, I believe, provides a unique learning experience for them in an institution with minimal diversity. Several students have candidly admitted to me over the years that I am the first non-white person with whom they came in close contact. As a matter of fact, when meeting new students in the beginning of a semester, I still occasionally find one or two uneasy looks, which, as my experience tells me, are most likely caused by my presence in a predominantly white classroom. Those individuals either become comfortable with me in a week or two or simply drop out. It is possible that while some of my students overdetermine me as an authoritative South Asian male, my balanced view of the gender discourse in a class such as "The Nude" challenges such a stereotype.

It would be too naïve to assume, however, that my teaching strategies make my racial and cultural difference completely invisible to students. Consider, for example, the following instance—an uncommon occurrence, though, in my student evaluations—where a lingering perception of difference leads to failed communication. This is a comment I received from the "Nude" in 2003:

Sunanda is wonderfully energetic teacher, whose strength is keeping his students interested in what he is saying. Talking to him outside of class seems like bit of a hard thing to do, but I suspect this is part of the way he was trained, where the teachers *did not* associate with the students.

It is interesting that this individual gave me an overall 5 (excellent) on a 1- to 5-point scale. She or he was apparently fond of me as her or his instructor but struggled to locate a possible reason for what she or he thought was my occasional abrasiveness. And this she or he found in my (early) educational background in the south Asian milieu, where students and teachers indeed hardly associate. This person, therefore, totally overlooked the significant part of my American education and essentialized me by referring to my racial background. Although a part of me, then, clearly appears as an Other in this student's mind, she or he felt quite comfortable with the rest of me that demonstrated expertise in teaching (I wonder how she or he would have explained a similar miscommunication with any of my American colleagues).

I suspect that it is primarily the nature of the discipline I teach that makes it so difficult for me to gauge student perceptions of me with greater clarity. Had I taught literature, history, or sociology, the likelihood of controversies on various issues related to the course content would have been high. In such a scenario, I would have an opportunity to test how much my race or gender intervened in my students' perceptions of my views or academic expertise, and building the "armor" of authority in the classroom would be a much more arduous task for me. On the other hand, it seems that teaching what I teach also has its advantages. It is precisely because contentious social and political questions are mediated by the peculiar traits of the visual arts and the thoroughly artificial character of the discipline, I have an opportunity to make students aware of vital issues without much unwarranted disruption. After all, I do not believe the gender, political, or cross-cultural awareness students acquire from "The Nude" or "Art and War" is much different from what they would get from a course in history, literature, or political science that covers the same topics.

Making art majors interested in theoretical matters and convincing them to see such issues as relevant to their work as practicing artists is a challenging task, with its dark, hopeless moments. But I have also learned that courses sufficiently critical in content and structure can meet that challenge effectively. The thematic, nonconventional, hybrid courses I offer would probably have come under unfavorable scrutiny in a conventional art history department. So in that regard, I find an art school milieu a much more productive arena, for its tolerance for experimentation and for the freedom it grants me to design new courses and use nonconventional teaching methods, such as an exhibition in an art history class. As my teaching continuously evolves in an academic environment that is challenging and supportive at the same time, I see myself as someone committed to making sense from the margin.

Note

1. See Kingston-Mann, Esther and Tim Sieber, eds. 2001. *Achieving against the Odds: How Academics become Teachers of Diversity*. Philadelphia, PA: Temple University Press. Also see TuSmith, Bonnie and Maureen T. Reddy, eds. 2002. *Race in the College Classroom: Pedagogy and Politics*. New Brunswick, NJ: Rutgers University Press.

PART III

Engaging Students in Learning

CHAPTER 8

The Whole Person in Front of Me: Toward a Pedagogy of Empathy and Compassion

Robin A. Robinson

Genuine communication involves contagion; its name should not be taken in vain by terming communication that which produces no community of thought and purpose between the child and the race of which he is the heir.

(Dewey 1991/1920, 224)

The basic categories of human mental life can be understood as products of social history—they are subject to change when the basic forms of social practice are altered and thus are social in nature.

(Luria 1976, 164)

My name is Jane ___ and I am a social worker in a limited community center, focused quite specifically on helping mostly post-incarcerated women. We provide wraparound services in a unique program that unites post-incarcerated mothers with their children immediately upon release, rather than make them "earn" their children back. We have had flexible seed money that so far, in a pilot program, has reunited families and led to more stable living and employment situations more quickly, and provided services to reduce everyday stressors for mothers and children, and to increase nutrition, sleep, and everyday health. We now seek funds to expand this program in the region. Please refer to the briefing memo I have distributed, and allow me to explain.

> University of Massachusetts Dartmouth student,
> Mock testimony of an imagined program
> for the course Female Crime and Deviance.

Introduction: Creating a Collaborative Mood

The course is Female Crime and Deviance. Thirty students, more or less, sit up or slouch on black, plastic desk-chair combos, an utterly generic university scene on an utterly typical mid-semester afternoon. Some talk quietly, some bolt a sandwich or chips, and some check their cell phones or finish a text message. As I enter the room, most put away what they are doing and shift into class mode. They are respectful, mostly, patient, ready for the lesson. The lesson I have prepared for them is this: to embark on a six-week project that will push each to embrace and explore an alternative identity associated with a communal social concern, and, in small groups, to merge these constructed identities into teams of collaborators who will research and design organized and detailed responses to social problems. They will prepare testimonies to convince a mock legislative committee to fund their inventions. They will take on problems of mental illness, of family and community violence, of reintegration following incarceration, and of health care, education, training, and employment. Bearing their adopted personas of constructed histories and challenges, they place themselves in others' shoes, walk a mile, and work to understand, from the inside out, some of what social policy means and does. And in these mock enactments, as students create and advocate social welfare policies and services, they enter the worlds and identities of their imagined alters: contrived at first, perhaps, but nearly always genuine and internalized in the end. In so doing, they grow in compassion and empathy.

The lessons I have prepared for them originate in the many years of community work that were my professional—and in some ways, personal—life before I became an academic. I worked in neighborhoods with throwaway kids and their thrown-away parents, in psychiatric hospitals and clinics, in programs for adolescent mothers and their children, and in quite a few other venues to serve, and sometimes to segregate, what are called, politely, vulnerable populations—true enough—but also are subjects of racism and other vicious biases, and bearers of unconscionable social burdens. I worked at the most local levels of social policy as well as in federal offices in Washington,

DC. When I prepare lessons of social policy for my students, I pass along substance and processes I have gathered and gleaned along the way. But most of all, my intellectual energy and compassion in the classroom—and students' learning and responses, loud and clear in their work as well as their evaluations of my work as teacher—reverberate with my determination to make lessons of social justice intellectual, visceral, and irrevocable.

Toward a Pedagogy of Compassion and Empathy

My job is to contribute to the enrichment of human minds. Implicit and explicit in the nature of what I teach—policy and justice studies—are worlds of facts and dynamic models of individual and group interaction; so, too, there is a realm of social identification that has as much to do with the Other as it does the Self. My academic home is the University of Massachusetts Dartmouth, a public institution whose roots are in textile training programs situated in the historical continuum of the Industrial Revolution in southeastern Massachusetts. The university serves, too, the sons and daughters of those whose families, for generations, have worked the largest commercial fishing port in the United States. Though the university has diversified in recent years, through intentional outreach, quality and volume of faculty research and programs, and value in times of economic uncertainty, the student population remains largely that of first-generation college students from middle- and working-class families, including those of immigrant diasporas of several national identities.

This chapter describes, in brief, methods that I have developed in order to integrate didactic learning with the development of compassion and empathy for differential experience with subject material that I cover in courses about social policy and social justice. What follow are methods I use, for example, in Women and Social Policy, pedagogy I employ to help students engage in learned knowledge through (simulated) personal experience. I approach collaborative learning efforts using two techniques in particular, one for first-year students and the other for upper-level students. The exercise with first-year students is a semester-long series of assignments for Introduction to Crime and Justice Studies that I call, collectively, The False Accusation Project (described in the appendix to this chapter).[1] In this chapter, I describe and discuss more fully the upper-level exercise that I have created for students in two courses, Women and Social Policy and Female Crime and Deviance (a course that explores and identifies social constructions of female deviance in contexts of social control of women and girls), which leads them to focus on the development of their own policy responses to social problems, culminating in The Mock Legislative Testimony. (Currently, I am developing another upper-level course, Religion and Justice in Society, which will culminate in a Mock Truth and Reconciliation Commission.)

An approach that concurrently addresses the subjective/reflective and the objective/didactic is likely to touch emotional experiences among students, and so a second purpose of this chapter is to address, or at least to raise, a psychodynamic perspective of the undergraduate college classroom, with attention to fears and anxieties that arise and/or are exacerbated by differences, real, and socially constructed.[2] My claim here is that the use of empathy-building exercises in the classroom, through group work, writing, readings, film, and other exercises, may alleviate such fears and anxieties and promote inclusiveness by underscoring, examining, empathizing, and creating ways to resolve and/or support difference as well as to promote connection.

To Locate Myself in This Work

The substance and process of the work I describe in this chapter flow from personal challenges and responses that I have described elsewhere (Robinson 1996, 2000), and that, suffice to say here, involved circumstances that led to labels I carried for a long time, impeding for a time my young adult dreams and ambitions, among others, of higher education. Social challenges and labels, for me, related to real threats to survival. Processes of working my way through each of these revealed clear patterns of ignorance and injustice among those who judged me and others like me: false constructions of character and ability, false accusations, false assumptions of what might help, or—for better or for worse—unwillingness to help at all.

I write this as one who enters the classroom with a clear vision of how my early experiences inform how and what I teach. The dynamics in my classroom echo the intensity of my early struggles, and at the same time inform my work with students who have had struggles of their own. The personal transformation that initiated these innovations in pedagogy was this: I came to understand that the labels and injustices perpetrated by some, ignorance and clumsy assistance by others, were much more products of their fear and powerlessness than facts or judgments specifically about me. Had they asked me what I needed, I would have told them. Their expressions of fear and powerlessness precluded my voice in a dynamic of social problem solving. When I became a teacher, I knew that one way to challenge labels and injustices, false assumptions, and faulty conclusions was to provoke—or, in fact, require—students to transform substantive materials into living social problems and to assume roles of real stakeholders in the issues to seek solutions. And the way to facilitate that was to push them to enact the real social processes that I had learned, long ago, drive policy responses to social constructions of the Other.

This methodology, of necessity, requires considerations of psychological safety and respect of students' privacy and agency as I prompt them to manufacture and then to engage, with compassion and empathy, visions of suffering and struggle. I know what personal meanings and responses such images hold for me, but I do not know those they may have, or not, for each of the students. I have come to think of this construct of awareness as *ethical empathy*.

To Conceptualize Ethical Empathy

Engagement in this intentional task of growing compassion and empathy among students requires awareness that there are multiply-determined microdynamics of solidarity and resistance beneath more obvious student-teacher dynamics. Some faculty engage in a pedagogy of empathic exchange with students as equals, but I am still thinking about boundaries, conflicted about the protective space between the personal and the public when working with students and colleagues. Using the personal in attempts to embrace those who may seem most alienated may very well be projection on the part of some faculty who have not yet resolved their own discomfort in the academy or who seek to create a comfort zone by blending with students of backgrounds similar to their own. On the other hand, empathic exchanges in one-to-one encounters may support students who are facing challenges similar to some I have known. Some of this is a measure of common sense but goes beyond that to real questions of exposure, reserve, introspection, and whom each serves: a question of pedagogical ethics. This matter may be a direction to continue a concurrent conversation, one that proceeds in its own domain and, at junctures of faculty-student connection, weaves through a pedagogy of empathy.

How do I create safety in the classroom for students to engage in dynamics of empathy and compassion? What is my voice in guiding them to find their voices in expressions of empathy and compassion? Daunting and perilous though it may be, if a central tenet of my pedagogy is to lead students to transformative experience, what processes do I develop to provoke, to promote, to support, to nurture, and, finally, to sustain the empathic perspectives I value—and yearn for them to value—as a product of the time they will have been with me as their teacher?

I teach lessons of the social fabric, of human interaction, of human suffering and want, of valorous work to alleviate misfortune, of plodding work to serve the deranged and annoying because they are human, of making the law a tool of service with models of compassion and processes to achieve empathy. Implicit in my most fervent efforts to infuse these lessons is a core of recognition on my part that each of my students arrives in the classroom with an inventory of experience, unknown to me. The pedagogical task, and the ethical pursuit then, for me, is to design a fifteen-week program of information and stimulation to reach the whole person in front of me, in ways that make sense to that student. I must not make the mistake of assuming I know the student because I have been one or any other faulty assumption of identity or experience. At the same time, I must model empathy and compassion. Perhaps my credo should be, to paraphrase Anna Freud (1969, 239): "I shall remember not to confuse my own with the (other's) appraisal of the happening." Perhaps it is the goal I should teach: to recognize and respect individuals' interpretations of their own experience.

Fear, Anxiety, the Unconscious, and the Freeing of Compassion

The genesis and manifestations of conscious and unconscious fears and anxieties are present from birth, and when mild—in normative conditions— produce, in a sense, tools for the individual to build adaptive thoughts, feelings, and behaviors, given any social situation. The story is a complicated one, but I suggest that driven by fears and anxieties promulgated by judgments from peers and authorities, by performance expectations, and by internal dynamics of common fears of childhood,[3] students' defensive thoughts, feelings, and behaviors may impede the development of empathy and compassion, of experiences of inclusiveness, and of possible responses of individuals and collectivities to injustice. Such fears and anxieties may recapitulate those of childhood, and as the student seeks, consciously and unconsciously, to create defenses to cope with such fears, obstacles to learning may develop and present in the classroom.

To fail at one task is to come perilously close, psychologically, to failing at others. The prospect of unchecked failure, of course, would lead to the individual's annihilation—of the ego, the sense of a competent self, at least. To put this in the language and spirit of the classroom, to fail at one task is to create just cause to defend against failure of another or risk loss of regard (i.e., love) from authority (professor, *in loco parentis*) or even expulsion from the class or university (conscious and unconscious fantasies take off!), where such abject failure may represent annihilation. So what do students often do when faced with tremendously challenging material, especially that which engages the emotions as well as the intellect? They may back away, look for the short cut, evade critical thinking and emotional response, and withdraw from the course. Students who have little or no contextual map for a placement of self in the academy (e.g., first-generation students) may feel especial pressure to avoid all but that which is reasonably safe and predictable. The addition of emotional material to didactic challenge may be overwhelming. Furthermore, anything that makes the student different from others promotes anxiety. The result of this combination may become a constellation of unconscious fears driven by fantasies of failure and subjugation, which manifests as resistance to do the work, let alone resistance to emotional engagement in the subject matter. A further manifestation of this constellation of fears may be the coalescence of likely or unlikely peers who come together in a dynamic of defense against common fears, expending finite emotional resources.

My method is to structure didactic learning to have purposeful elements that recognize student fears, that address the fears in the approach to classroom material, and that extend beyond the didactic to form a pedagogy that promotes relational aspects of learning, such as empathy and compassion. To underscore common experience is to ameliorate difference and attendant anxiety and thus to promote inclusiveness. It is this modeling of empathy in the classroom that may promote a truer community. I seek to bring students to perceive and to understand how they are as individuals in the context of community. Here, I find my own compassion and empathy in dual engagement: modeling possibilities and modalities of concurrent learning and feeling and bearing witness to students' responses to my pedagogy of compassion and empathy.

The Mock Legislative Testimony

To promote these goals and values, I created The Mock Legislative Testimony to be the final and major group exercise in two courses called "Women and Social Policy" and "Female Crime and Deviance," at the 300 or junior/senior level. The project presents students with the challenge and opportunity to create group membership in a common cause as they prepare testimony to support a new program, of their group's design, to serve the needs of women and girls who face issues in a policy area previously studied in class. Students meet in working groups to discuss and determine what service they will put forward and to adopt roles of stakeholders to support that service, followed by weeks of focused literature review about the specific policy area. Finally, by group, each student presents a five-minute testimonial talk, in the role of a stakeholder, to describe the need for the service and/or (depending on the role) how the service will address the need and be implemented.

Before students receive this assignment, for the course Women and Social Policy, for example, we have spent ten weeks working on concepts and substance of basic and perceived human needs, after the model suggested by David Gil (1992) in his classic work, *Unraveling Social Policy*.[4] We have applied this model to fictional and actual accounts of women in social contexts, of juveniles, working women, mothers, the elderly, and other groups. We have tangled with multiple sociopolitical models of power and policy analysis and the social policy process. We have struggled with the limitations and possibilities of needs assessment instruments in the formulation of human services and the reformulation of policy. I infuse this potentially overwhelming amount of sociopolitical theory and method with real stories of real women in need and in peril[5] and imagined stories that make the policy spheres of women come alive.[6]

Perhaps the most searing critique I would make of social policy in the United States today is an adherence to technocracy by so many policy makers, with little direct experience with women and girls in the social margins, in their determination of what such women and girls need, and what they will receive.[7] And because most of my students with majors in Crime and Justice Studies or in Sociology will be entering professions in law, policy, or human services, I want them to *feel* their social policy education as well as understand the substance.

Much of the substance in this course—violence, sexual assault, domestic violence, child sexual abuse, substance abuse, poverty, neglect, and others—can upset students in any of several ways: heightened fears, identification with a known victim and/or survivor, reflections of frightening experiences, flashbacks, and nightmares. For this reason, at least, I believe students benefit tremendously as they become compassionate and serious learners of this profound material through the most effective and responsible methods I can design to help them find room to project their fears, anxieties, and conflicts while learning challenging substance. The mental room to speculate about disturbing material through immersion in fictional accounts and memoirs, case studies, and in The Mock Legislative Testimony also prompts students to generate questions and debate about the issues, thus stimulating critical thinking on these topics, rather than passively adopting media clichés. The Mock Legislative Testimony includes ways to help students identify the learning and relational skills they have developed and to practice and imagine ways to apply these skills across disciplines, throughout their education, and into their work lives.

Over quite a few years of assigning and refining this exercise, I have found that the most effective way to develop the groups is on the first day of the course. Right at the beginning, I have the groups count off—ideally six in a group or four groups in a class of twenty-five or so—with no exceptions for roommates or dating couples who want to be in the same group. Though at first I wondered if I would alienate them by laying down such a rule, rarely does anyone object. My reason for the randomness of the groups (and that is the result, as friends usually sit together, and by counting off I break them up) is to create the opportunity to build new community, to raise awareness of familiarity and difference, and to challenge them to experience the newness of others' personal and cultural perspectives—all in the service of increased inclusiveness. I ask each group, on the first day, to come up with a group name; in this, I push them to work together for the first time, to create a new identity each will carry through the semester, and that they will carry as a newly formed group.[8] This first-group effort also serves to break the ice and to ease the establishment of group dynamics with nonthreatening content.

By the time they reach the first stages of developing the mock legislative testimony, they have been working to build relationship within their groups through discussion of profound subject content (about which they may differ wildly!). I have taught them and they have read about and they have engaged with each other about myriad perspectives of women in society. They have worked with me to understand and apply concepts and analytical approaches to stakeholder analysis, social class location, sociopolitical and philosophical models of power and influence, consciousness of culture, social problem definition, historical perspectives of social policy, women in the polity, theoretical models of troublesome women's behaviors, and relationships between social policy and social control. Then, I give them The Mock Legislative Testimony assignment about five weeks before the testimonies begin in class. I assign each group a very broad policy domain and charge them with the task to define a niche topic for which they will design an innovative policy response to a perceived social need in the community.

Through collaboration and consensus building on all matters of the exercise, each student in each group assumes one of several roles, to sustain throughout: a member of the target population to be assisted, a professional in the chosen niche of the assigned policy domain, an advocate, an expert witness, and others of their choosing. Each student develops a testimony to represent his or her interest in the establishment and funding of the policy response, and students in each group work together to coordinate the overall testimony to be delivered to convince a mock legislative committee (another group of students) of the worthiness of their proposal. Each group of students participates twice, in the delivery of their testimony, and as mock legislators hearing and questioning another group's testimony.

Quite often, students comment on final course evaluations that The Mock Legislative Testimony was the most valuable part of the course. Nearly all the students embrace their adopted roles for this project, some to the extent of dressing the part on the day they are to deliver their testimonies.[9] They have prepared the material for this exercise in the figurative shoes of another, while engaging in a rigorous academic exercise of research and needs assessment.

They present their testimony in three forms: (1) in a carefully condensed version of all their research into a one-page briefing sheet of bullets (a preparation for real-world presentation of an idea or proposal to a busy administrator or committee); (2) a spoken testimony based on the bullets in the briefing sheet and embellished with connective narrative; and (3) an annotated bibliography of the substance and narrative they have prepared. Though a few students take the path of least resistance and deliver polemic, most students prepare carefully researched, responsible testimonies to support their claims and proposed policy remedies. Moreover, the quality of the ideas they generate for policy responses to social problems overall compares quite favorably with those of practitioners in the policy domains that students are emulating. Furthermore, students demonstrate empathy, compassion, and substantive understanding of salient issues as a result of their work on this project. And finally, students engage, with their own voices, in the synthesis of substantive material with experience and communicate that to an audience effectively.

Some Testimonies

At the beginning of this chapter is a quote from the testimony of Jane, a student in Female Crime and Deviance, whose group decided to propose an innovative program that would bring together just-released women prisoners and their children. We had studied through several sources and viewpoints the perils to family of such separations; most students were not only distressed by the suffering of the innocent children but also understood the limitations of extant social services as they were currently organized and funded. Jane's testimony began the description of what students imagined, with compassion for such challenged families, might be an alternative means to bring together mothers and children. Besides Jane, the social worker, members of the group assumed roles including the eleven-year-old daughter of an incarcerated mother, a community advocate, a holistic healer, a teacher who organized an after-school component to the program for the children, and a parole officer.

Another testimony project grew from concern about rape counseling specifically for teens, who are admonished from all directions not to have sex and who may not report or admit to being raped, fearing blame and retribution. I had read accounts of such assaults aloud to the students from several quite effective works of fiction, including Dorothy Allison's *Bastard Out of Carolina* (1993), Maya Angelou's *I Know Why the Caged Bird Sings* (1983), and Georgia Savage's *The House Tibet* (1991). We addressed this social problem from several perspectives, deconstructed and reconstructed causal stories and traumagenic effects, and discussed etiologies of later behaviors including alcohol and other drug use, violence, mental illness, early pregnancy, sexual acting out, eating disorders, and other possible consequences. In a group that I charged with the task of designing a program to address any form of violence against women, this group—which called itself after a woman with a horrendous abuse history, at that time on trial for murdering her children—decided to address rape counseling designed for teens. One quiet student from a rather conservative immigrant family, Anna, introduced herself as a police officer who works "with teenage victims of rape, females, to divert them from engaging in predictable sequelae." She described in swift but effective detail her plan of her own design that would "integrate police officers in community settings to model safety in going to police and reporting rape," noting that 61 percent of rape victims are under eighteen years, and 22 percent are under twelve years. Richard's testimony of an imagined father whose sixteen-year-old daughter committed suicide following a rape enriched his own and others' perspective of this experience:

> My daughter, Kathleen, experienced all the symptoms they describe of rape trauma syndrome, and she even recorded the rape in her diary, which we found after she died. She complained of soreness and body aches, and pain that could have been physical or psychosomatic. She became really isolated, and didn't want to be in school much. That was probably because she was raped inside the school by an old friend who transferred to another school but then came back. She wrote in her diary that her stress dramatically increased, and she had what they call sensory memories from the incident, like the guy had beer on his breath, and later when she smelled beer, she had a panic attack. I am here because of what happened to my daughter, and because very few teens would feel comfortable telling their parents about a rape. I want there to be a responsible and respectful way for teen rape victims to get the help they need.

Richard was able to take a good deal of factual clinical and policy information and make it come alive and in so doing, evoke compassion and empathy for the imagined characters and the personal tragedies that drive the clinical and policy stories.

Another stunning testimony was the work of Jorge, who had come to the university from Puerto Rico to study and who intended to return. Jorge was a little older than most students and was married. His presentation gripped us all, as he testified in quiet, emphatic tones, softened at times by tears, of the effects on him and his wife of an assault she had suffered a few months before. His plea as a man, feeling shut out from the services offered to his life partner and beloved, feeling guilty and responsible for what had happened to her, having no solace sent his way, deeply affected the students and me, and indeed, it took a reality check when Jorge finished talking to recall that he was speaking as a fictional character, in some ways, perhaps, and not others. Moved beyond mere words to respond to Jorge's presentation, students and I mobilized to bring the director of the university Rape Crisis Center to class to discuss and recommend supports for partners of rape victims. Jorge went back to Puerto Rico, with a master's degree in social work, and the last I heard was teaching social work students.

Facilitation of the Personal

I have neither cajoled nor invited students into this exercise of simulated personal experience of thorny policy dilemmas and services to vulnerable populations. Rather, I have required them to participate in these activities as a condition of passing the course, and for most of them, for gaining credit in a required area of their academic progress. In a sense—and I must acknowledge responsibility for this choice—I use my authority to influence personal engagement with the didactic. This stirs in me compassion for students about whom I may know little, they who may be assuming or witnessing—under my tutelage—roles mildly or terribly close to some experience or person they have fled or have tried to flee in some near or distant past, for whom this exercise provokes discomfort or retraumatization. And it has happened. I must balance this risk with substantial benefit. None of us can know the effects we may have on the whole persons in front of us, and so we should proceed, I would argue, with expectation that we might cause inadvertent harm, and with preparation that we might transform that harm.

I demonstrate empathic anticipation on the first day of the course, when we review the syllabus, when I stand in front of my students who do not know what to expect, really, and I admit that I, too, am in the dark. I am in the dark not about the material I am about to teach them, but I acknowledge that I do not know to whom I am speaking, I do not know their life experiences, frames of reference, beliefs, points of pain and gladness, and sensitive subjects that could shut them down. I issue a caveat that we are about to study material that may be troubling, that may cause physical and/or psychological distress, and I tell them that if that should happen, they should seek counseling support, and that I can and will help them to find it if necessary. And I always follow through. Most students have a low threshold for faculty disrespect or disregard of them, and to ignore this aspect of the lesson is to risk a backlash of disdain or mistrust that may go beyond the immediate. This is critical, I believe, to the truth of my intent in working with a pedagogy of empathy and compassion.

Also, on the first day, I assign students to keep a semester-long reflective journal of intellectual connections and personal thoughts and feelings; I grade this only on effort and completion, not substance. I include this as a contemplative practice in support of my pedagogical goals.

And so, I seek to create a safe container for students to work with disturbing material on several levels at once: to build a knowledge base of the subject area, to project applications of the learned material to extant social dilemmas, to grow in relational strength among themselves in the endeavor, and to develop empathy and compassion in specific and generalizeable ways.

Transformative Education: Empathy in the Classroom and Beyond

How powerful it is for a student to write in her journal that this course changed the way she thought about women and distress. Perceptions change. "I thought I knew" is such a common first sentiment in the last journal entries of the semester. At this point, students will have read hundreds of pages of theory, research findings, speculative essays, and illustrative supplemental texts, and all that has contributed mightily to their new working knowledge of women in social context. But it is quite clear that much of what they have learned lies in the realm of engaging with texts and exercises that evoke the challenges that real women and girls face in the public sphere. They have learned through empathic engagement in mock testimony, through small collectivities of sustained and focused interactions around troubling social dilemmas. They have coalesced quickly in temporal efforts to imagine solutions to social problems that come alive for them quickly because they are founded in the real-world policies they have studied.

The first transformation of this pedagogy may be that empathy for others alleviates fears that others intend to harm the self. If I have compassion for you, perhaps you reciprocate compassion. I have argued that to fail at one task is to come perilously close, psychologically, to failing at others, and so to disturb equilibrium and to provoke fears of collapse of a competent self. The competent self is internal and task oriented as well as external and relational, and so the perils of failure—substantive and relational—may manifest in tandem, according to the nature and magnitude of the fears and anxieties any one individual must defend. In the classroom, such fear of collapse of the competent self may impede the student's ability to engage in the collectivity of the classroom and thus *to learn*. The structured practice of collective engagement in common cause in the classroom provides a place of normalization where such fears can be contained for the while, and perhaps processed, going forward. So the alleviation of students' self-perceptions as Other may be a step in empathic development, and it comes from within as internal fears and anxieties of intellectual failure approach equilibrium with external fears and anxieties of relational failure.

Perhaps specific to the provocative material I teach in this course, students may recoil from or deny deeply traumatic possibilities of women's lives, because these possibilities seem too awful, or the truths too unbearable. Emotional disturbance may impede learning. The structured use of collaborative work of this nature in the classroom brings students of differential experience and perspective together in the service of solving, together, troubling social problems. I can report that a great exchange of individual experience occurs within groups (which in filtered form occurs among groups in the testimonies students create). In this, they may find relief from individual fears and anxieties, spoken or not, as they experience empathy and compassion for each other.

I bear witness to the transformation of so many of my students as they grow in empathy and compassion for populations who previously had been often, to them, objects of scorn, ignorance, pity, or disdain. Each semester, I stand humble in the face of the testimonies students produce for this assignment: I see so much more of the whole persons in front of me. A contemplative pedagogy of reflection through collective and collaborative enterprise provides, I think, another face of empathic development: as students work together, with similar and mutual fears of failure and loss in the presence of their peers and as witness to traumatic substance, they gain mastery over what had been, to them, possibly unknown and are able to sustain a measure of compassion and empathy, extending it forward to work and to love, however defined.

Appendix

The Mock Legislative Testimony

Group Project: From Theory to Policy to Praxis
    Services to Women and Girls as Policy Responses to Social Problems
    Project Objectives

- To use what you have learned about elements of social policy and social responses to address social needs of girls and/or women related to the policy areas of work, violence, and health/sexuality.

- To work within a group to identify, to research, to recognize the importance of, and to convey the roles of various stakeholders in the creation of services to address such needs, such as victim/survivor, advocate, helping professional, administrator, legislator, and community support;
- To learn to write and to practice writing a briefing that explains your role, position, testimony, and request in a succinct and effective manner;
- To articulate your position before a group of questioners—both skeptics and supporters—in an organized, brief, and coherent speech.
- To learn to listen to the positions of others and to ask pointed questions to clarify their intent.

Group Assignment

This assignment should be demanding, enlightening, collaborative, and fun (really). You will have the opportunity to create group membership in a common cause as you prepare testimony to support a service of your group's design to serve the needs of women and girls who face issues in a policy area, as we have talked about so far this semester.

1. You will meet in your groups to discuss and determine what service your group will put forward and to adopt roles of stakeholders to support that service. I am available by e-mail, phone, in class, and in my office during office hours to assist you in any way I can. Since coordination of meeting times seems to be something of a difficulty, I will provide an hour of class time, total, to meet on two days, so that I can be available to consult with your groups in class. Additional coordination among the members of your groups can happen through e-mail, phone, or whatever works for you.

2. For the group presentation/testimony, each group will:

   - receive from me an assignment of a service area of need;
   - research the area of need as it applies to women and girls in communities and/or correctional facilities, such as employment and training, education, housing, medical and/or mental health needs, community reintegration, and others.
   - assign/decide stakeholder roles for each group member and carry out stakeholder analysis;
   - organize the group presentation—one group member presenting a brief introduction to the service that the group is presenting/supporting, and a five-minute presentation from each group member, each in her or his role.

- prepare a one-page briefing sheet for the group's presentation, in bullet form, that summarizes the key points of each person's testimony and clearly presents the need and how the service will address the need.
- give me the briefing sheet the class before your presentation, so that I can copy it and distribute to the questioners and to the class before your presentation;

3. For the group receiving the testimony, each group will prepare one question per group member to ask the each of the presenters.
4. Each of you shall:

- prepare a one-page briefing sheet that summarizes your testimony;
- give me the briefing sheet the class before your presentation and distribute to the questioners and to the class before your presentation;
- prepare a five-minute testimonial talk, in your role, to describe the need for the service and/or (depending on your role) how the service will address the need and be implemented;
- respond to a question during the testimony.

Evaluation

I shall evaluate each student on:

- the quality of your one-page briefing sheet;
- the quality, creativity, content, and organization of your presentation.

Peers within each group will evaluate each group member on their collaborative experience with each, on numbered scales and with comments.

I understand that some people are uncomfortable or even worse talking in front of groups, and I will not take away from your grade for hesitation, stumbling, or other sign of anxiety, as long as you show in your presentation that you are organized and have put effort into researching your role and the issue. (I was the kid with the knees knocking during oral book reports in fifth grade—I understand stage fright.) We have all been together for the last three months, you will be part of a group, and students generally get into this assignment, so *relax and enjoy.*

Here is an example of one group's briefing sheet to address the policy needs of women reentering the community after jail or prison. (Students are restricted to one page with bullets, to simulate a real-world policy briefing.)

Group 1—Los Unos
Statement of problem: Education and training are imperative for women who are coming out of prison or jail and need extra supports to get back into a productive and independent life.

Background: Every year (number of) women in (name of jurisdiction) are released from prison and go back to the community, often to children who have been in the care of someone close to the mother or state-sponsored foster care. In many cases, children are returned to the mother if she has made certain that she can provide them with safe and adequate housing, food, child care, and a healthy home environment.

For life to begin again on the right foot, a decent job is imperative. For a decent job to be attained, the right education and training are imperative.

Policy proposal: We propose a policy for women released from prison. These women have just finished their sentence and may be free to move back with their children, provided they have housing. They need a job, but because they have been in prison, they are unfamiliar with current education and training requirements. They wish to go back to school to get the education they need but are also in need of childcare. These women will be permitted to attend school part time and also work part time to provide their children with food and shelter.
We are:

- (Names: testimonials from target population): One teenage mother who has been put in jail for prostitution, and one mother in her thirties who has been put in prison for theft. Each single mother has given her children to a close family member to be taken care of. Once out of prison, they would both like to get back into school to get a better job than they were in before.
- (Name of childcare director): This director runs a childcare service that is state funded. Childcare is given on a needs basis; families are evaluated by their financial status and physical needs of childcare. Those who are in greater need of services will be given subsidized childcare, funded by the state.
- (Name of career counselor): This counselor is found within the institution of learning that the single mother attends. Once education and/ or training is complete, this counselor will help the mother find a job that suits her lifestyle: allowing her to work full time but still take care of her children.
- (Name of financial aid counselor): This counselor assesses the financial needs of the single mother wishing to attend school. He will assess

the cost of her both attending school part time, working part time, and taking care of children, mainly full-time.

- (Name of psychological counselor): This type of counselor will assess the mental health needs of the mother who has just finished her sentence in (jail) prison. He or she will also work closely with the children, as poverty and separation may cause depression in both the children and the single mother. He or she may also report back to the Department of Social Services (DSS) and comment on the living environment, which makes it imperative that the single mothers stay in school and work as well.

Summary: Our policy proposal is designed to fit the needs of single mothers leaving the prison system, going on transitional assistance, taking care of children, while at the same time trying to get the proper education needed for a substantial career.

The False Accusation Project

The False Accusation Project consists of five essays throughout the semester that reflect upon introductory text issues on constitutional law, criminology, social constructions of deviance, social movements, and gendered justice, as well as supplemental texts and films. Works have in common a theme of false accusation, to which students are asked to relate with a sustained, semester-long thesis associated with a personal experience; I make the reasonable assumption that nearly *everyone* has been falsely accused of *something*. The essays, to address the goals listed above, are as follows:

1. Describe a time you were falsely accused. (The purpose here is to establish as a text students' accounts of their own false accusation story, as an exercise in self-empowerment, producing legitimacy for a personal experience through the creation of a narrative. The classroom context for this exercise is the storytelling and alternative narratives of the Salem witch trials, including testimony from the trials, reading from Arthur Miller's *The Crucible*, and several other texts.);
2. How did it feel to be falsely accused? (The development of this essay requires the introduction of the affective element—I am particularly emphatic about the use of first person active voice rather than passive voice. Because of the case study provided by the text, students examine the nature of landmark Supreme Court cases that address rights of the accused and other aspects of constitutional protections, as well as threats to same. We consider the Scottsboro trials and appeals, the

historical context and dynamics of the Scottsboro trials and appeals, including socioeconomic and political factors of the Depression period, racism, and the Jim Crow era, xenophobia, anti-Semitism, the strengths and weaknesses of labor solidarity, and other contextual phenomena. I ask students to write about how it felt to be falsely accused, giving the context of the situation.);

3. What was it about you or the situation that caused the false accusation? (At this point, students have been learning about and discussing issues of demography and identity, and with this essay, they locate the markers of each that may have caused the false accusation. To accompany this exercise, we watch and discuss the film *In the Heat of the Night*, and they discuss study questions about the film in larger consideration of contemporary aspects of race, class, and gender in the criminal justice system. I encourage students to maintain the first person and affective elements of their reflection on identity and dangers of stereotypes, scapegoating, circumstance and association, and other elements of false accusation.);

4. What was the process that led to the outcome—sanctions, exoneration? (Students learn concepts and terminology related to the courts, the jury process, and intrapsychic as well as interpersonal dynamics inherent in such processes. Together we watch the film *Twelve Angry Men*, and together we discuss in detail the character development of each member of the jury, observing, too, the nature of dynamics among the jurors. I encourage students to engage in a reflective process of considering the nature of their "conviction" or exoneration, the feelings, reactions, and cognitive processes they engaged in through the experience. Here, too, we address the respective structures and characteristics, history, and cultures of retributive and restorative justice practices.);

5. How can you or others use your experience of false accusation? (Though not on my original syllabus, students in my class the first time I taught False Accusation Project asked if I would show the film *The Shawshank Redemption*, a film about the false conviction of a man, who in his revenge against the system that imprisoned him, breaks the law and triumphs. I told them I would do so if they agreed to write an extra essay: this became the fifth essay, the final exam for the course, and asks students to incorporate all five questions into one integrative essay. Here students write subjective and objective perspectives of accusation, relative and absolute determinations of guilt and innocence, social constructions of crime and criminality, processes of law and justice, correctional control and community reintegration

issues, and the continuum of responses to social constructions of crime and deviance.)

Notes

1. The False Accusation Project is an innovation for Introduction to Crime and Justice Studies, to encourage a broad and deep exploration of issues in the field, beyond students' preconceptions of criminal justice and law enforcement topics. Often, students enter this course expecting material that might appear on popular "ripped from the headlines" television programs, with serious crimes discovered, investigated, and solved in neat packages of compressed time. Here, I seek to challenge students to think critically about justice issues and assumptions of race, class, ethnicity, and culture, to think comparatively across cultures, nations, and eras. Inherent in these challenges are theoretical constructions and systems of thinking from several disciplines. Goals I identified for this method included the following: confidence building (through writing and speaking); anxiety reduction (through writing and speaking); empathy building (through the use of challenging supplemental texts); identity marking (through supplemental texts, writing, and speaking); trust and critique of process (through writing, supplemental texts).

2. Many of my students are first generation, that is, first in their families to attend college; in 2007–2008, 65 percent of students at the university where I teach, the University of Massachusetts Dartmouth, were first-generation students. Most are working at least one job to pay for their education. They represent many ethnicities and cultures, and many are immigrants or first-generation, hyphenated Americans.

3. Anna Freud determined from her work with children in World War II, and following, defense formations of children (Freud 1966, 1969). From this work, she discussed a general outline of the three basic fears of childhood, fears that underlie conscious and unconscious formulation, and motivation throughout life. The three fears of childhood are as follows: (1) fear of loss of love object, (2) fear of loss of love from love object, and (3) fear of annihilation. These fears produce anxiety, for which the individual organizes defenses, so that fear and anxiety do not overwhelm the individual's conscious and unconscious thoughts, feelings, and behaviors that are adaptive and productive.

4. Gil's model suggests the organization of basic and perceived human needs by use of the following domains: biological/material, productive/creative, social/psychological, security, self-actualization, and spiritual.

5. See, for example, Nancy Lee Hall's *A True Story of a Drunken Mother* (1990) and *A True Story of a Single Mother* (1994).

6. For example, I assign Anna Quindlen's (2000) novel of domestic violence and escape, *Black and Blue*, and Margaret Atwood's (1998) speculative novel of militaristic control of women's bodies, *The Handmaid's Tale*, among others.

7. See, for example, my articles "'Crystal Virtues': Seeking Reconciliation between Ideals and Violations of Girlhood" (2004) and "'It's Not Easy to Know Who I am': Gender Salience and Cultural Place in the Treatment of a 'Delinquent' Adolescent Mother" (2007).

8. Group names reflect diverse references among students and have included, among many: Athena, Gold-diggers, Sexy Six, Outnumbered (five women and one man), Revolution, News at Six, Child Savers, and *Los Unos*.

9. Outstanding in my memory is the student—amiable, bright, responsible, and vocal in class—who assumed the role of a pregnant teen in need of various services. She came to class on the day of her testimony with a substantial bulge under her sweatshirt. I was appalled—at myself!—for neglecting to notice all semester that she was pregnant. At the end of class, when she removed the pillow from under her shirt, we all laughed—at me.

CHAPTER 9

Teaching Ethics through Multicultural Lenses

Janel Lucas

Introduction

Teaching demands that we constantly assess who we are, who our students are, and how these reflections relate to what we do and how we do it. As an African American woman, my experiences with racism and oppression form a lens through which I experience and view course content, student interactions, and student-faculty interactions. As a teacher, my concern is to move students along the path of cultural competence (the ability to recognize and empathize with a wide range of human feelings, needs, and desires, despite the cultural barriers and challenges that various relationships may present) (Kiser 2008). The teaching of ethics—my major specialty—similarly calls upon us to explore who we are within the contexts of our experiences and suggests a developmental process, especially for students like mine, who are preparing to become counseling practitioners. In the following discussion, I will explore the ways that particular approaches to pedagogy can support the work of moving students toward ethical and cultural competence.

The Role of Faculty Identity

I came to teach at a university level after many years of practicing clinical social work, primarily with populations of color. I worked primarily with troubled adolescents in inpatient and group settings. Throughout my teaching career, I have continued to maintain a small clinical practice working with chronically mentally ill adults. These two identities come together in keeping with my university's broader educational mission as well as my own approach to teaching and learning: the integration of theory and practice. This is essential in an institution such as ours, dedicated to preparation programs for educators and human service professionals.

My training and work as a clinical social worker form the basis for my teaching. One of the most important guidelines for the professional clinicians is to start where the client is. In the classroom, the same rule applies. I constantly assess and reassess my course goals, student needs, and responses and modify my approach where needed. Clinical skills also play a role in my understanding and responding to student experiences and to the emotional challenges that arise in the classroom. For example, the ability to connect with students, empathize, and de-escalate disagreements between students requires skills similar to those used in developing a relationship with a client. Facilitating classroom discussion calls into play skills similarly required to facilitate a psychoeducational group, where you attend to the emotional as well as the educational needs of the group participants. Just as locating and providing the correct service requires knowledge regarding eligibility, program requirements, and so on, teaching clinical skills requires similar knowledge bases. Remaining up-to-date in the field and aware of the challenges students encounter during their internships or as they enter the field permits the professor to engage students in discussion of an applied approach to the provision of human services.

Just as my students' identities play an important role in the classroom, my identity as an African American woman impacts the learning environment on several levels. Every class I teach involves social justice teaching. It involves such reflective practices as "processing," "debriefing," and "feedback" (Adams 1997, 31). Although these may be (and should be) inherent in any course, they are particularly critical in a course on critical ethical thinking and decision making taught by a woman from a disenfranchised population.

In the field of counseling, it is expected that practitioners be at least one stage beyond their consumers with respect to their identity development, and I have similar expectations of myself in the classroom. As a faculty member of color, I have to be able to deal with questions, statements, reactions, or actions that may be naïve, discriminatory, prejudicial, and at times racist. Instead of being offended, I need to know how to turn it into a "teachable moment" and continue to work toward the education of the student(s). One approach is to rephrase a comment or question or clarify a concept: for example, specifically educating a student that we do not use the word "colored" anymore and how offensive that is to people of color. Or, frequently students will refer to an inner-city community in globally pejorative terms (ghetto, run down, etc.). A useful technique is to redirect the comment or question back to the class or to ask other students for their experiences and observations. Usually, there is someone in the class who is willing to contradict the student's perception either through direct experience or second-hand knowledge, or who will begin the process of critical discourse. Often the most direct approach of confrontation is the last approach used, resorted to only when other techniques have failed.

While at times it is important to directly confront or address students' comments, sharing my own experiences within a clinical context also provides an apt parallel process to similar comments in the classroom. In discussing cultural competence, I often give examples of challenges I have faced in the field. For example, a common approach to diversity is to pair clients with therapists of similar ethnic and racial identities. This occurred in one of my former professional work settings. As the only professional of color on staff I was assigned to work with a young African American woman for whom it was felt I would be a good role model. However, she resisted working with me, feeling I was an "oreo" because I had "made it," and it took us several months to work through her resistance.

On the other hand, some clients initially present that they are comfortable with a professional who is of a different race, ethnicity, and so on yet continue to drop suggestions that this is an issue for them: for example, "all of my providers are black" or "I've never worked with a black provider before," and so on. Again, within the clinical setting, it is important to pick up on these cues and readdress the issue at hand. Such examples provide an opportunity through direct experience to model for students the importance of open discussion regarding differences and clinical techniques, set the tone for open dialogue in the classroom, and demonstrate the importance of sharing what can be painful or difficult experiences. They also serve to put on the table what may indeed be a similar experience for them, that of having a faculty of color who is in a position of power.

For all students, my identity raises issues of power and authority. However, for some students, there is a resistance to my authority in the classroom environment, where instructors generally are the consummate authority figure. In this institution, we are a small group of faculty of color, and we are diminishing in size. We are supportive of each other and find it imperative to process our experiences, in some cases more formally than in others. One issue that is frequently discussed is that of the dismissive attitudes and behaviors of many students toward faculty of color. For example, "If that had been Dr. X...," would that student have responded in that tone, asked that question, perused that magazine in class, made that comment, or reacted in that way? Or, the fact that some faculty feel it is critical to have students use the title of "Doctor" as a way to maintain a minimal standard of acknowledgement regarding their role and status. These are just a few of the more subtle ways in which faculty of color have to contend with their authority being undermined in the classroom.

In an earlier work focused on the teaching experience of a black faculty member and a white faculty member coteaching (Havas and Lucas 1994), we addressed how white faculty are accorded more power, consistent with the "status and roles assigned within the group or the larger society" (Pinderhughes 1989, as cited by Havas and Lucas 1994, 46). We were initially impressed that students eagerly addressed issues of race and class more readily when we cotaught than when we taught individually. Students made assumptions regarding my own experience (assuming I was raised in a predominantly black community, when I was not) and similarly saw my coteacher as coming from a privileged background (though she did not).

Although initially the students viewed our power differential as consistent with our minority/majority status, at times my own lack of power as a woman of color was compensated for by the fact that as a practicing social worker, I often taught the "more interesting" clinical component of the class. In this instance, in fact, my former coteacher, the program director, actually did have more power as she was responsible for the program and the overall content that impacted students' learning, and I was a new faculty member.

Given these dynamics, we agreed that as a white woman she would take on the role of addressing student comments that were inappropriate, as students (and others) are more likely to hear information that is inconsistent with their self-perception from those whom they perceive to be most like themselves. She modeled for white students the ability to be white and to engage in antiracist work, while my role began to challenge conventional stereotypes that students had of African American women.

The attempt to abrogate power holds true at times for students of color as well. For example, there appears to be the nonverbalized or even at times the verbal expectation that faculty of color should somehow give special dispensation to students of color. This is complicated by the fact that white students often believe that this is the case. On the other hand, my observation is that faculty of color are also perceived by students of color as being "harder" on students of color in comparison to other students. In more than one instance, I have been asked by students of color why I "was so hard" on them. Although this is not the case, I do find it important to discuss with students of color the realities they will face as professionals of color. Thus, in some instances, I become an informal mentor as they may not be as readily chosen for mentoring by other faculty.

Finally, my identity plays a significant role in what may be viewed as challenges to my authority. As an African American woman and social worker, my ethnic and professional cultures revolve around the constructs of collaboration and mutuality. Thus, my approach in the classroom is to come from that stance of collaborator and working toward consensus. For some students, the importance placed on involving them in classroom decisions and valuing of perspectives may be viewed as my attempt to compensate for a lack of knowledge or confidence in my approach.

The Undergraduate Context

I teach within a school of undergraduate studies focusing on professional studies. Thus, students in my courses aspire to be counselors, social workers, human service workers, case managers, advocates, and policy makers. My courses generally focus on helping students to understand the wider context of service provision and within that context, to develop generalist helping skills. As all students complete three significant internship experiences, my courses integrate knowledge and experiences from the field. Course expectations are that students understand themselves in relation to others on a micro, mezzo, and macro level.

Over time, our student body has become increasingly diverse. Once an institution primarily attracting a fairly white, middle- and upper-class female population, currently approximately 25 percent of our students are students of color (indigenous and international) who represent the range of socio-economic statuses and backgrounds. However, the representation of faculty of color appears to be decreasing, with very few administrators of color.

Although generally supported by my colleagues and administrators, there is an isolation and responsibility that is inherent in one's role as a minority faculty member in a relatively small program with a small number of faculty of color. A curriculum of particular interest to you or the small group of minority students is unable to be developed or offered. Also, there is the additional need to be a mentor to students of color either formally (e.g., as the African, Latino, Asian, Native American (or ALANA) advisor) or informally and to be supportive through attending ALANA or other diversity events. Occasionally, this need is parallel to the need to informally mentor faculty of color as well, to support their endeavors, to serve as a sounding board, or to come together as one of the few. It is a critical survival mechanism to gain support from that which you give. Within the context of institutional dynamics, there are the pedagogical challenges inherent in a variety of courses. Contemporary Issues is a course that most extensively challenges the coexistence of identity, pedagogy, and culturally relevant teaching.

Contemporary Issues in Human Services

First defined by Gloria Ladson-Billings as cited by Adams (1997, 34), culturally relevant teachers "see knowledge as doing, discuss their pedagogical choices and strategies with their students, and teach actively against a 'right-answer approach.'" Similarly, the overall focus (ethics) of this course, Contemporary Issues in Human Services, the senior capstone course for students in two of our professional majors, Counseling and Human Services, and the students' personal and internship experiences provide an additional impetus for the role of culturally relevant teaching. Students leaving this program will enter graduate programs of psychology, social work, or mental health counseling, or begin entry-level human service work as counselors, child welfare social workers, mental health aides, or after-school counselors. This course is the last gatekeeping course that students face as they prepare to join the world of professional helping. When they leave this course, we want to know that they value and have integrated the voices of multiple perspectives (cultural competence) and have developed the skills required for lifelong learning and service to others.

Integrating Social Identity Models

As educators, it is important to understand our students and the learning environment. Understanding students' social and cognitive developments become critical tools in this process. Although these processes often involve an informal process on the part of the instructor, in this course, two social identity models take a more formal role. In general, social identity development models describe developmental processes in which an individual's internalized stereotypic or negative beliefs about themselves can be surfaced, processed, and transformed into an identity that moves beyond subordination (Adams 1997). This course focuses on identity models such as Helms's racial identity models and models of homosexual identity development. Generally, the models refer to "stages" or levels of awareness that are flexible rather than fixed. All of the models include acknowledgement and inclusion of a group's sociopolitical history and move from a position of internalized racism, privilege, or homophobia, to a self-affirming inclusive perspective. Discussing these models provides an opportunity for students to assess their own growth and development as well as to understand how they relate to and impact their work with others. Thus, we are able to simultaneously work on the development of self and others. As racial identity is linked to what is usually one of the most powerful experiences in this course, a brief synopsis will be included here.

Racial Identity

Racial identity theory states that an individual's experience of race in the community and in society influences their self-concept and worldview (Cross 1991; Helms 1990, 1994). Helms's work has its roots in Cross's seminal theory of nigrescence, based on a process viewed as a "Negro to Black conversion experience" (Cross 1991, 189). Helms has articulated models of identity development for people of color and whites. The model regarding people of color assumes the experience of oppression and the recognition and transcendence of internalized racism. In Helms's models, statuses are beliefs, values, and behaviors that shape an individual's approach to and functioning in the world. Similarly, one's experiences in the world affect one's racial identity formation or status functioning. Thus, there is a dynamic process between the individual and their social context.

Racial identity is integrated in this class in several ways. First, students read articles that briefly define racial identity development and apply racial identity theory to counselor development (Trickett et al. 1994) and that integrate the constructs of racial identity and homosexual identity development (Akerlund and Cheung 2000). Class discussion articulates the constructs, and students begin to apply the model individually to their own identity development. Although this is not a stated goal of class discussion, it spontaneously occurs as students critique the model and begin to consider how it relates to their own experiences and where "they fit" along the continuum.

There is evidence that racial identity is related to the classroom and is a critical component of clinical work. For example, one's racial identity is related to a student counselor's course work or professional development (Ponterotto and Mallinckrodt 2007). Similarly, Day-Vines et al. (2007) relate a counselor's stage of racial identity to the ability or interest in broaching the issue of race in discussion with clients. Thus, the literature provides a basis for integrating theory and practice and demonstrates racial identity as a critical component of clinical work, an area of development that students highly value.

The Pedagogy of Multicultural Lenses

Within the context of ethical and multicultural identity development, this course focuses on models of homosexual and racial identity development (but more specifically on racial identity) for several reasons. First, I feel it is important to recognize and validate the often-invisible minority that lesbian and gay students comprise. Differential power issues related to gender are frequently discussed, but those related to sexual identity are often overlooked. Students also need to understand and be prepared to work inclusively and to recognize parallels between racism (sexism, homophobia) and internalized racism (sexism, homophobia). Second, students of color and lesbian women are the two largest minority groups in the class and most likely in the institution. Third, as an African American woman, I have felt it necessary to move students in this course beyond what often feels like diversity 101. Despite a program that "infuses multicultural content throughout its curriculum," anecdotal student comments suggest that students often do not recognize that they are just beginning their journey toward competence and that this is a lifelong learning process.

Although students have studied racism and homophobia, they seem relatively unaware of the developmental processes related to racial identity development or homosexual identity development. More specifically, racial identity is viewed as an important component of culturally competent counselor training, and counselors are expected to function at least one level higher than their consumers (Watts et al. 2002). Fourth, as an African American woman and a social justice educator, I concur with Adams and see it as my role to help students make connections between their awareness and action, to discuss the risks involved in challenging discrimination or oppression, and to help them identify personal or small group actions for change (Adams 1997). Finally, I strive to consistently model for white students and students of color cultural competence, the first tenet of which is that you must not be afraid to raise, discuss, confront race, racism, and so on. For example, when asked directly about the comfort level of working with an African American therapist, one former consumer denied that this was a concern. However, this same consumer continued to mention that all of her providers "were black." This example highlights the importance of raising the issue of race and racial differences and the importance of listening for indirect references or opportunities to discuss race.

Challenges in the Classroom

This course presents multiple challenges for faculty and students. Recently, the course has become increasingly diverse. In one class of twenty-three students, ten (43 percent) were students of color, whereas another class consisted of twenty-four students, eight of whom (33 percent) were of color. Although there is the occasional dilemma related to pedagogy, the central challenges revolve around classroom dynamics as they relate to issues of race and power. In other words, the classroom itself becomes a laboratory of developing identity, cultural competence, and ethical relationships. As such, developing safety in the classroom takes on a heightened importance.

Despite the "power" that one holds as an instructor, as an African American woman, the changing dynamics of the course enrollment lends support to what can frequently be a lonely position—that of being one of few women of color in the room. However, although a critical mass is important, in this course, larger numbers of students of color did not always translate into a more "positive" learning experience. For example, in one class with a larger group of students of color, discussions regarding race and racial identity were frequently tense. More specifically, one student of color who shared her own struggle with racial identity felt painfully abandoned by her peers of color, resulting in her emotional withdrawal from the course and effectively shutting down substantive discussion. Intervention required addressing the silence and "elephant in the room" and engaging in considerable discussion after class with the student who was wounded by her peers' actions.

Although a critical mass is important for some students' sense of safety, more central is the composition and development of the entire class and the multiple dynamics that support or impede their development as a cohesive group. This can be accomplished by using exercises that provide an opportunity for students to explore their own value bases and share those perspectives with those who hold contrary positions, engaging in activities that place them in the perspective of "the other" (such as a debate position opposite their own), and encouraging group development through consciously manipulating small group activities and group memberships (perspective, race, and professional interest).

Small group work can be a powerful way to begin to develop classroom safety. Group work allows students to discuss and discern their similarities and differences, and consensus is often more readily achieved. It is more difficult to remain anonymous, and many students find it easier to take risks regarding their perspectives with a small group of their peers rather than with the entire class. Groups also provide an opportunity for students to take a leadership role, or this role can be manipulated, supporting students' personal growth. In short, group work nurtures the opportunities for students to deepen their self-exploration and enhance their knowledge of each other, critical aspects of sound pedagogy.

Cultural competence is a foundational concept in the professional literature and is a component of all the professions' code of ethics. For example, being culturally competent is an ethical mandate for counselors (Kocet 2006), and counselors must first understand how culture affects their own view of self and others (Sue and Sue 1999). The latest revision of the American Counseling Association's Code of Ethics takes particular care to "ensure that multicultural and diversity issues are incorporated into key aspects of the counseling practice" (Kocet 2006, 230). As ethics and cultural competence are key components of the helping professions, they are central to this course and are central to the challenges of teaching these constructs.

Pedagogy of Ethics

An overarching pedagogical approach in this course is based on Kolb's Experiential Learning Model (Kolb 2006), using a variety of pedagogical techniques that help students engage in self-inquiry and potential growth. In this model, learning activities move from concrete experiences to observations and reflections, toward the formation of abstract concepts and generalizations, concluding with testing implications of concepts in new situations (Kolb 2006).

One particularly effective technique I use is to ask students to construct their own "hierarchy of values" (personal, agency, professional, and client). In this exercise, they construct and glue to paper the abstract entities representing the values they hold, the values a client may hold, the values of the profession that they have learned throughout their education, and the values that an agency demonstrates through its mission, services, and so on.

This exercise has been a particularly engaging and powerful experience throughout the course. An early lesson of teaching is that when students struggle or grapple with material they are engaged and get more from the experience than when just "fed" material. Students "struggle" on several levels as they attempt to concretize their own abstract compass. In this exercise, they struggle with the exercise of placing one value in relationship to another, what they have learned about ethical choices, where their own values should come into play in the professional arena, and consequently, they struggle with themselves.

They are then placed in small groups to discuss their hierarchies, similarities, and differences. As they begin to share their constructions with each other, they of course begin to recognize that these hierarchies ask them to confront their assumptions about themselves and their classmates. For example, in one class, one student loudly commented on her very good friend's hierarchy and she (jokingly) proclaimed that this person should not be allowed to work with others. The student had developed a hierarchy that placed the client's values above her own. Much to the surprise of the student who commented, as a group, we discussed the student's perspective, and as a group, we concluded that her stance was indeed consistent with an approach to sound helping practices.

My approach to this course is informed by my identity as an African American woman who was raised and educated in a majority environment, began her professional development as a social worker and as the only or one of a few workers of color in majority social service and mental health settings, and teaches in an institution with a minority of students of color and faculty of color. As an agent of sociocultural change, I bring my own experiences (clinical as well as those regarding race) into the classroom. For example, I share with students my own challenges to be viewed by those similar and different as a competent clinician, or as a faculty member. Some of my experiences include that parents *still* are often surprised that I am a faculty member and in conversation upon finding out may comment "good for you" or that a student described me to her mother (with whom I was speaking on the phone sight unseen), that I was "cute," a comment that devalued my status and role as her advisor. This example seems to resonate with students who may themselves have had these same thoughts or heard similar comments in their own homes, which they sometimes share.

Classroom Techniques/Student Responses

The values hierarchy experience begins to break down barriers between students and reinforces the individuality of members of the class. At the same time, it provides an opportunity for class members to discern commonalities as well, building classroom cohesion. The level of self-disclosure in this exercise provides an excellent foundation upon which to base other substantive and difficult class discussions. Students experience the changing nature of values, ethics, and racial identity and use these frameworks in their understanding of themselves, their peers, and their clients. The exercise draws parallels between the exploration of ethics and cultural competence and thus the relationship between ethics and social identity.

As a way to concretize constructs of the model of racial identity, I show a video, *The Color of Fear* (1994). *The Color of Fear* is a video by Lee Mun Wah, which depicts an encounter group of eight men who spend a weekend discussing race and racism. The men are of Asian, African American, European, and Latino descent. One particular white male of European descent (David) engages in behavior that is recognizable as racist while

176 • Janel Lucas

denying that he is a racist ("I have several good friends who are colored"). Other examples of David's comments include the following: why do others identify themselves as African American or Japanese American, why don't they just identify themselves as American? He further states that he doesn't understand what you "coloreds" want and consistently invalidates the experiences of oppression that the other men describe. On the other hand, Victor, an African American, vigorously and emotionally describes his experiences with racism and continually challenges David. For example, he angrily declares how "sick and tired" he is of those who suggest that blacks can join whites, and that he is barred by "coming over there" due to his skin color, hair, and so on.

Although most students watch the video attentively, students have been observed to put their head on their desk closing their eyes, check their calendar, or otherwise engage in behavior that can only be interpreted as ranging from nonengaged and dismissive to openly hostile. In such instances, it is important to immediately intervene by addressing individually the student's behavior to interrupt the message their behaviors give to their fellow students.

Generally, class discussions regarding this video are among the most substantive and moving that I have experienced throughout my years of teaching. Although student responses certainly vary, most students clearly recognize David's racism, and both white students and students of color recount their personal experiences. In one more memorable instance, a student reacted strongly to Victor's tirade, recounting her father's experience with what she described as reverse racism. Many students were visibly upset, and although I attempted to address/have a discussion regarding her perspective, this occurred at the end of class, and it was clear that it was not enough. What I did not know at the time was how upset many students were by her comments. Several white students and students of color approached me out of class to discuss their concerns. I enlisted them to join with me in the classroom process, asking that they address their feelings and her comments, in short, that they engage in antiracism work. The following week (upon the conclusion of the film), as a class, we processed what we had collectively experienced.

Challenges to Creating Community

Although the social construction of each class and student/faculty identity play a primary role, pedagogical approaches also play a critical role. Tatum (1992) as cited by Havas and Lucas (1994) refers to four strategies that facilitate student development: creating a safe classroom atmosphere, the power of self-generated knowledge, providing a framework for students, and empowering students as change agents. As demonstrated in this discussion, it is extremely important to develop a classroom culture of trust and mutuality. Although it helps to begin with a group of students that seem to like each other and to be a more cohesive group, from the beginning, we engaged in a considerable amount of small group work. The small group work was frequently structured to provide opportunities to work with those holding different viewpoints: for example, working together toward resolutions with others who hold a different values base as demonstrated by their different constructed hierarchy of values. Students learned a lot about themselves through this process. Their ability to be open with each other enhanced my own approach to classroom instruction. I was more open and frequently engaged them in my own dilemmas not only regarding prior professional ethical dilemmas and experiences but also with respect to course content and delivery.

My empowerment also stems from the fact that I have become more skilled at facilitating discussions focused on race and allowing everyone's voice to be heard and their perception to initially be validated, thereby working toward a new understanding of the actual experience. Here my clinical training also supported my skill development. Despite many positive contextual changes, it is clear from course evaluations or student comments that question my authority, grading, and so on, that some of our students are challenged for the first time in their lives by having a minority member in a position of power over them, and that I have failed to move some students as far along the path of cultural competence as I would have wished.

A specific approach was used to facilitate the more difficult discussions regarding *The Color of Fear* after fearing an extremely contentious classroom atmosphere. I began by asking each student to say a few words that described what they were feeling immediately following the film. I began and addressed my own feelings of anger, helplessness, but hopefulness. This technique provided an opportunity for us to hear from everyone and provided a starting base for our discussion. I next asked students to put their reactions in writing, but within the context of a framework that I hoped would serve the purposes of allowing them to gain some distance and perspective on their thoughts and feelings as well as to bind some of their anxiety, potentially allowing for a more thoughtful discussion. This appeared to be extremely successful, as while there was an abundance of emotion, students were able to listen to each other and respectfully challenge each other regarding their experiences, perspectives, and assumptions.

Would students of color and white students have experienced my comments as authentic had I not been African American? Would I have thought of this approach had I not been an experienced clinician? Would I have recognized the seriousness of the classroom climate and thus the need for an intervention had I not been an experienced faculty member? Would I have taken the risk if I did not have peers with whom I could process this experience or potential disaster? Would I have shown this video if I did not feel that students come to it with a base understanding? I suspect the answer is "no" in all instances.

Student and Faculty Learning Outcomes

So how do we know that students have progressed in their quest to achieve ethical and cultural competence? What has been learned by the faculty in her quest as a social justice educator? As mentioned earlier, students self-report that their understanding and perspectives regarding race and racial identity have been enhanced and they observe this in their peers as well. Course papers were generally well done, class discussions were lively, and students seemed to be readily applying course concepts. Although personal encounters with ethical decision-making dilemmas in the field appeared to be few, students genuinely seemed to be more prepared to encounter these challenges.

More importantly, students took some ownership and interest in course content, and they were satisfied to grapple with ambiguity recognizing that there is not always a right answer and that there is more than one truth. Students have expressed a desire to show the video to others, suggested that I show the video to other student groups, or have been spurred to develop/participate in a racism workshop.

Students also readily commented after class and to others regarding the usefulness of the course. More specifically, they report sharing the readings with others, discussing class materials with their peers or field instructors, and raising with other faculty that exposure to some concepts in the class such as racial identity or professional identity was critical and that they would have appreciated these constructs earlier in their development.

Over time and through this course, my approach to teaching has evolved on several levels. I initially believed that one's identity was shaped primarily by race, and while I have not abandoned my focus on race as a powerful determinant in one's life, I have come to understand the role of multiple identities and the sociocultural construction of identity. I have engaged in work to develop my own racial identity including participating in an Undoing Racism Training for faculty. These experiences have supported and developed my ability to more openly address the range of diversity issues and to more fully integrate my identity as an African American woman first, and faculty second, whereas initially, I may have seen both identities as more parallel, or even at times, as faculty first and African American woman second. As the coteaching model is no longer used, individually I must model antiracist work for minority and majority students, address students' stereotypes, and model for all students competent teaching and clinical skills. My approach is less linear than formerly, or actually circular, and is adapted according to the group. More specifically, in some classes, I may have students begin with the personal meaning, move them to the content and critical thinking, subsequently moving back to personal or professional meaning. This shift is important as I strive to provide a parallel process in the classroom for young women (and now men) developing their own identities.

Conclusion

Students come to this course expecting to learn about the application of ethics to professional practice. Through this process, they encounter themselves and each other, constructing their identities in the context of other students; in other words, what Henriksen and Trusty (2005) define as multicultural education. Through the pedagogy discussed in this chapter, influenced by my lenses as an African American woman and clinician, my approach to teaching this course is a vehicle for social justice teaching and learning, as there are multiple opportunities for processing, debriefing, and feedback, and experiencing knowledge as doing (Adams 1997). My lens as an African American woman shapes the content and process, which is readily shared with students. Modeling my own growth and experiences as a change agent supports students in this endeavor. In the end, I believe that we all became more culturally and ethically competent human service providers. Just as important, through each class, I learn more about my multicultural lenses and its relationship to teaching, clinical work, and pedagogy, recognizing it is a lifelong process.

CHAPTER 10

Hearing Students' Silence: Issues of Identity, Performance, and Recognition in College Classrooms

Carolyn P. Panofsky and Lesley Bogad

Over the past several years, we have spent many lingering moments outside of one another's office doors debriefing the events of our classrooms. This chapter was inspired by some of those conversations that led us to read and write and talk about the *silence* that we witness in our classes, both undergraduate and graduate, at a mid-sized, predominantly white, working-class state college in New England. When students are silent, we might imagine that they are shy, or disinterested, or unprepared, or perhaps hostile. But we want to suggest that students' silence may be something different from any of these. In this chapter, we turn a reflective eye to our own classrooms to explore questions of identity, performance, and recognition—our own and those of our students—as significant factors in college students' success.

The examples we draw from in this chapter are situated in an undergraduate education course that we both teach entitled *Schooling in a Democratic Society*, a required course for all undergraduates who want to enter the teacher preparations programs at our school. This course enrolls twenty-five students per section, with approximately ten sections and multiple instructors each semester, and includes content on the history, philosophy, and cultural context of the American school. But importantly, the course also serves as an introduction to social justice pedagogy and practice, so issues of power around race, class, gender, sexuality, ability, and the like are at the center of the curriculum. Like all classes in the School of Education on our campus, the course is approximately 75 percent female and predominantly white.

In one classroom activity that contextualized issues of marginalization in K-12 schools, undergraduate education students wrote in bold markers across sheets of butcher paper hanging on the classroom wall in response to this prompt:

> *People can be silent in schools for many reasons. Are there times when YOU are silent in school? When do you lose your voice? When do you feel comfortable speaking in the classroom?*

Their responses speak to our hunch that students' silence is complex and rooted in issues of identity and culture (as we will discuss below), rather than mere resistance. Students said,

- I am silent when I don't know/understand the assignment.
- I am quiet only when I do not understand what we are discussing in class. I feel comfortable speaking in class when I do have a clear understanding of what the topic is and I know what I am talking about.
- [You lose your voice when] You don't want to be embarrassed by saying the wrong answer or not understanding the question.
- [I am silent when] I am scared that my answers are wrong or when they are wrong and the teacher puts you on the spot in front of a large group of people.
- I sometimes don't know how to exactly start something off if I haven't grasped full [*sic*] enough.
- [I get quiet when] I have the feeling of walking in and not knowing what to expect.
- [I am comfortable when] Goals and expectations are clear

These comments show how students use silence when they feel unsettled, unanchored, and unsure. In these moments, students cannot recognize themselves as a part of the community of learners—the content, but more importantly, the *context* is uncertain. Such silence is a point of misrecognition, of not seeing oneself in the reflection of the class norms or process. As one student notes above, "I have a feeling of walking in and not knowing what to expect." These students are strangers in a strange land, without a guide or interpreter to translate form and function. In this sense, their silence comes from an unknowingness about when to speak, how to speak, and what to say: "I sometimes don't know how to exactly start something off if I haven't grasped full [*sic*] enough." Silence is a strategy that avoids risk taking when there is too much to lose. Silence, then, is not a form of resistance but rather a clue into an identity of marginalization. This interpretation runs counter to the assumptions that many faculty members make about what that silence says.

In the context of a predominantly white, working-class state college, we suggest that students and faculty often don't share the same assumptions about the purpose and outcomes of academic discourse and practice or the same understandings of academic culture. Students and faculty have different ideas about what makes a "good student," as well as different experiences that inform our expectations of teaching and learning.[1] In this chapter, we seek to uncover and denaturalize the cultural assumptions that characterize many of us in the privileged position of faculty and explore how our classroom practices may promote or impede students' performance as successful college students.

Theoretical Contexts and Frameworks

We begin with the premise that a college class, like any cultural setting, is a site of cultural practices and values that may be transparent and largely "out of awareness" to cultural insiders, while opaque, unintelligible, and disorienting to cultural outsiders (Hall 1972). We suggest that talk and dialogue are cultural practices of such unquestioned value in college teaching that few of us even think about them at all, much less understand them as cultural. Because the value of talk is taken for granted and the process of talk in dialogue is assumed to be integral to class participation, college faculty rarely, if ever, address the issue of teaching students how and why to engage in this practice. At the same time, many people who enter higher education as first-generation college students may have neither the tools to help them understand the "ways with words" in classroom talk nor any models to help them imagine and integrate an identity as college student (Heath 1983). The fear of being exposed as an imposter can lead to a persona of quiet disengagement, frustration, and alienation. We must work against such outcomes: as participants ourselves in disciplinary discourse communities, we have acculturated and become master practitioners of the academic discourse of our disciplines; as teachers, our task is to apprentice our students to the discourse practices of these communities.

Our focus on the importance of talk is echoed by Janet Galligani Casey (2005), who argues that certain elements of the educational process—such as talk and dialogue—are, to college faculty, "self-evidently important." Of first-generation college students and students of working-class backgrounds, Casey writes,

> For a population [i.e., working-class students] likely to see higher education as a means to an end rather than an end in itself, this emphasis [on the process of education, on the experience of education—as much as the outcome] can seem surprising, disorienting, and even downright absurd. I have had students from less privileged backgrounds confide that they are at a loss in seminar-style courses, notably in the humanities: the model for such courses, based on dialogue, seems pointless to them... The quiet student, then, may not be shy or intimidated so much as stymied by an implied value system that is entirely unfamiliar, and that remains unarticulated. (n.p.)

How can we understand this value system, one that is barely or not at all visible to most of us? What is going on that can make the same activity— classroom discussion—seem so valuable to some and pointless to others? Pierre Bourdieu (1984) identifies valuing "for its own sake" (as in "art for art's sake") as an aesthetic of the "pure," reflecting a life of (comparative) ease and "distanced from necessity." This aesthetic contrasts with valuing the "functional" and practical, reflecting a life controlled by necessity (with comparatively little ease). Talk for its own sake, in this view, is an exemplar of middle-class expectations that seem frivolous to those who expect talk to be, as Patrick Finn (1999) has pointed out, practical, pointed, and functional.

To be clear, we are not suggesting that faculty today live lives "distanced from necessity" in a literal sense, but that the institutional culture of higher education reflects that historical condition. Nor are we suggesting that talk "for its own sake" has no purpose. Rather, making our purposes visible to and understood by our students is a challenge we must recognize and address. In relation to the historically constructed rules and codes of the academy, to be a first-generation college student is to be not-privy-to/not-privileged-to-know about the values, practices, activities, and assumptions of this institutional ethic and aesthetic, not inculcated with what Bourdieu (1986) would call the "habitus" of this privileged ethos. For students who are "ends-oriented" like those mentioned by Casey, the process of education and the talk that is part of that process can be inscrutable and meaningless in their apparent lack of function or practical purpose for those whose ethos is to go to college to prepare for a career (as compared with the more privileged process-oriented goal of "becoming educated").

Nor is it the case that the ethos of ends-oriented education is learned only in the home, for researchers have clearly documented that children schooled in different "tracks" or living in communities with varying degrees of privilege are afforded vastly differing school experiences. Anyon (1980, 1981) and others (Finn 1999; Fine et al. 2000; Oakes 2005) have shown that both *what* students are taught and *how* they are taught tend to be strongly differentiated by academic tracks and residential strata. Despite its label, the "college prep" curriculum typical in most high schools today does not provide the kinds of experiences college faculty might like to assume: in college prep classes, it is typical for students to do little talking about texts, little to no analytic writing on tests, and to understand writing as the "five-paragraph essay." In a recent discussion in one of Carolyn's upper-division teacher preparation courses, only one of seventeen students recalled ever writing anything longer than a five-paragraph essay in high school, yet all were enrolled in "college prep" courses. Another upper-level student at our institution recently remarked after reading Anyon's research about low-level curricula in working-class schools, "I never heard the word 'concept' before I came to college" (Schuster, personal communication). Both anecdotal and research sources suggest, then, that many first-generation college students are schooled in cultural practices unlikely to produce a habitus of talk-for-talk's-sake or other college-like "ways with words," and, perhaps even more importantly, their K-12 experiences rarely afford access to the values and practices of more privileged schooling (such as honors or AP classes).

In her oft-cited discussion of cultural capital, social reproduction and the requisite tensions that arise around teaching other people's children, Lisa Delpit (1995, 24) suggests that "being told explicitly the rules of the culture of power makes acquiring power easier." In what follows, we explore this issue to show ways to make explicit the value we place on "talk" and our expectations about it in our classrooms. We look specifically at the tensions that are produced when first-generation college students who have experienced education as a *skills*-based activity of knowledge and discourse *consumption* meet up with faculty who expect students to participate in education as a *process*-driven activity of knowledge and discourse *production*.

A View from Somewhere

We come to this project as two white women—each of us raised in communities of relative privilege, though not wealth. Our own histories of negotiating higher education and social class produce a particular "view from somewhere" (Haraway 1988) that informs our understanding of our students and their lives. We are both faculty in a school of education where we teach undergraduates in teacher preparation programs, as well as graduate students seeking master's and doctoral degrees in education. We also share academic interests, having earned our doctorates in social and cultural foundations of education. Yet we are of two generations: Carolyn Panofsky had been in higher education for several decades when Lesley Bogad arrived.

Lesley Bogad: I came of age in the 1970s and 1980s in southern California where my childhood was infused with the politics of second-wave feminism and shaped by the intense value placed on education by my parents who were both teachers and principals in elementary schools. By the time I was fourteen, I had already visited colleges and universities all over the country in preparation for my own pursuit of higher education, *which* was as much a "given" in the context of my life as was brushing my teeth every morning. While my family always had fewer financial resources than many of my peers who vacationed in Europe, or went on exotic spring break excursions, I was enveloped in a culture of privilege that taught me how to navigate the world around me.

School was a comforting place for me: my values and identities were generally affirmed there and my academic success furthered my feelings of belonging and connection. College life was demystified for me at an early age as I spent three summers at "geek camp," living in a college dorm and taking college classes designed for "academically talented youth" when I was a teenager.[2] My academic, material, and cultural capital allowed me the opportunity to spend my undergraduate years at a Seven Sisters school 3,000 miles away from home. Here I was surrounded by successful women—faculty, administration and peers—who helped me further nurture my voice, my confidence, and my sense of self-efficacy. Later, my academic interests in diversity, feminism, and institutionalized oppression led me to question my own privilege that went largely unnamed in my youth. Like my students, I cannot leave my history at the door so I have to consistently renegotiate my memories, assumptions, and experiences with both the content I teach and the students with whom I share the classroom.

Carolyn Panofsky: I grew up in the 1950s and 1960s, also in southern California. The images of border crossing and living in two worlds seem emblematic of many of my experiences. I was inspired by the civil rights movement and a sense of social justice that often collided with the political beliefs and values of my parents. Neither of my parents graduated from college, but many in my extended family were college educated, and the ethos in my family included engaging in practices of privilege such as visiting museums, attending plays, and the symphony. My economic background was similarly mixed, with a modest level of comfort in our home, but wealth in some more distant parts of the family, and enjoyed by many peers, especially when postelementary schooling took me beyond my neighborhood. So I grew up with many windows into privilege, but typically feeling "outside," moving between different worlds, sometimes not quite knowing the local customs or language. I grew up with the unquestioned expectation that I would go to college, but with little sense of what that meant or would be like or what choices I might make.

In a state university setting, I was relatively sophisticated in intellectual and cultural matters compared to many of my peers. Still, I was often puzzled by professors' lectures: I wondered, what were the questions that all that talk was about? What was the underlying structure that accounted for the invisible connections between points? I rarely asked a question because I didn't know what or how to ask. My efforts to approach faculty outside of class were usually unsatisfying, and after completing my bachelor's and master's in English, I often wondered how different my experience might have been if I had had the opportunity to study with women professors.[3]

During my undergraduate experiences, I spent a lot of time trying to decrypt the structures and processes behind the content of a professor's lecture. Fortunately, I was reasonably successful at this decryption activity and my insights served me well when I became a peer tutor and, later, a professional in the emerging field of academic assistance. So while I share some part of the first-generation college student's dislocation in college, my many experiences "over the border" had alerted me to search "behind the scenes" or "below the surface" to make sense of academic life and work. In this, I suspect I was considerably more privileged than most of the students I teach. Certainly, my own discomfort in straddling two worlds had attuned me to these issues. Similarly, my experience as a woman in the academy, as well as in earlier schooling, has afforded many insights into the experiences of students, such as ours, in less privileged schools and tracks of being ignored, silenced, or dismissed by the person at the front of the class.

In the context of our lives, and the lives of our students, there are many ways to untangle the dynamics of silence. It can take on a variety of meanings across lines of power. Silence can be a manifestation of invisibility just as it can signify the "luxury of obliviousness" (Johnson 2001). Silence can be a mode of resistance, a thoughtful space of reflection, a performance of acquiescence. In the limited space available here, we use lenses drawn from scholars such as Delpit (1995), Johnson (2001), Bourdieu (1973/2000), Anyon (1980, 1981), and Casey (2005) to explore three examples that illustrate how silence manifests in our classrooms in order to hear that silence in new ways.

What Silence Looks Like:
Recognition, Performance, and Identity

Recognition: What Counts as Learning

An early experience that alerted me (Carolyn) to the difference between my and my students' understanding of classroom activity occurred by chance. One of the classroom strategies that I use regularly in my classes is partner and group work. I think of this collaborative activity as a way to help students feel safer, more comfortable, and more at ease given the lower risk of a more intimate setting. The need for safety is especially important in our undergraduate Foundations course that addresses difficult issues of difference, including race, class, gender, ability, and sexuality. As important as creating safety, I also see collaborative talk as creating a space for students to share language and build discourse together and to engage in the social and discursive interaction that Vygotsky (1978) argues is required for higher learning to occur. At the time of the event to be described, these ideas about collaborative activity informed my thinking, but I did not make them explicit for my students.

Around the middle of the semester, there was a particularly lively class session when students met in small groups to discuss a shared text they had read before class. The room buzzed with their conversations, and as I walked around the room, occasionally stopping to ask or answer a question, I could hear the students engaged in rich dialogue about the text. This session seemed particularly successful to me, and the written work that students collaboratively produced appeared to support that impression. The next day, as I walked across campus, I found myself behind two students from the class. One had been absent the day of the small group discussions, and she was asking the other about her notes and wanted to know what she "had missed" in class. The other student replied, "Nothing. Just groups."

That response has echoed in my memory for years and I have spent a lot of time thinking about it. In my doctoral studies, I had studied and researched education as a cultural process, but early in my college teaching, I hadn't thought about the talk in my own classroom as a cultural practice to which I was an insider but my students might be outsiders. The meaning and purpose of these "ways with words" was, in anthropologist Edward T. Hall's (1972) term "out of awareness" for me, a naturalized part of academic culture; as with so many aspects of any culture, it is difficult to make such norms explicit for "outsiders." What I saw as rich discussion in the class was seen by my students as "not counting." I came to realize that for them what did count was filling notebook pages with copious notes from a professor's lecture. The process of talk, the insights produced during engagement with text and questions, the negotiation between conversational partners were all ephemeral, not a worthwhile use of time compared to filling notebook pages with content to be "studied" and "learned." Most students did not recognize the activities of talking and of coconstructing responses to questions as a *meaningful process* worth their time and didn't see the written product of their collaborative work (which I commented on and made photocopies of to supply all participants of a group with a copy of their collective responses) as *meaningful records* of their activity.

So if the students did not recognize the activity they were engaged in as worthwhile and thought the class was doing "nothing," one may ask, "What was going on?" Perhaps, one might speculate, the activity had a kind of formlessness that made it seem like "nothing." But I doubt this accounts for the student's perception; I used a fairly structured approach, based on cooperative learning models that I explained and for which I provided a rationale. I always prepared a series of questions, designed for students to engage with a text in an "exploratory" fashion, not to "find answers" but to construct one or multiple readings as a form of inquiry, of sense making. Each small group would collaboratively prepare a single set of responses to the questions, always with my reminders (sometimes oral, sometimes written) "to include all voices," meaning to incorporate multiple perspectives, rather than a single response, that "there is no one right answer," and that "the activity isn't about writing what I (i.e., the professor) want, but about figuring out your own ideas, testing them against a text, and using evidence to support claims." The writing assignment was "low stakes" to encourage participation and decrease grade anxiety. The questions attempted to "apprentice" the students in the practices of the academic community of discourse by asking them to use the writer's discourse and analytic frames as lenses for connecting with students' own experiences in their field placements, or with their own schooling, or with other texts we had read in the course.[4]

Yet the structures of this activity, so visible to me, must have remained invisible to many of the students, unrecognized as "real learning." I saw myself as trying to apprentice students to the academy's "ways with words," with the expectation that in time students would break through the silence to take up a speaker's position in whole class discussions, as Vygotsky's (1978) theory would predict. Yet only a few students engaged in whole group discussion on occasions when it was not preceded by the structured small group work. More recently, I have been working to make the "ways with words" more explicit in my classroom, to make the process of talk recognizable as a valuable learning activity. I have found that asking students to reflect on this activity, asking them to write, informally, on what they've "gotten out of" the activity, and then to share these thoughts with the class, helps to make the talk more recognizable and may spur some students to break their silence. It also helps me to tune in more quickly to problems and to establish an open channel for discussion about the reasons for our activity and in this way to shift students' *recognition* of *what counts* as learning.

Performing Disagreement: The Production of Knowledge

Like Carolyn, I (Lesley) also teach *Schooling in a Democratic Society* in the Educational Studies department. In a recent semester, I watched two students delicately negotiate a space of intellectual disagreement in this course. Two white women, both traditional-aged college students, had strong opinions about the ideological content of Disney films and the pedagogical implications these animated classics have on our understandings of race, class, and gender. Kelly, having read and discussed the racial politics of Disney films in another class, argued that the film *Aladdin* presents a racist and ultimately problematic reading of Arabs, Arab culture, and the Middle East (Giroux 1995). Gianna wrinkled her forehead as she listened to Kelly, and with a scrunched up nose wondered out loud why we were complaining when "at least there are not just white people in the movie." Kelly quickly nodded and smiled and opened her eyes wide in affirmation. "I totally agree with you. I am not disagreeing with you, but..." Gianna reponded with a nodding head before Kelly even had the chance to finish her thought. "I am not disagreeing with you either, it is just that..." Each woman, seemingly unpracticed in negotiating respectful intellectual disagreement, trailed off in silence for fear of upsetting the other. I interrupted the pause. "But you *are* disagreeing. It is okay to disagree. That is how we learn things!" I laughed and reassured them that they could disagree, even engage in a heated tangle over an academic point and still "be friends." Both women smiled at me, and the class chuckled a bit. When the laughter subsided, the conversation pushed forward in gentle debate.

In the face of explicit disagreement, both of these women retreated from the opportunity to take on the performance of knowledge maker. As a well-rehearsed academic, I could feel their quick exchange pulse with a tension of new ideas and expanded possibilities. I was excited and energized to see their intellectual conflict emerging—it signified *learning* to me. But for the students, that same tension was foreign and unrecognizable as productive. Far better rehearsed in their roles as consumers of information—much like the students Carolyn notes above—neither of these young women was comfortable performing as a producer of knowledge in our classroom.

In part, we read this as a gendered dynamic, where the politics of "nice-ness" between women (Adams and Bettis 2003) deflates the tension that often fuels learning. But furthermore, we suggest that moments like these illustrate students' inexperience with debate, discussion, and talk-for-talk's-sake. Without an explicit understanding of the rules of engagement around academic dialogue that can include respectful disagreement, the students above reveal the fear and discomfort that silences dialogic interactions and the production of ideas. In fact, when I asked students in this same class to write about their voice and their silence, one student wrote, "Sometimes if it is a heated topic and maybe I don't agree or something; I won't speak up just so I don't get caught in the crossfire."

For many of our students, having spent years in schools that valued sit-still-and-be-quiet over stand-up-and-be-heard, the performance of being a "good student" is wrapped up in quiet acquiescence, not boisterous word play. It was only with explicit permission to proceed in conflict that the dialogue I discuss above continued and that Kelly and Gianna could begin to take up the performance of disagreement in a new way. This example illustrates how we think of *performance* as fundamental to first-generation college students' acclimation to and success in their higher education.

Building Identity in Language: The Silenced Dialogue

The example above touches on the dynamics of silence in our students' lives; for many of them, the performance of being a "good student" is wrapped up in silent deferral—listening, taking good notes, nodding and smiling, and consuming vast amounts of information. But as they gain the tools of language, thus breaking the silence, they are able to build identities as think-ers, knowers, critics, producers, and ultimately, we hope, reflective practi-tioners. To this end, I (Lesley) often begin my undergraduate Foundations of Education course with a few chapters out of Alan Johnson's book called *Privilege, Power and Difference* (2001). In chapter 1, Johnson (2001, 11) makes an argument for breaking the silence around issues of privilege, power, and difference. "We can't talk about it if we can't use the words." Finding the language to speak about racism, sexism, classism, and homophobia is central to confronting the injustice they sustain. He goes on to say that at times "I feel like a doctor trying to help a patient without ever mentioning the body or what is wrong. We can't get anywhere that way—and we haven't been. Our collective house is burning down and we're tiptoeing around afraid to say 'fire!'" (2001, 12). This premise leads us to the "Silenced Dialogue" chapter out of Lisa Delpit's widely cited text, *Other People's Children* (1995). Students—particularly liberal, well-intentioned white students—are often resistant to Delpit's work because it makes them feel culpable for the racism that is produced by our unexamined assumptions about power and schooling. They are often alienated by the language in this text, as it talks directly about race, racism, power, hurt, and blame. These are not the kinds of things that many of these students talk about over the dinner table at home or "around the water cooler" in other spaces they inhabit.

In my class, students work in small groups to name Delpit's central claim and then we work from these statements to build a collaborative argument statement on the board that fully captures Delpit's position. Each semester, this exercise teaches me so much about what Delpit calls "the silenced dialogue" produced by a culture that practices erasure and/or careful negotiation around topics that are contested or considered taboo. Our students have been shshh'ed repeatedly and told to ignore our differences: "Don't stare at the person in the wheelchair," "Don't call him 'black,'" "That's auntie's 'friend'—don't say 'lesbian.'" The weight of these experiences leaves a strong resistance to an instructor's reversal of all they have learned. They have no words, and even when they do, they fear that those words are not the right ones, that they will "say it wrong." So, when we work on Delpit's chapter the students often reflexively retreat into a space of discursive avoidance, enacting the silences named by Johnson.

Delpit (1995, 45) argues that white, middle-class teachers must explicitly teach students who are not a part of the culture of power about "the codes needed to participate fully in mainstream American life" while encouraging those students to maintain and be proud of their cultural backgrounds. Delpit's is a powerful position about the responsibility that (white) educators have to make visible those dominant tropes of speech, dress, interaction, and practice that not all students will learn at home. However, when my undergraduates first attempted to articulate this position, they came up with the following: "Delpit argues that different students need different things from their teachers." Such a statement includes no mention of race, no mention of power, and no words to name who is different and how. This is a silence that comes in part not only from being unpracticed and insecure about using academic language but also from living in a society where "we're tiptoeing around afraid to say 'fire!'" (Johnson 2005).

With practice and time, however, the students are able to see themselves as a part of this new discourse community, to use the words, and to take on the identity of one who is "unafraid to raise questions about discrimination and voicelessness with people of color" (Delpit 1995, 47). This comes from explicit efforts throughout the semester to name the unspoken and rehearse new identities. In the class discussion, if a student refers to "we" or "they," I always interrupt gently: "Who is the 'we' in that sentence?" to push them to articulate. When someone stumbles over the words—"People who are...colored...I mean, black or um, African people who...," I step in to offer up an alternative without judgment. "You mean people of color?" Red faces start to drain and we move on. By the midterm, many students toss around phrases like "dominant ideology" or "white privilege" like they have been at it for years. As one student noted in comparing two pieces of her own writing from the beginning and end of the course:

> Looking at them [my work from the first day and last day of class] side by side, I noticed a difference in the vocabulary I used. At the beginning, I was using words such as "us," "we," and "equal." I have now been able to use words like "privilege," "culture of power," and "codes of power." My views have changed greatly and I have the vocab needed to help me express what is wrong with the education system today.

While the student identifies the shifts here as being about "vocab," we are suggesting that this is a larger shift in identity that comes from not only having the tools of language, but also knowing how to use them in new ways. As James Gee (2005) argues that discourse is a kind of "identity kit," we suggest that in taking up a new "vocab" students are also taking on a new identity.

Conclusion

We see, then, that much of this work is about language—the codes that Delpit speaks of. But it is also about practices, about taking up the language of others, of working for intertextuality in the sense that students learn to appropriate the discourses of the authors they read, to interact with texts, and to allow the authors' voices "to speak through them," as Bakhtin (1981) would say. In this way, successful higher education is an intertextual accomplishment in which the student learns to speak the words, the discourses, the texts of the authors as a way to engage in analysis and critique. If students are silent because they don't "understand the assignment" or don't know "what to expect" or because they "don't know how to exactly start something off," then they will be deterred in learning to speak in these new ways.

How, then, do we as faculty in a predominantly white, working-class state college work to create spaces of possibility where our students can find these "ways with words," gain the competence to see themselves as successful college students, and perform the active participant's identity with confidence? We can start by thinking the best of our students—resist psychologizing them as "shy" or seeing them as merely unprepared, lazy, uncaring, or apathetic when they don't participate. Not unlike our students, we need to learn new cultural meanings in academic activities, to see through their eyes, to make the familiar strange, to practice a kind of auto-ethnography in/on our own classroom practices. We can do this by telling our students that every classroom has a culture, and explaining explicitly what the culture of our classroom is. As we explain the culture of our classroom, we need to tell our students *why* we have them do what we assign, whether it's talk in the classroom or outside writing assignments. We need to help students understand that the process of these activities and practices is at least as important as the products (especially if the student sees the product as the grade). We need to find ways to support our students as they learn *how* to engage in these activities: we can't let ourselves forget that activities that seem natural are actually cultural, so we need to acknowledge that successful acculturation to college takes time and that cultural newcomers need to be welcomed and supported by caring mentors who act as cultural guides.

Delpit argues that K-12 teachers must be explicit in teaching the rules and codes of power to students who do not have access to them at home. We suggest that college teachers need to do the same. When our students fail to recognize the modes of school success, we must come to see that failure of recognition on their part as a failure of recognition on our part, as well. As the insiders who are privy to the culture of power, we know (as Delpit again reminds us) that being told the rules of codes of power makes acquiring power easier. Our work then becomes a challenge of naming the things we take most for granted, bringing into the foreground the unspoken expectations we have, and guiding students into a more comfortable place to be able to recognize the cultural practices of power in teaching and learning. When we do these things, we are hearing our students' silence in new ways as they are learning to *recognize* what's going on in our classrooms, to *perform* in our cultural practices, and to build an *identity* of one who competently engages in the academy's "ways with words" and can use the rules and codes of power. We, as well as our students, need to use our voices in new ways: in our case, as in theirs as future teachers, teaching must communicate the rules and codes of power if we seek to work for equity and justice in education.

Notes

1. Students at our institution are predominantly the first generation in their family to attend college, and 40 percent have transferred from a community college. All but 10 percent live off campus, 25 percent are married, and 80 percent work off campus; the median number of work hours for all students is twenty-one hours per week.

2. For more information, see http://cty.jhu.edu/.
3. Strictly speaking, I actually had two women instructors, both in my freshmen year: one was a T.A. who taught the weekly discussion section in my first semester of freshmen English; the other was the lecturer in an art history survey course of 175 students. I never saw a woman at the front of the class again, until I shifted my focus to graduate programs in education.
4. In a seventy-five-minute class, each four- to five-person group might have twenty minutes or more to discuss four or five questions, with each student taking a designated role (e.g., a recorder to compose the groups' written responses; a reporter to speak for the group in whole class discussion; a timekeeper to keep the group on task to finish on time; an ombudsperson to identify differences of opinion and to assure that all voices are heard and represented; each student was responsible for taking each role at least twice during the semester and to note their role on the response form). The small group discussions would be followed by a whole class discussion in which groups shared their responses, led by the "reporters" but with the freedom for others to speak as well.

CHAPTER 11

Exploring/Exploding the Boundaries of Inclusive Teaching: Social Class Confronts Race and Gender

Phyllis Charlotte Brown

Ms., what do you think of a teacher who tells her student she asks too many questions?

(Donna, 14, personal communication, July 2004)

It was supposed to be just a one-time, short-term community service assignment that I had accepted, connected to my faculty work in training teachers at Lesley University. As I prepared to teach study skills for the Alternative Education Program (AEP) in Providence, Rhode Island, I was both anxious and resistant—not only because this was a new challenge but also because I had resolved to act in a way that was completely at odds with the values and perspectives that I usually teach my Lesley University student teachers. I was determined not to concern myself with the sociopolitical backgrounds of my AEP students. My focus would be on teaching study skills: that was all they were going to get from me. Diversity, social class, personal, or school issues would not be my concern. By taking this unlikely stance, I was betraying my own long-held belief that a teacher should care about where her students come from, who they are as individuals, and what they have faced in life.

These feelings were rooted in the disappointment and frustration I had experienced in my professional life as a black woman with a doctorate in education who teaches in a predominantly white institution. Now, as a college professor whose field of specialization is Teacher Education, I was coming to terms with what it meant to be one of the few professors of color in an otherwise white school. I teach primarily white students and I was experiencing heightened visibility and a growing reputation as an "angry black woman." My despair about the increasing failure of public education to provide all learners with a high-quality education also left me feeling as if I were colluding with a corrupt and bankrupt educational system. For the first time in my career, I experienced a sense of profound invisibility, on the one hand, and hypervisibility, on the other. Particularly impatient with prevailing diversity rhetoric that did not make a significant difference in pedagogical practice, I wanted nothing to do with it at my own university and certainly not with the young people I had agreed to teach in the AEP.

When Mr. Leo D'Maio (founder of the AEP and my own former mentor) called to suggest that I teach in a summer program for young people who had failed eighth grade, I was sympathetic to the idea but not interested in participating. He, however, was determined, and I finally acquiesced. I couldn't say no to "Mr. D," who had been a source of unwavering support and encouragement when I was an undergraduate in his Talent Development Program at the University of Rhode Island (URI).

Once I said yes to Mr. D, my feelings of resistance grew. At my university, I was already burdened with more teaching responsibilities than I thought I could handle; but even more importantly, my experience of racism in the education profession was alienating me from my work as a teacher.

Purpose of the Program

The AEP, Inc., was established and incorporated on February 26, 2001, with a mission "to facilitate the access and equity of targeted/underserved racial, cultural, economic and socio-linguistic groups into educational pursuits" (AEP 2004). I would be teaching in the subdivision of the program called the Junior High to High School Transition project. It was created by "Mr. D" and Raymond E. Gallison, because in Gallison's words,

> [We] realized that students going from junior high to high school were unaware of what it was going to take to be successful in high school. The highest drop out rate happens between the 8th and 9th grade. Between the 8th and 9th grade is also when young people begin to get involved with the criminal justice system. Young people enter the criminal justice system through the truancy court and this is often the beginning of a

lifetime of encounters with the criminal justice system. (personal communication, May 5, 2005)

Students who successfully completed the project were given the opportunity to enter high school and promised admission into a College Readiness program after they graduated. These students are tracked for their remaining time in school (AEP 2004).

Program Structure

AEP is a three-week summer school program designed to provide struggling eighth graders with the knowledge and study skills they will need to be successful in high school. The program is run from 9:00 A.M. to 12 P.M., Monday through Friday during the month of July. AEP is located in the high school that these students will be attending in the fall. The day is divided into two sessions. The first session focuses on social issues that may confront the students. Guest speakers come from the community, high school, URI, and law enforcement agencies. The second session focuses on skill acquisition, including study skills, time management, and goal setting. Both parts of the program are meant to help students think more deeply about their life choices and learn how to avoid making costly mistakes as they go forward.

All of my new students that summer came from families that were economically disadvantaged. They lived in housing projects, apartments, and single-family homes. They were white, African American, Latino and Asian, biracial, male and female, whose ages ranged from fourteen to sixteen years. A number of students spoke English as their second language. Some were parents of small children or were soon to be parents. All of them had been identified as potential high-school dropouts or as individuals likely to engage in criminal or gang activity. Some were already in the judicial or the foster care systems. Many came from single-parent homes. Some came from dysfunctional and abusive homes. Many knew someone who was incarcerated, involved with a gang, or who abused alcohol or drugs. Some had a relative or someone else they knew who had been murdered.

All of the students struggled academically, refusing to go to school, or acting out when they are in school. The reasons for this are varied—most had difficult home lives; others acted out because they were deficient in English language comprehension, basic math, and study skills. Ignored, dismissed, and neglected by the school system due to circumstances beyond their control and to their own behavior, they were youth who had been betrayed, sometimes by their families and sometimes by their schools. In school, these kinds of students are always the learners labeled "at risk" for school failure.

In the first class, I introduced myself and asked the students if they had any questions for me. The first question students raised focused on the judgments I had about them—because they "knew I have seen their records." They were surprised when I told them I had not, and that the only judgment I made about them is that they are smart and capable of being academically successful. I could tell from their expressions and sighs that they did not believe me. I knew that I would have to prove that I truly did believe that they were smart and capable. However, I did acknowledge that they were in this intensive summer school program because they needed to learn how to be productive learners, capable of negotiating their school experience. I chose to see past their troubled educational experiences, preferring to focus on the fact that they are "at potential" for success and personal triumph. It is from this perspective that I explored the concept of inclusive teaching in a school-based summer program.

Inclusive Teaching

Going beyond superficial views of inclusive teaching requires us to recognize that inclusive teaching and learning practices and strategies must include white students as well as students of color. I wished to broaden traditional definitions of inclusion to encompass the following:

> The philosophy behind inclusion is simple: Every individual is an equally important link in the social chain. For schools to include everyone, teachers must accept diversity in the student population. In an educational context, diversity refers to students who have disabilities and impairments, students who are of ethnic minority status, students who speak English as a second language, and students who are of low socioeconomic background. (Johnson 1998, as cited in Johnson 1999)

When I began teaching study skills to eighth graders in the AEP, I fell headfirst into the trap of believing that working with "at-risk" students always pertains to students of color, of African American and Latino descent. I assumed that my students would all be students of color. To my surprise, they were not. In fact, the majority of my students in the first summer were white males.

When I recall this first summer, I can vividly remember my own shock when I walked in the classroom door. I was surprised to see so many white male students and imagine they were surprised that their teacher was a black woman named Dr. Brown. All the students were in this program because they had failed eighth grade. Yet it was the presence of so many white male students in my class that made me realize that without inclusive education, schools are also failing the very people they were established to educate. What these white male students had in common with the students of color was that they were all from socioeconomically disadvantaged backgrounds. Another factor that stands out in my mind was the attitudes and perceptions of the students of color in response to the question, "Who will be successful in this program?" As they saw it, students most likely to succeed in the program were the white students. Even though they were all in the same academic situation, students of color believed that they were less likely to succeed in this program than their white counterparts. I was surprised by their comments, because I had assured them all that I believed in their ability to be successful in this program and school. Yet students of color who believed that whites would outperform them met my assurances with skepticism. They had internalized the pervasive message that they were destined for failure.

Program Activities

Two field trips were also part of the first-session curriculum. The first of two trips was to the Rhode Island Boys and Girls Training School, a juvenile detention center. The students spent half a day at the Training School. They toured the unrestricted areas of the facility and heard from inmates about life there. They saw the conditions that inmates must live in and that they have no freedom of choice. One student poignantly stated, "It's a place no one would want to live in...they have no rights, no say in what they want and what they need" (Shane, personal communication, July 20, 2006). Students had to follow some of the rules that inmates have to follow such as walking with their hands clasped behind their back. According to AEP student Miguel, "I know now for a fact that I am not going to any sort of training school. I'm going to change some of the things that I do that can get me into the training school" (personal communication, July 20, 2006). These were the reactions that we hoped students would have after their trip to the Rhode Island Boys and Girls Training School.

A second field trip was to the URI main campus in Kingston, Rhode Island. At the university, students toured the campus, talked with current students, and were introduced to the university's admission process and to the Talent Development Program where I was myself a student. This program offers tutorial, financial support, and advising to students who are first-generation college students and/or are underprepared for college (AEP

2004). My students of color reported that they were surprised to see students of color who are in college and began for the first time to visualize themselves as college students. Unsurprisingly, students found their experience at URI more positive than their experience at the Training School.

Akisha was one of a number of students whose reflections on URI and the Rhode Island Training School revealed that she had already been exposed to the criminal justice system. After visiting both institutions, Akisha, at thirteen years already a mother, writes,

> We went to the URI and to the Rhode Island Training School (RITS) with the AEP. I have a choice...at first I wanted to go to the RITS because my friends were there, but when I went there I was about to cry because of the tragedy it is. No freedom, they make choices for you. In URI you get to make so many choices for yourself, and you get respect even if you are Black or white...I decided to go to college after seeing what college is about...I am not going to let [anybody] drag me down. And, [I want to] give my son a better future. (personal communication, July 2005)

These field trips gave students an opportunity to see how their decisions and choices will determine where they will go in life. Once they see the difference, most of the students recognize they need to make good choices. As Joseph stated, "I choose to go to college because I want to be somebody, not a bum" (personal communication, July 2005).

The second session of the transition program, as noted, focused on intensive instruction in study skills such as reading comprehension, reading strategies, note taking, time management, goal setting, test taking, and acquiring certain "habits of mind." One important type of "A Habit of Mind" we focused on, for example, is that "you know how to behave intelligently when you don't know the answer" (The Institute for Habits of Mind 2010) and begin to think about what you need to do to discover it. Beginning in summer 2004, the study skills curriculum was also redesigned to integrate and align the study skills students learned with content areas of the high-school curriculum. In addition to learning study skills, students were encouraged to consider what attitudes and behaviors they would need to be successful in school. These behaviors had to do with "habits of mind" they would need in order to excel in high school and in life.

To assess student needs and engage them in taking responsibility for their own education, students completed and analyzed the results of two online self-assessments. The first assessment is an online study skills self-assessment, and the second is an online multiple intelligence test self-assessment. These self-scored assessments helped students identify what study skills they were lacking and their preferred learning style. The results of these assessments were used (1) to modify the study skills curriculum to emphasize the skills in most need of attention (frequency, reading comprehension) and (2) to help students understand how they best learn and study.

Content area specialists in math, science, and English were then invited from Lesley University to teach AEP students strategies and perspectives intended to help them to be successful in these subjects. Students got hands-on experiences applying their new skills in these subjects and learned behaviors expected of them in ninth grade. In 2006, filmmaking was added to the content areas required for AEP students. Working with Reel Vision, a Boston-based youth filmmaking project, participants learned media literacy skills—in particular, how to write and produce Public Service Announcements (PSAs). Special projects such as developing PSAs about student-generated issues were incorporated to foster collaboration, public speaking, media literacy, critical thinking, and technology skills.

To acquaint them with the high school they hoped to attend, students met with a school counselor who works with AEP staff to ease their transition to the next level of their education. They toured the school and learned about high-school graduation requirements and a typical high-school student's daily schedule. They were told about the rules and regulations that all members of the school community are expected to uphold and the consequences for those who do not. The counselor encouraged students to come to see her when they have a question or a problem and told them that she would also seek them out.

The Students

As I see it, the academic failure of these students is due in large part to a school system that has not provided them with the type of education that encourages and expects all learners to succeed. Many of the teachers in the schools they have attended are unprepared to teach to a racially and economically diverse student body. In addition, few teachers receive sufficient training in their education to effectively teach English language learners, students with special needs, or students from economically disadvantaged backgrounds. In this way, the structure of school reinforces the inequalities that these students and their families face daily. Tatum's research (2003) provides insight into how teachers who participated in a semester-long professional development courses, came to understand what a mistake it was to try to embrace all their students without seeing their color. As long as schools continue to blame the victim, to avoid self-examination, and to put the least-qualified teachers in classrooms with diverse learners, the system of privilege that benefits those with economic resources and who speak English as a first language will continue to prevail, and the cycle will not be broken.

Inclusion

For me, inclusion has come to mean exploding the concept to take into account the failed school experiences of many students from a wide range of backgrounds. Inclusion that has traditionally focused too narrowly on people of color and people with disabilities needs to be expanded to include youth of all racial backgrounds who have in common the socioeconomic characteristics of poverty and government dependency. All of the young people that I taught in this project have been largely excluded from the possibility and the potential of being successful in school because of their academic performance and their behavior. To avoid prejudging my students, I declined the opportunity to read their school records. I knew that most of them contained only negative reports that documented their failures. I believed in their potential to overcome even the most insurmountable odds.

I concur with researchers who have denounced the use of "at risk" as a covert mechanism for labeling students who are outside of the mainstream. For example, Martin Haberman

> argues that terms such as *at risk* become code words for students who are perceived by educators and the public to be "problems in the schools." And, it is not coincidence that status characteristics such as race, class, and linguistic diversity become equated with "at riskness." (as cited in Ladson-Billings 2001, 15)

Moreover, I would advocate dispensing with the "at-risk" label altogether, because it makes it more possible for educators to view struggling students as "at potential" (Greene 2000). This could be the first step toward changing students' perception of themselves as school failures. The next step is to teach them how to actualize their potential.

In a review of successful programs for "at-risk" students, Nieto (2000, 50) found that a key factor in predicting academic success for students of color, English language learners, and those with socioeconomic disadvantage was for teachers to treat students "as if they were talented and capable." When teachers treat their students with respect and challenge them to do their best, they motivate students to reach their highest potential. When I asked my students, "What motivates you to do your personal best in school?" they responded that family, teachers, fun, sports, and meaningful work were key factors. For example, George stated,

> Something that motivates [me] to do my work is something I am interested in, like sports or other interesting things. Another thing that motivates me is, if the teacher is nice to me in class—that kind of gets me motivated (personal communication, 2004).

Donna, whose quote appears at the beginning of this chapter, had a different view of what motivates her. She stated, "What motivates me to do my personal best is people around me telling me I can't do it. It makes me want to do it really good so I can say HA! I did it" (personal communication, July 2004).

Donna's thinking resembled other student comments. Some reported that "Haters" motivated them to do their best. When I asked them who they were referring to as "Haters," they said they were the teachers who don't like them and expect them to fail. According to Gallison and D'Maio, this is one of the ongoing complaints about school that they hear from students year after year:

> All the kids kept saying to us that teachers don't care…it is the most difficult thing to break them out of that mind-set…We talk to them about why teachers have to do what they have to do…we defend the teachers even when we know that some of the teachers are the problem…We show them how to take responsibility (personal communication, May 5, 2005).

Gallison's and D'Maio's statement reinforces the argument that students who struggle in school are doing so partially because their teachers do not expect them to succeed. Student responses illustrate that students know when a teacher does not like them or does not believe they can learn, and that they are motivated to do their personal best when teachers are nice to them and the schoolwork is fun and meaningful. Even when their teachers are "Haters," some students want to show them that they are wrong. Yet it is difficult to imagine how anyone could be successful in a class where they believe that the teacher expects them to fail and hates them. This situation is a tragedy particularly when we know that "no other intervention can make the difference that a knowledgeable and skillful teacher can make in the learning process" (Darling-Hammond as cited in Linek et al. 2003, 3).

An incident during my first summer illustrates how students who are labeled "at risk" often get mistreated in school. I came to class one morning and found that school administrators had given my students an unannounced math quiz. The students were visibly upset. Furthermore, they assumed that their failure on this test meant that they were going to fail the summer program. All but one student had failed the test.

Although "pop quizzes" are given in many classrooms, this unannounced test given to students who were already struggling with school was perceived as a hostile vehicle to eject them from the program. Additionally, because none of the AEP staff was notified about the test, the quiz was further experienced as an indication of a lack of respect and collaboration for the program itself. When I asked the students to tell me how they felt about this situation and what they would like to do about it, to my surprise they were angry yet unwilling to confront the administration because they felt that they did not have the right to do so, even though they felt that what had happened to them was wrong. Once they learned that they would not fail or be dismissed from AEP, they were complacent with their failure.

I was enraged about this situation because I knew that my students had been set up to fail, understanding clearly that if they had been students from privileged backgrounds, the school would never have done this for fear of parent and even student retaliation. In response to this unconscionable act and determined to show students that with support, appropriate instruction, and high expectations, they could all achieve success, I invited one of my graduate students to teach mathematics to AEP learners. The outcome of Gina Achin's instruction (the students referred to her as the "Math Lady") was evidenced by students' successful completion of assignments, a positive shift in their attitude toward mathematics, and their increased self-confidence about quantitative reasoning. Caroline's letter below expressed what many students felt about the math lessons Gina taught. She wrote,

Dear Math Lady,

You have helped me to see that math can be fun... You made math fun in ways that no other teacher of mine has ever done. Actually I really never had a teacher actually care enough to make a lesson fun, even if it was intended to make us learn better... Thank you for giving us the opportunity to be better in school. You didn't judge us even though you knew we weren't the best students in school, you didn't doubt us either. You gave us a fair chance. You treated us as [if] we could do anything we put our minds too. You gave us the confidence that we can do anything... and that means a lot. (personal communication, July 2005)

The impact of her success was best summed up by one student who responded when asked to evaluate the mathematics instruction stated, "I learned more mathematics in two days than I have learned in all the years I have been in school" (Kathy, personal communication, July 2004).

Study Skills

In addition to skillful teaching of content and high teacher expectations, students must also be taught the study skills that they will need to be successful in school. According to Gettinger and Seibert (2002, 1), "Study skills are fundamental to academic competence. Effective study skills are associated with positive outcomes across multiple academic content areas and for diverse learners." The students' reaction to learning study skills validated the research: "I have improved my study skills and hope to learn a lot more in life [because] of this program" (Paul, personal communication, 2004). "Capable students at all grade levels may experience difficulty in school, not because they lack ability, but because they lack good study skills" (Gettinger and Seibert 2002, 2). Teachers cannot assume that students know how to study and should be prepared to offer them instruction on how to study effectively.

Furthermore, study skills are particularly important for middle- and high-school students to learn because, "Although problems with study skills are evident among elementary school children, weak study skills are generally ascribed to adolescents and older students, largely because expectations for independent study increase substantially in middle and high school" (Deshler et al., as cited in Gettinger and Seibert 2002, 4). The self-efficacy that study skills can engender in students was highlighted by one student who stated,

> This program helps kids in their study skills and reading and test-taking and math skills...this program has made my work a lot easier so when I go to the high school next year I will not have any trouble doing the work. (Ronald, personal communication, July 2004)

The reality of high school is that this student would encounter difficult material that might give him "trouble"; however, he would start high school motivated to succeed, because he believed, "I can do it and I should never give up, and I will be successful in my life if I keep doing what I am doing" (Ronald, personal communication, July 2004).

Student Voices

There were some success stories in the AEP over the past three years. Donna, whose words we heard at the beginning of the chapter, became an honor roll student in the ninth grade. Most students successfully negotiated that difficult first year of high school. Yet there were students who did not fare well in high school; at least one student, Andrew, ended up in the Rhode Island Training School, and some have dropped out of school altogether. However, when these and the other students completed AEP, they did so with feelings such as Ronald's:

> I have learned that you should never give up, keep trying. I also learned that nobody is stupid and we are all intelligent and smart...We should set our goals...my goal is to go to URI (University of Rhode Island). Thank you Ray, Mr. D., Tiger, Dr. Brown, Aubrey and Sulee you have shown me that I can do it...thanks again for teaching me the better side of life. (Ronald, personal communication, July 2004)

This student's words are a particularly powerful testament to the program's positive impact on students' attitude toward their education. When Ronald started the program he had a poor attitude and was angry that he had to be in summer school. As the program progressed, his behavior and attitude began to change. His work improved, as did his thinking about going to college.

Although students in AEP between 2004 and 2006 began the program reluctantly, even complaining that they had been "tricked" or "forced" to participate, by the end of the program, unanimously said that they were glad they had come to AEP because as one student put it,

> This program was great and I learned a lot from it. [I] learned [that if you] make the right choices...you will succeed in life. But if you make a bad choice you will end up in the training school. [I learned] that you should get a good education first before you do anything and once you get your college degree your life will be a lot easier.

My Evolving Understanding

As stated at the beginning of this chapter, I began to do this work reluctantly, as a short-term, voluntary community service that would not make too many demands on me. When I met my students, however, and they said to me, "You expect us to fail, right? We're losers!" I realized that these students had given my work purpose and passion. These are the students that Ladson-Billings points out are "school dependent" because they need the guidance and direction of the school to be successful in education and life. I discovered that these students were often the victims of their own inappropriate behavior, because they did not understand or know the rules of engagement for operating successfully in school. I taught them how to negotiate the "culture" of high school. I taught them that part of the strategy of negotiating high school successfully was to recognize danger zones and to identify shields for their self-protection.

The students learned to analyze and understand their study skills and habits. They developed strategies for looking at math differently and learned how to use a reading strategy to comprehend difficult material. The study skills that they developed provided them concrete approaches for how best to study, take notes, and improve their comprehension and test-taking skills. Most importantly, they learned that they have choices in life. In three short weeks, the AEP transformed students' beliefs about themselves as learners. It would be naïve to believe that this program alone would sustain them in high school. If they did not receive support and nurturing in high school from their teachers and counselors, the likelihood that they would hold on to these gains might be diminished.

Until I began working with the AEP students, I was in despair about public education, a serious obstacle for someone like me long professionally engaged in teacher education. But my community service with the AEPs has radically changed my understanding of the experiences of the struggling learner and of the strategies we can use to encourage students to "turn-on to learning." I have become more empathetic toward the "at-risk" learner, and more understanding of the challenges that face the instructors who face them in the classroom. It turned out to be possible to make a significant impact on the lives of students "on the margins" in a relatively short period of time. Perhaps this possibility is realizable in other schools across the country.

The anger, invisibility, and hypervisibility that I experienced as a professor of color reflected in part what my AEP students experienced in their schools. My summer students, who lacked many education skills, also felt discouraged and disconnected in their institutions, as I did. However, my AEP summer experience showed us all—my students and me—that there was hope and the possibility of success. The identification of danger zones and the use of shields that I taught my AEP students were also reflected in my work at Lesley University. I learned that by employing "tempered visibility" strategies, that is, blending or alternating invisibility "staying below the radar" and hypervisibility "standing out from the crowd," I was better able to be in control of my own success in my institution, both personally and professionally (Smith 2006, as cited in Blake-Beard and Morgan 2006).

Most important and directly related to my teaching of graduate students at Lesley University, my AEP summers have enabled me to better "teach" teachers how to more effectively reach students from diverse backgrounds in their own classrooms. This "community service," which I highly recommend to my colleagues, has provided me with many case studies of students and their school experiences that I have shared in my classroom with graduate students to help them understand how what they are learning at the university will aid them in becoming better teachers of diverse learners in the inclusive classroom.

The transformation for me that came as a result of my time working with AEP youth allowed me, in Payne's words,

> to grieve and go through the grieving process as one teaches or works with the poor. The Kublier-Ross stages in the grieving process are anger, denial, bargaining, depression, and acceptance. As one meets and works with a particular family or individual, there is such frustration and, ultimately, grieving because many situations are so embedded as to seem hopeless...Yet the role of the educator...is not to save the individual, but rather to offer a support system, role models, and opportunities to learn, which will increase the likelihood of the person's success. Ultimately, the choice always belongs to the individual...But it is the responsibility of the educators and others who work with the poor to teach the differences and skills/rules that will allow the individual to make the choice. As it now stands for many of the poor, the choice never exists. (1996, 145)

My hypervisibility as a professional of color has added value to the discussion and the learning in our own increasingly diverse classrooms. One of the positive benefits of my hypervisibility in the front of the classroom in both AEP and the graduate School of Education at Lesley was the value-added impact of a professional of color, particularly a black woman whose position as an expert, authority figure, and role model encourages and inspires students of all colors. Contrary to the prevailing wisdom discussed often in the literature about the presence and experiences of professionals of color in classrooms of all levels but particularly in higher education, my presence was as instructional if not more for white students than those of color. As a person of color, I was and am cognizant of the need to create a safe and nonjudgmental space for teaching and learning because "I have felt unsafe in many classrooms" (Jones and Smith 2003).

As for me, once I began working with students in the AEP, I came to realize that inclusion was not a topic I could or should avoid. My own initial personal despair over the value and authenticity of the "diversity" discourse was an issue for me to struggle with in my own professional and scholarly world, my own institutional setting, not in theirs. My own anger and alienation receded and my tempered visibility strategies increased. I recognized that for my AEP summer students, this program meant something very important: it was the last opportunity they might ever have to turn their lives around and to plan for a future that could only be acquired through success in education. My students had never experienced the privilege of being fully included in their own education primarily because they were labeled "at risk," without the benefit of being seen as an individual from a family living in poverty. According to Payne (1996, 16), "To better understand students and adults from poverty, a working definition of poverty is [defined here] the extent to which an individual does without resources (e.g., Financial, Emotional, Mental, Spiritual, Physical, Support Systems, Relationships/Role Models, Knowledge of Hidden Rules)."

These serendipitous summer experiences gave me new purchase on my work with students at different locations and levels within the educational system, including my work with preservice and in-service teachers in the graduate programs at Lesley. Working with the AEP struggling middle-school youth made me reflect on my school experiences good, and bad, through a new lens. Working with AEP students was like a mirror of my own life. I was that poor kid, not labeled "at risk" because I did my work, but was on the margins of everything because of my race, gender, and the economic status of my "working-poor" family. Reflecting on my own educational experiences through this new lens, I realized that I had the power to transform the students' lives using my own education and skills. I knew they didn't have to buy into the "at-risk" or "loser" labels of the "haters" and could teach them how to succeed. Comer says the way out of poverty is education and relationships and I had had both educational and personal mentors and was able to be both to my students.

In conclusion, there is no happy ending to my struggle as a black woman in the educational setting. In exploding the definition of inclusion, I have become aware of another aspect of diversity since I first wrote this chapter. Since 2009, I have worked as a program director of elementary education in a proprietary institution in the South. As a "token" and "only" in my position in a southern white school, I was both invisible when it came to my knowledge, skills, and abilities, that is, my accomplishments were ignored and hypervisible, again labeled as an "angry black woman." I was finally able to make sense of a senseless experience by understanding the cultural clash between an accomplished and outspoken black woman in a white southern institution who did not know her place. Institutional structures and cultural and geographical diversity are therefore another aspect of the explosion of the concept of inclusion that needs to be added to our national conversation of diversity and inclusion.

Flawed as the educational system is, it remains a pathway out of poverty. I have used my education that taught me I have "inalienable rights" to fight back against injustice for my students and myself. My experience teaching and my relationships with the AEP students transformed me into a better and more reflective teacher, testimony to the transformative power of education for both teachers and learners.

CHAPTER 12

Building Agency through Writing

Marjorie Jones

Introduction

Children's games, the ones children create for themselves, can often be an indicator of passions they might pursue in the future. That seems to be true in my case. My mother often told the story that, as a child, I would "play school" and be the teacher, gathering both the willing and unwilling into my classroom. I don't recall these early experiences, but her recounting of them helped me to appreciate that I may have always believed that a teacher's role was to help a student learn, and that there was great fulfillment for the teacher in this role.

I grew up in British Guiana (now Guyana), where high academic performance at the elementary level, measured by success at a Secondary School Entrance Examination (SSEE), was critical to determining the types of jobs and professions one would pursue. Students preparing for the SSEE attended school during the day, as other students did, but received additional instruction at the end of the school day. During one of these classroom sessions, I had completed my assignment, shown it to my teacher and returned to my seat. I had free time until the next assignment, so I decided to imagine myself as a clerk in a large department store. As a child, I often witnessed how in the town department stores the clerks would procure the merchandise for the customer, calculate the cost, and prepare a bill, then call, in a very audible voice, "sign a bill." The supervisor or storeowner would sign the bill as a way of verifying its correctness. As I was playing store, I unintentionally called out, "sign a bill." My teacher turned her head toward me and sternly said, "Don't ever let me hear you saying that again." Because education and employment determined one's socioeconomic status, my teacher did not want me to claim a place beneath what she expected of me.

Success at school helped me to develop a sense of self-worth and assured me that I could realize my fullest potential and contribute to the development of society. As a student, my sense of wanting to be recognized as one of the "smart" students has informed my role as a teacher in supporting students to develop to their highest potential. There were aspects of my identity that often made me feel inferior in the class-conscious society in which I lived. I lived in a village, which though it was only three miles outside of the center of the capital city, did not have as high a social status as other sections of the capital city. Another social stigma was that I lived in a female-headed household. It was the accomplishments at school that built my self-confidence and my self-worth. Overcoming fears about both ability and possibility were critical to my academic achievement and sense of place in society. Individuals harbor doubts about their ability to achieve, but encouragement and appropriate environments can support them in achieving what may have appeared to be out of reach.

Now much later in my career as an educator, I reflect on the work that I have undertaken in developing writing courses in the Adult Baccalaureate College/Adult Learning Division (ALD) at Lesley University. Our courses are designed to develop learners' skills in relation to the writing requirements of the programs and to seek to address capacities related to citizenship engagement. For me, the classroom is not simply an enclosed space in which teachers and students interact over what is in the formal curriculum: it is also a deeply public, civic space in which all participants develop important critical, moral, and political understandings and practice them through their dialogue and collaboration. Over a period of twenty-five years, I have worked with different adult populations, each of which has benefited from experiencing a safe environment to learn and grow, ultimately finding a sense of agency and transformation in the educational encounter. Both teaching and learning are fundamentally collaborative activities that build on mutually affirming social relationships, creating temporary communities that emerge during the educational encounter. Some of these relationships, both between students as well as between me and former students, are more long-lasting than others.

It is this reciprocity, the experience of seeing the teacher as a learner, as well, that allows for pedagogical insights for all the participants and thus does not limit learning to a fixed space, the classroom. Learning involves authentic dialogue, self-reflexivity, the forging of social relationships, community building, humanistic concerns, and even love. My own childhood experiences exposed me to shifting and dynamic systems of power, and I share this personal context with students to begin unpacking dimensions of their identities and power dynamics that play out in all our lives, regardless of what roles we might have as teachers or students. Despite the differences among us, I share much with them. Similar experiences and feelings as my own as a young person are often brought up by students in the adult classroom as reflected by an African American female student, aged thirty-two years, who noted, "No one in my family ever went to college, so no one in my family expected me to go to college."

Twelve years of my professional career were spent with practicing teachers who had acquired a teaching certificate and were continuing their education focusing on equipping themselves to be better practitioners in the classroom. Course content focused on theory and practice in education, but it was mastery of the theory that frequently caused anxiety. Because they had attended a teacher training institution after high school and had not entered the university directly from high school, they harbored feelings of being less capable than students who had entered the university directly from high school. Their concerns focused on their ability to read and comprehend educational theory that would then inform their practice as teachers. Because many of them had had at least five years of experience as practicing teachers, I would match their experiences with the various theories to demonstrate that the instructional process could be approached either from theory to practice or from practice to theory. Beginning with their knowledge and expertise in the use of appropriate classroom processes was the strategy used to help these teachers recognize and experience what was possible for them. "Adults have enough life experience to be in dialogue with any teacher about any subject and will learn new knowledge, attitudes, or skills in relation to that life experience" (Vella 2002, 3).

Teaching and Learning at Lesley University

The program that has provided the experiences embedded in this essay is a degree completion program in the ALD of Lesley College. The program is designed for working adults who desire to complete an undergraduate degree. The program structure is guided by a theoretical position that believes that the aim and purpose of education is to promote significant learning enhanced by examination and deeper questions of one's self and place in the world (Daloz 1999, 243).

The age of the ALD student population ranges from twenty-five to thirty-eight years. The adult learners are mostly female and represent a wide variety of cultures and ethnicities. A significant number of the students pursue a major in Human Development. Often they are paraprofessionals working in school classrooms and seeking to become the designated teacher in the classroom or the director of an after-school program. Others are seeking qualifications to establish their own home-based childcare facilities or to work in the field of counseling. Some students are seeking to change careers in the business and corporate sectors to professions that "care" for people. The second-largest number of the population pursues an individualized major that allows them to fashion their own degree.

Students come with a sincere desire and commitment to complete their course of study, but this is in many cases accompanied by anxiety and concern about their ability to perform satisfactorily and complete the process. My belief is that education must equip adults for the complex task of sustaining their own individual growth and of contributing to the growth of others for whom they provide care in the family and outside it, in community and society at more collective levels. Many adult students, either for reasons of poor preparation in foundational skills or for lack of practice, require additional writing support when they return to college. Hence, I developed courses in the ALD Writing Program to focus on both foundational skills in writing as well as academic writing. To achieve these goals, I personally connect with each of my students and develop a relationship and a learning environment that motivates and supports student learning. Building agency through writing is the major goal and theme of my pedagogical practice with students.

Adult learners come to the teaching/learning experience in higher education with a wide variety of educational, professional, and personal experiences. Yet among a significant number of the population resides a gnawing message that "I can't do this" and "I'm not good enough to do this." This fear and self-doubt often paralyze student progress or impede the pace at which and the level to which some of the students are able to experience success. Sally, a thirty-five-year-old white female student who had attended two two-year institutions before coming to Lesley, noted, for example,

My first class, I was filled with anxiety, fear and apprehension. I was walking into the building and my heart began to race rapidly, my ears were pulsing, and I began to sweat. My mind was racing with questions: Do I belong here? Am I making the right decision to come back a second time? Am I smart enough? Can I do this? And why is this happening again? I thought I was over my anxiety.

Fear and apprehension often accompany the adult student despite visible accomplishments. One student remarked, for example,

I was accepted at Lesley University, for the first time, two years after I graduated high school. It was a huge accomplishment for me, considering that I was told in high school by one of my teachers that I was not college material.

Sally had completed high school despite the messages that suggested that she could not. Yet she continued to carry the messages of self-doubt and inadequacy as she continued her education as an adult.

The anthropologist Sherry Ortner, in her article "Thick Resistance: Death and the Cultural Construction of Agency in Himalayan Mountaineering," argues that it is crucial to look at cultural forms and practices in terms of their "effects" rather than their "meanings." She is concerned with how issues of culture, history, and power can be mutually defined and elaborates on Clifford Geertz's description of cultural forms as "webs of meaning" and introduces the concept of agency as "thick resistance." She states, "I view agency as a piece of both the power problematic and the meaning problematic. In the context of power, agency is that which is made or denied, expanded or contracted, in the exercise of power." "It is the (sense of) authority to act, or of lack of authority and lack of empowerment" (Ortner 1999, 147). Sally's decision to return to the academy was an act of agency, a step forward in her taking action to empower herself in an arena where she previously had none.

Writing Courses as Vehicles of Agency: Establishing the "Learning Community"

The first two courses in the degree completion program are designed to help students to transition back into the academic setting. As Norgaard writes,

> When you enter the university, or enter advanced course work in your major, you are entering the sort of parlor that Kenneth Burke describes. While the conversation can certainly be engaging, and the ideas stimulating, the experience of entering a new setting can be quite unsettling. (2007, 1)

My colleagues and I developed the courses, in order to acknowledge, first, the anxiety and unsettling nature of the resumption of studies and, second, the need to develop skills in literacy and critical inquiry. The first course, Writing Skills I, is designed to develop and promote writing abilities through integration of personal and public voice for a variety of purposes. The course provides examples of writing from many types of rhetorical patterns: narration, description, exemplification, definition, classification, comparison and contrast, analogy and extended metaphor, cause and effect, process analysis, and argument and persuasion and encourages consideration of a variety of writing strategies. This variety acknowledges the range of interests and the variety of learning styles of the population.

The first meeting of the course is essential in setting the tone and assuring each student that individual contributions are essential to the overall outcome of the course. Trying to set a relaxed atmosphere, I tell the class that I welcome their presence because without it I would not be able to practice my craft. Some planned activities at the outset of our meetings are designed to establish a relationship among all the learners in the room.

We begin by discussing how we might become a "*learning community*" and attempt to define the meaning of that phrase. I write the word "learning" on one side of the board and ask students to brainstorm all the words that come to mind when they think of the term learning. Next, we record on the other side of the board the words that come to mind when students think of the term "community." We then review the words that have been brainstormed, and using those words, write one or several "definitions" of a learning community. One of the definitions developed was, "A learning community is a group of people with a common purpose who have come together to collaborate and share knowledge by supporting each other." In further discussion, students are invited to consider the learning community more broadly, focusing in particular on how individual members see their role in contributing and receiving knowledge from the community, and in being supported as a member of the community. Students begin to raise questions and make comments more freely. Some comment on their understanding and interpretation of the definition and begin to share with the class the hesitation with which they entered the class. Some students observe that they were now less fearful of the academic learning process, because they now know that they will be able to work with others to develop their skills.

To further the building of a learning community, I ask students to name the attributes they bring to the process. Responses such as curiosity, being a good listener, and nervousness help student learners to acknowledge each other as individuals with traits that may be seen as strengths or challenges, but nonetheless human traits that can complement one another and enrich the group's capabilities overall. In addition, students are invited to compile a class roster that includes contact information and encouraged to use it to contact each other for whatever reasons they determine necessary. They often use the roster to clarify course-related information and strategies for completing assignments, and in so doing, they extend the concept of community beyond the classroom.

Students inevitably carry memories of earlier, often painful experiences with writing into their present work as new students. Only if students feel a sense of safety in the classroom community can they share and reflect on their past disappointments and frustrations to more positive expectations about current academic challenges. The principle of safety enables the teacher to create an inviting setting for adult learners. People have shown that they are willing but also ready and eager to learn when they feel safe in the learning environment (Vella 2002, 8). Safety is critical to the learning experience, so that students can share and reflect on their past and sometimes painful experiences and then determine ways of moving from these disappointments and frustrations to more positive expectations about current academic challenges.

Allison, forty years old, for example, pursuing credentials that would allow her to leave her corporate job and establish her own home-based child-care facility, reflected in this way:

When I think about the history of my writing, my writing personality, I think about my struggles. Despite what I think to be very strong writing skills...I have had relentless difficulties that seem to plague me through the years. I love to write. It is rare that I can write something and keep it simple and concise. I am tirelessly wordy. This was brought to yet another undeniable realization of mine when attempting to write an application essay that absolutely could not run over 500 words. Hah! My first draft was 1500 words.

Self-reflections like these are crucial for building agency because they allow students to identify problems they have struggled with and to focus in making new, more concerted efforts to improve in directions that they choose themselves.

Building Confidence and Recovering from Wounds

Why does being in a group build confidence, after all? At the beginning, when we talk about expectations and concerns, some say "I never know what to write," "I have always been a poor writer," and "My teachers told me so." Whenever someone relates one of these stories, there are always many others who say they heard the same comments, so that the initial speaker says, "Oh, that happened to you too!" They are thus writing with people who have had similar experiences to theirs, and therefore, no one seems to be the expert in the group. Everyone is starting off with some hesitation.

Students become very comfortable sharing, and this helps them recover from hurtful experiences they had in school at earlier ages, where they were called names or humiliated. This helps them to see their own life experience as more of an asset, instead of a source of pain, a resource from which they can determine what they will now do as practitioners. Even as an adult they easily return to those negative feelings, which they remember quite vividly. In teaching, naturally, I try to not make my students feel the way they felt in the painful experiences that they share. We all realize what it has done to the "learner," for example, when one of the students confesses, "I hated going to school" or "the teacher made me feel bad."

The Learner as Contributor to the Pedagogical Process

A powerful strategy for fostering student agency is to invite them to contribute to the teaching-learning process in which they participate. It is important to prepare a course syllabus that reflects both the content and process of a plan, but the syllabus should also be a living document that can be adapted to the needs of learners. I provide an overview of the syllabus in my first class, noting that it is an agreement between the professor and the students. Students are invited to identify their *expectations and concerns*. I then use the list they provide to identify when and how the syllabus will address their particular expectations or concerns. I also suggest strategies and resources in the university that are designed to help the student address these issues, as do the students. Student input has a two-fold purpose: students see that others share their expectations and concerns; that they are not the only ones needing improvement in specific competencies; and that they are not the only ones who find the task formidable. Students begin to view each other as resources, the teaching-learning process as a collaborative activity, and the classroom as a community of support. I return to this list during the semester to note the progress that has been made on the items listed as expectations and concerns. Vella (2002) outlines a similar strategy.

> One of the first tasks I do in any course is to invite learners to work in small groups to name their own expectations, hopes or fears about a learning event or norms they want to see established in the large group. (Vella 2002, 9).

Two strategies used to provide a laboratory experience for students are (1) working in small groups to develop ideas and (2) peer editing. In the small group, students can interact with a peer, focused on the same assignment and working for a shared outcome. They can collaborate with peers as they explore the meaning of what they have read and determine ways they might write their own interpretations of the assigned reading. The assurance of safety and shared responsibility available in teams has always proved welcome, no matter what the cultural setting (Vella 2002, 22). The composition of the small groups varies throughout the course to expose learners to peers with a variety of perspectives, abilities, and learning styles, thereby providing the opportunity to work closely with as many of their colleagues as possible.

Another important group dynamic that affirms community as well as individual input is the continual process of peer editing during our class sessions. The majority of the essays selected for course reading are those that are derived from personal experiences or observations, to model for students that their own life experiences qualify as course content, and that the observations they have made or make presently on them can be the subject of critical reflection in their writing. The strategy is designed to demystify the process and product of writing. As faculty I use my own experiences in the academy and return to the concept of agency. This concept is particularly relevant in the class context because of the need to insert oneself in the "conversations" and my role in providing legitimacy and motivational words to encourage student experimentation with writing. I teach with conversation, and as one student described our class, "Our talking is our writing."

Students write all of their essays in two drafts. Before writing the first draft, there is a whole group discussion. After writing the first draft, students read their drafts aloud in small groups and receive feedback from their colleagues. This activity gives learners the opportunity to "hear" their own writing and listen to the writing of others. This activity is not devoid of anxiety; one student noted that she was reluctant to share her writing with others, because she was fearful of their criticism. It was important for me to discuss the distinction between criticism and feedback and to model the difference in the classroom.

A thirty-year-old woman, who had immigrated to the United States from South America when she was eighteen years old, noted her sense of feeling ill prepared for the college experience but being willing to face the challenge of the task when she wrote that "as an ESL student, I lack confidence in writing and communication skills. I did make some effort with my teacher's encouragement. I did benefit. I discovered new words, new meanings, new styles to express an idea."

Not a native English speaker, this student was attempting to equip herself with skills to serve the educational needs of the urban immigrant community where she works. Her appraisal of her experiences in the course acknowledges her challenges and her own efforts to overcome them. Identifying what she has accomplished is evidence of the exercise of her own power to chart and manage her learning.

There are other strategies that can be used to engage adult learners as active collaborators in the teaching and learning process. Posting an agenda at the beginning of each class is another good step in making the class transparent to their understanding. The agenda, after all, relates the day to the syllabus plan and identifies a sequence of activities for addressing course content.

> Trust in the sequence of activities builds safety. Beginning with simple, clear, and relatively easy tasks before advancing to more complex and more difficult ones can give learners a sense of safety so that they can take on harder tasks with assurance. (Vella 2002, 9)

Sometimes, the agenda includes a "Thought for the Day" contributed by either the teacher or a student. This thought can come from something that the student has read or could simply be a saying or an idea composed by the learner. These "thoughts" are ways of beginning of the work of the day, allowing the voices of various members of the community to set the tone and provide content and context for the day's work.

Collaboration as a Pedagogical Approach: Breaking Down Unnecessary Hierarchies

I always talk to my students as people, not in a too formal "teacher-student" manner. It is important to engage them and provide a level of comfort to break barriers. The new connection that results can best be described as collaboration. As a professor, it is not important to exercise the power over them that you have. It is necessary to bring them from a feeling of being on the margin to a place that is safe where they can approach you personally. You share your power in order to mentor them (Finkel 2000).

Some of them come into class even thinking I do not like them, and it is important for me to try hard to examine this power dynamic and not make them feel more powerless. I take much time and reflect on their work, in order to provide feedback, putting a great deal of time into helping them think about the revisions. It is important to avoid presenting this as punishment, instead of as encouragement to improve work. Often I ask them first if they want me to provide feedback and only then do it. Of course, almost everyone asks for it.

Through observation of my teaching, I have seen what strategies work and I build on them. My teaching is full of humor, and we laugh, we really laugh in class, which is an aspect of making people comfortable and spontaneous in what they say and write. When my students take risks, that is my reward, and it is easy to show them my pleasure. We talk about how our classroom is not about "getting it right," but that it offers a place and a time to "try out new things." The tone of the classroom is personal, and I call people by their name. When I speak with students, I make a point of looking at them directly, making eye contact, and at times physical contact. In my own environment as a child learning and growing, everyone wanted you to do well, and when you did well, everyone celebrated: all of that is still a part of who I am. I know how to celebrate others, as it is a part of where I came from. My success was never only my own. That is how, in return to others today, I teach and live, and the students pick that up. I celebrate their presence in my classroom and their success.

The Learner as Knower

During class, we also grapple with common myths about writing, ones that have discouraged many of my students in the past. I post myths about writing on an overhead projector; then a student or I read the myth out loud, and this stimulates a discussion about what the more complex reality actually is. After one or more responses, I suggest what the consensus actually is among composition scholars about the issue. In the majority of instances, the students' critical responses have been consistent with the scholarly consensus. Once they recognize this, they have to reflect on the reasons that they might have believed that they were not capable of writing or learning to write as successfully as they would wish. They begin to see that many of these beliefs are related to the myths we have just deconstructed, and this leads them to start identifying ways in which individuals become competent writers. These are some of the myths and realities we tackle.

> *Myth*: Good writers work alone.
> *Fact*: Good writers frequently rely on others for suggestions and help, and writers often collaborate to share ideas and work out their writing problems.
> *Myth*: Good writers quickly get their prose correct and polished, the first time they write it.
> *Fact*: Although experienced writers can sometimes produce good prose on the spot, for important jobs, professional writers usually write many drafts.

We have another activity, called *What Writers Say about Writing*, designed to give students the opportunity to hear what established writers have said about their own writing process. Students can see that everyone does not have the same writing process, but that everyone can write something they can be proud of. I use Nobel Laureate John Steinbeck's famous quote, "I suffer always from fear of putting down that first line. It is amazing the terrors, the magics, the prayers, the straightening shyness that assails one," as a place to begin the conversation. The surprise that accompanies the reading of the various quotes prompts students to share their own writing experiences and doubts.

In my second writing course for adult learners, similar pedagogical dynamics are also at play. Writing Skills II is an advanced-level college writing course focusing on the development and expansion of logical, analytical, and research skills to enrich academic writing. The course readings are essays related to government, justice, education, feminism, wealth and poverty, culture, and morals and ethics. Students engage with the civic and policy issues raised by the readings and learn to take their own critical stances toward the issues as both writers and citizens. "An essential part of your college education is not just learning facts but also learning how to make sense of and join that conversation—a conversation that is not limited to classrooms but also extends to larger civic spaces" (Norgaard 2007, 1).

Loretta, a teacher aide in her thirties, spoke of the impact of the assigned readings and discussion:

> I am even becoming interested in politics and how it influences the laws protecting the environment. I even want to learn about the candidates for President! I was never interested in this area before! This course has stimulated my sleepy, comfortable mind to begin the journey to political awareness as well as the rights of our citizens for justice, education and their well-being. I feel more responsible for the way things are run in my part of the world.

One of the results of providing models of writing through the various assigned essays, working in small groups, participating in peer editing groups, and receiving support and feedback from the instructor is that students actively practice strategies for improving their writing and increasing their sense of agency as critical thinkers and citizens. To demystify critical thinking, I always try to locate the roots of my own agency, like theirs, in conversation and dialogue by linking them directly to writing. Some days, I refer to myself as a "scribe" and ask them how can we make our writing as exciting as our talking? If we have a conversation about describing an object, I will be the scribe and write on pieces of paper what they say, then we will go back to the paper or board and ask how can we write this in a way to make it more vivid, to give it more imagery where the grammar is corrected. We do the revisions together, first in small groups of three, and then as a whole class.

In our class discussions, students often reflect on their growth and confidence due to their being part of a community of learners and thinkers, and they do not feel the anxiety and isolation of the writing process that has often paralyzed them when trying to formulate their thinking. One day Rosalyn, in her late thirties, for example, spontaneously burst out to the class with the comment that "we are collaborators. I am not alone!" Another student wrote in a response journal,

> My voice, my agency, has already grown during our six weeks together. My confidence in reading and comprehension of the material has multiplied threefold. I am talking about society's issues with classmates, my partner and whoever else is willing and able.

By making thinking, talking, and writing interconnected acts in the classroom, any of the aforementioned activities can be considered an act of agency, an act that makes a statement about the actor's power in relation to self as well as others. These acts are important because of the need for "the reconstruction of regimes of power/knowledge" (Ortner 1999, 158).

Generating student participation, in speaking, active listening, and writing is not always easy. As Juanita said to me in an office conference,

> I still haven't participated in the class conversation because I keep feeling, what if I am wrong on some topic I was totally unaware of, like justice and government? But I know I want to make an effort to participate in conversations because I learned that ideas are not simply wrong or right, but it is how we understand them that matters. The class has helped me to learn how to think critically, which I haven't done before.

Students may have experienced models of teaching where they were expected simply to be receptacles, rather than contributors and collaborators. In our classroom, the emphasis is on cohesive learning as a community, and my role is to listen carefully to responses and incorporate student ideas into my remarks throughout the class. This affirmation of students' knowledge and my posture both as a learner and as a fellow class member allows active engagement and thoughtful exchanges, leading us all to construct a deeper understanding of the issues we are examining. One student remarked in her log that my encouraging words in guiding the class discussion, such as "as we read and think together," helped her find strength in being part of the group and seeing the work of the group as a collective social contract for everyone to strive for improvement in critical thinking and writing skills.

Writing Can Build Agency

Once students can write out their thoughts and reflections from their experience, they can then receive credit both for their professional practice and also for being able to write and talk about practice at more critical levels. As a result, they can participate more actively in their own professional community. This allows them to move beyond simple practice, that is, simply doing their jobs, to a position where they can be one of the speakers at the PTA meeting in their school or one of the facilitators at a workshop for other teachers. They learn to explain what they do, they learn to match what they do with what theorists have said and done, and thus they see themselves as being able to theorize.

Next, they can transfer these capacities to other areas of their life. It is a transformative experience that has repercussions throughout their lives. They can write and express their ideas in other classes. The writing class is not a class onto itself, a closed world, but is designed to teach writing, so that you can think and write in other classes, on the job, or wherever you might go. My former students now write editorials, send comments to newspapers, and have become active change agents in their communities.

Agency is considered to be "a more active projection of the self toward some desired end"; it is that dimension of power that is located in the actor's subjective sense of authorization, control, and effectiveness in the world (Ortner 1999, 147). Fear and self-doubt about the presence of "voice," and their ability to be successful in higher education, often impede the students' appreciation of their own levels of achievement. The goal of instruction in writing, we must remember, is not only the development and enhancement of communication skills but also the building of agency on the part of the learner. Agency says to the adult learner, "What you do matters; what you do has an impact on someone or something." This sense of agency can be carried from one educational setting to many other sites in a person's professional, personal, and civic life.

Conclusion

Adult learners come to the academy with a significant amount of experience as people who have raised families, served as heads of households, been employed, spent many years in a profession, and participated as active citizens in community affairs. No longer "young" people, and sometimes out of school for many years, they also come with doubts about their ability to achieve the academic goals they set for themselves. Courses in writing can provide content that echoes their interests and experiences and pedagogical strategies that acknowledge that they bring valuable knowledge and experience to the teaching-learning encounter. These strategies provide for the right pacing, the sense of safety, and the inclusion of each learner's voice. Adult learners, if treated in pedagogically encouraging ways, identify and consolidate skills that they have learned and apply in other courses; transfer new senses of hope and possibility to areas outside the classroom; and learn to see "weaknesses" not as a deterrent to learning but as a marker of the starting point for development of skills that enable them to meet academic and life goals.

My own experiences, in life and as a facilitator of learning, have shown me the way to work toward a more effective and collaborative teacher-student partnership. The conditions that need to be provided are clear, I believe, and especially for adult learners. They include a safe environment that honors the learner's experience, engaging the learner in the construction and application of knowledge, using a variety of methods to encourage participation, and recognizing the adult learner's valuable contributions. All of this results not only in successful mastery of course content but also can give voice to the life of the learner, within the classroom and beyond.

CHAPTER 13

Words Matter: Vocabulary in a Diverse Precollege-Level Writing Class

Richard Pepp

"Nurse, I have to see the doctor right now! My husband is shrinking!"
"Well, he'll just have to be a little patient."

I was once told that one should always begin with a joke. I chose this joke, not because of its significant social burden of the stereotypical creation of the hysterical wife, nor because of the hierarchical doctor-nurse relationship and whatever gender associations go with it, nor even because of its implied criticism of health care in America. I begin with the joke because when I tell it to my Introductory Writing class at Massasoit Community College, not everybody gets it. (I am not talking about those who get it and don't think it's funny, or those who don't allow themselves to be amused in a classroom.) Not everybody gets it—I know, I've asked. Native speakers and English language learners alike don't get it. And I love this joke.

I teach at Massasoit Community College, a comprehensive community college in Brockton, Massachusetts, on the northern edge of Plymouth County, about twenty miles south of Boston. Massasoit offers transfer, career, and mechanical-vocational programs, with open admission for all qualified students—those with high-school diplomas, GEDs, and a variety of equivalents. I have taught there since 1974. Over the past thirty years, changes occurred in me, Massasoit, and the world. I started teaching at Massasoit at about the same time that busing began in Boston, accelerating (but not initiating) white flight from South Boston and Dorchester to the suburbs and rural communities around Massasoit. Although Massasoit is in racially diverse Brockton, its student body did not reflect its city for many years. Also, thirty years ago, America was still in the early stage of the economic change to two-parent working families earning one-parent salaries. Back then, American factories still made things.

Massasoit grew and grew, from a tight-knit little community in 1966 into a large, two-campus comprehensive community college. More and more students have come from Brockton—and Boston—with increasing numbers of Haitian and Cape Verdean immigrants. From 1976 to 2006, the percentage of minority students increased from 2 percent to over 25 percent. All students seem to read less and work more hours. Over 50 percent test into one or more developmental courses.

Through all this, for five days a week, teaching four and five and six courses each semester (and nights, and summers), I have worked with students on reading, writing, thinking, speaking, listening, and changing by doing these activities differently, critically, and, I hope, with more strength and energy and consciousness.

In many ways, it has become harder to teach. Now, more and more underprepared students have come to the school; technology and the technology divide play an increasing role both in student preparation and lack of preparation. This year, for the first time, two students used "u" in writing their papers: text messaging has arrived. The media-driven world has driven reading into a corner; the high-stakes test world has displaced curiosity; the income divide and the high cost of education, transportation, and housing have pushed paid work in front of the delayed gratification of reading, thinking, and learning. Of the female students attending freshman registration in 2003, 9 percent were single mothers. Learning becomes something that students need but barely have time for. My classes seemed full of mysteries to be contemplated—especially Introductory Writing, a precollege-level writing course.

In the spring of 2005, Massasoit Community College sponsored a faculty-driven seminar whose mission was to investigate "the two worlds" of student and faculty culture to develop inclusive teaching and learning. I was to be the facilitator, but I also wanted to participate in the seminar. I was looking for a topic. One day early in the semester, in an Introductory Writing class, I talked about the thesis sentence as carrying the concept of the essay—and I heard a dim silence around the word "concept." I asked, "What does concept mean?" No one answered. There was some nervous shifting. No concept for "concept." I kept asking: no concept for "thesis" other than "main idea." I said, "That's sort of true in the context of an essay." I heard the silence: no concept for "context." No operating vocabulary for the kinds of college language that students would need to think with. I had found a great absence of critical, abstract, and formal vocabulary. I had assumed too much, but I had found my area for research.

I assumed a threefold task: to research college-level vocabulary or vocabulary acquisition in general; to listen for the moments of vocabulary-induced silences in class, especially where I would tend to assume understanding; and to find my ways not so much to build student vocabulary as to work on student vocabulary building. Then, maybe, they would laugh at my jokes.

I had assumed too much. First, I had to acknowledge the historical difference between my younger students and myself. (My older students are such an incredibly mixed bag that no generalization can hold them.) Because of the spirit of the times and because of my family history, I was significantly different from most of my students. However much I might think of myself as a poor Jewish kid from Philadelphia, I am in fact an over-sixty-year-old, liberally educated, monolingual white guy. I look just like a teacher. Although neither of my parents attended college—I started life over the grocery store in Philadelphia—I grew up reading and being read to. Many of my early favorite books were Victorian poetry. I knew A. E. Milne's poetry books before I knew *Winnie the Pooh*, and, in the Little Golden Book edition, I read Robert Louis Stevenson's *Child's Garden of Verses* over and over. These straight-haired, sentimentally illustrated children in these books were so very much **not** me: they did not go to synagogue, they did not live in the North Philadelphia ghetto, and they did not have a big brother who occasionally beat them up. Yet these books spoke to me. Unlike my students, I was a bookish kid in a bookish time.

One starting point for my investigation was a piece of "knowledge" that asserts that fifty years ago, the average fourteen-year-old had a vocabulary of about 25,000 words, and today's fourteen-year-old has a vocabulary of about 10,000 words. This finding has been published in *Harper's*, in the "Index" (August 2000), and in *Time* (February 14, 2000). The *Time* item suggests that the numbers are true for "vocabulary," and *Harper's* specifies "written vocabulary." Whether the demise of vocabulary is documented truth or, as some have argued, an urban legend, in talking with my students I have learned for sure that language has changed with the world. While many students have extensive computer vocabularies, the names of farm implements and hand tools have vanished. (Ambitious students sometimes wanted to "home" their skills.) Abstract words and words of emotion seem to go missing, hidden behind general judgments of "sucks" and "excellent." More chillingly, Orwell was right about how language can shape politics, and vice versa. I teach a journalism course, and for five years, I have asked my students on a quiz what is meant by the phrase "public interest." No student under forty has understood the phrase "public interest" to mean anything other than sports and gossip. I wanted to learn how to fight Big Brother—the hydra-headed Big Brother of Big Government, Big Consumer Capitalism, Big Industry, Big Technology, Big Instant Messaging, Big Gossip, and so on—with vocabulary.

One of my efforts at Massasoit, many years ago, was to help to design our precollege writing course. Many popular textbooks for basic writing courses focus on sentences and paragraphs. At Massasoit we decided that Introductory Writing should be, first and foremost, a writing course; that while teaching sentence skills was often necessary, sentence skills are not necessary unless somebody is actually going to write something. We also decided that while many underprepared writers have to be told and shown what paragraphs are for and what they do, in practice, for college work, nobody actually writes a single paragraph. We understood that writing essays is the way to prepare for writing essays. My personal sense of the course is that Introductory Writing should be the first three or four weeks of English Composition I, done very thoroughly. Students should be introduced to writing and should become writers.

The classes are limited to twenty students. Brockton High School is our main feeder school. Brockton High's numbers are huge, over four thousand, with an extremely diverse community of students. It has a strong tradition of academic excellence and produces wonderful graphic artists, but it has all the ills of large urban schools, including gangs, and it serves many students who are just learning English. Brockton is, like Lowell, Lawrence, Fall River, and Holyoke, an old mill town that continues to serve as an entry point for immigrants but without the jobs that made the mill towns vibrant. Our other feeder schools are in commuter towns south of Boston and in the rural towns of Plymouth County—being a city kid, I think of them as cranberry bog towns—occupying the terra incognita between routes 3 and 24. Many of our students come from vocational schools. A middle-class student in the Introductory Writing class will often have a learning disability.

For the fall semester, my students came to a summer orientation and sat in a room and wrote an hour-long writing sample, assessed by at least two writing teachers. Then they went to a computer and took Accuplacer tests in reading and mathematics. Based on their writing, their reading scores, and a faculty decision about where they would be best served, they were placed into Introductory Writing, which does not count as credit toward graduation and which is for them a prerequisite for English Composition I. They fill up my classes fast because I teach in the coveted 9 A.M. to 12 noon slot. About a quarter are from Brockton High, and a couple of these are African American, a couple Cape Verdean immigrants, and a couple of students from Haiti. They sit next to kids from towns such as Lakeville and Middleboro. A girl whose father works construction and who has a swimming pool shared with relatives who live in the same suburban *cul de sac* (or "cold sack," as one student wrote) sits next to a kid who lives with his cousin in a basement apartment in Mattapan Square in Boston. A couple of older students, with kids of their own, wonder how they fit in. Some students love to read and write, some hate it, but all have some writing issue. They have one thing in common: nobody knows what "prerequisite" means.

The classroom is likely to look different in the spring term. Now perhaps half of this class has emerged from English as a second language (ESL) classes. Most of Massasoit's English language learners come from Haiti and Cape Verde (so their first languages are Creoles, not French or Portuguese), but there are Spanish speakers, Vietnamese and Chinese, Eastern Europeans, and so on. The mix of ages and experience is richer than in the fall class. I have always argued that Introductory Writing is a writing course, not a language course, but this spring class threatens to make the distinction meaningless. Of the younger students, many came through the bilingual programs at Brockton High, and they have somehow passed the Massachusetts Comprehensive Assessment System (MCAS) writing test. Even though none of my students know what "prerequisite" means, they all know that essays have exactly five paragraphs.

Although the profile of every class is different, every class presents the same problems: how to teach to many individuals working at many levels in many ways all at once and how to draw students past the culture of passing and getting over into the culture of learning and practice, which in this class means achieving some level of mastery of written communication. It also means that students who have struggled with language have to become willing to engage with language. Most of their writing indicates a limited vocabulary, for a number of reasons: English is not their first language; English is not their parents' or community's language; they are burdened with learning disabilities; they come from language-poor backgrounds.

Much of the research into vocabulary relates to its impact on reading.[1] According to the reading research, socioeconomic status (SES) plays a major role in vocabulary development. Hart and Risley found that "disadvantaged homes provide little support for vocabulary development" (Lehr, Osborn, and Hiebert 2001). The testing of reading skills presents what is known as "the fourth-grade crisis": reading skills may stay even across SES lines up to grade three, while children are still learning to read; but in grade four, the child's vocabulary plays a significant role in more challenging reading, and a reading score differential sets in. (Significantly, the same phenomenon is not seen in mathematics, a subject more dependent on what is learned in school.)

Thus, to catch up, vocabulary-disadvantaged children need to acquire new words at above-average rates. But students who struggle with reading read less; therefore, they acquire fewer words, and so on. In terms of vocabulary development, good readers read more, become better readers, and learn more words; poor readers read less, become poorer readers, and learn fewer words. As Billie Holiday sang:

> Them that's got shall get
> Them that's not shall lose

And so it is for students who find their way into my class.

*　*　*

Apparently, there is much disagreement about two pieces of information: what a word is, and what is meant by knowing a word. As a result, counts of how many "words" a student might "know" can differ by factors of ten. However, a general consensus indicates that students going through elementary school might be expected to learn about three thousand words every year. Yet explicit instruction is effective for only about ten words per week. Do the math. Students may be expected to learn 2,600 words a year in other ways—or not. Most words are learned not by formal instruction but incidentally. Furthermore, words are not known all at once. A word can be recognized, even used, but with more use and acquaintance, more senses of its meanings develop. Carey (1978) argues that there are "levels" of word knowledge, from "fast mapping" to "extended mapping" (Baker, Simmons, and Kameenui 1995, 16). Bauman and Kameenui (1991, 16) distinguish among association, comprehension, and generation as levels of knowing. Carey (1978) estimates that about 1,600 words might be in the process of being learned at any one time.

Most studies in vocabulary acquisition limit their focus to early education; but ten or twelve or twenty years later, unready readers, students with learning disabilities, and English language learners have passed through the system and now fill the seats of my community college Introductory Writing classes. Most have struggled with school—but not all; few are pleasure readers—but some are; most fear writing—but some consider themselves poets and are working on their novel and cannot understand why they are in this class; and from the inner city, from faraway lands, from isolated rural communities, from the four thousand of Brockton High and from home schooling, from Dorchester and Lakeville, newly arrived from Haiti and Cape Verde, or descendants of earlier boat arrivals such as the

Mayflower, they sit next to each other, across from me, all of us separated by a common language.

I used to think that my role as a community college teacher was to compensate for a lousy high-school experience. In regard to vocabulary, as I mentioned earlier, I'd have to go back further than that. Students suffering from what Louise Moats calls "word poverty" start school behind and rarely catch up (cited in Baker, Simmons, Kameenui 1995, 6) At college age, a student with a rich vocabulary who confronts unfamiliar words acquires new meanings and new words by generating rough meaning plus an empty slot for further enrichment, that is, he or she will understand that, for example, *analysis* means taking things apart to look at them but will understand that there is more meaning to come. (This student knows how to be a little patient.) Students with poor vocabularies will have difficulty adjusting the meaning to the situation: for them, a word has and should have one clear meaning. Thus, I must teach didactically that words are "slippery customers."

One of my first insights into how tricky vocabulary development was going to be came from Alberto, a bright kid from South America. His English was quite good—it fits into my ESL category of "charming." I was having the class read and respond to a chapter about the writing process by Anne LaMott, an essayist and novelist, who has a very popular book used by creative-writing teachers, *Bird by Bird*. The chapter, titled "Shitty First Drafts," is about getting started writing, and LaMott advises writers to silence critical voices in their heads by imagining they are mice and putting them in a jar. She adds, "A writer friend of mine suggests opening the jar and shooting them all in the head. But I think he's a little angry, and I'm sure nothing like this would ever *occur* [my italics] to you" (1994, 27).

Alberto reacted with horror. Had somebody actually shot a jar of mice? What had *occurred*? Something *occurred* to Alberto. Here was a bright kid with adequate English horribly misreading this passage. It never *occurred* to me that this double meaning was a problem. We just had to discover it and then cover it. Alberto taught me that words are slippery, and that levels of meaning were extremely subtle. Furthermore, I realized that no instructional vocabulary scheme would have unearthed the *occur* confusion; most word list approaches are more interested in teaching words such as *pusillanimous*.

There are various approaches to word acquisition (Lehr, Osborn, and Hiebert 2001, 14–17). Mostly, words are learned incidentally, both from listening and reading. Usually, multiple repetitions do the job. Unfortunately, most of my students are not casual readers, and many live in environments that are poor in English vocabulary. So many classes take the way to vocabulary by explicit instruction. Most of my students have been subjected to this, badly. They have done the "look up ten words, write the definitions, use in a sentence, take the quiz" routine. They have hated it and claim to remember next to nothing. They all know a few big words, such as "procrastination," that find use in their academic lives. In fact, most are unfamiliar with any deep meaning of "academic." It was clear to me that, owing to the diverse backgrounds and career goals of my students, some sort of standard word list to memorize was not going to be effective.

In the world of vocabulary research, two word lists stand out. One is the *General Service List* (GSL) of the most frequently encountered 2,284 English words (Bauman 1995). In the GSL list, "the" is number one; "beak" and "plural" tie at 2,284. "Patient" ranks 703, and "patience" comes in at 1,882. These words are said to constitute 85 percent of the words that a reader is likely to encounter in books. A second list is the *University Word List* (UWL) of the 560 most common words used in academic writing that are *not* on the GSL (Coxhead 2007). This list is broken down into ten levels of frequency. I tested the validity of this list by looking over some of my writing assignment sheets, and indeed, my usage approximated the frequency lists.

The list of highest academic frequency includes some words that are to be expected—it ranges alphabetically from *analysis* to *variable*—but others come as a surprise—*approach, area*, and, wouldn't you know it, *occur*. It is apparently academic to ask, "What is your *approach* to your *area*?" My student is more likely to understand this sentence concretely as a reference to somebody driving into the neighborhood. I theorize (headword *theory*, list 1—but *thesis* is list 7) that if I use academic words frequently in class, talk about them, and encourage their use, I will help to bring my students into academic discourse. But it is a struggle.

In a beginning lecture, I emphasize two words from educational jargon: "metacognition" and "schema." These words become part of a conversation about learning. Part of the conversation is, of course, about self-knowledge and self-awareness, and part deals with how words are powerful and how naming can structure education. Also, there is a special benefit to using these words with so-called developmental learners. These are clearly *college* words.

Such highly unfamiliar vocabulary, ironically, serves to welcome the entire class: nobody, no matter where they are from, knows this stuff—except **us**, now. Their spell checker will deny them the use of "metacognition." It's a new language to everybody. By creating what is for them "exclusive" language, the new words—some of them academic jargon—lead to inclusion: *we* becomes *us*. These new words become the new language of our class. (Pedagogy can be dangerously close to pedantry.) But simply having a word can be powerful.

Words that are not slippery can be generative. My first major class assignment is a descriptive essay about a special place. My purpose in this assignment is not only to work with development, organization, and concrete detail but also to bring each writer to his or her expert area. Students share essays and are generally impressed with the writing and the people in their class. The limitations are not your room or your car, no Disneyworld or Six Flags, and no tourist brochures. Many students struggled getting their details out, because of blocked vocabulary—whether because of language or vocabulary poverty ("you know, like, whatever") or the difficulty of transferring receptive vocabulary to expressive and productive. Students needed names.

Kate was from Dorchester and the South Shore. She was smart and widely read, but she had problems with, or refused, punctuation and organization; thus, Introductory Writing. She thought of herself as a writer, but she did not seem to want readers. As a young, untraveled student, she also felt she had nothing to say, as other students wrote about trips or summer vacations or their childhood in Africa or the Caribbean. But she remembered fondly her grandma's house, although clearly, she said, there was nothing special about that. "Tell me the things in the house," I said. "Walk me through it."

She took me through the kitchen—nothing special, she said. In the hall, there was a bunch of stuff, including a piano that she used to play **with**. "You play the piano?" I asked. No, she didn't play. But there was a hole in the piano with a door, and there were these rolls you could put in and then the piano would play. I went quietly crazy. "That's a player piano!" I hissed. Naming it made it real and somehow transferable. She could write about this special object that she could name. She could write about the whole house and its specialness. In her last draft, she walked the reader through the house, awash in memory, and when she arrived at the player piano, she wrote, "I liked to watch the paper roll down. It was like watching a movie written in Braille."

The naming of the player piano seemed to free up Kate's writing, but I encountered a different problem with Raynauld: who has the authority to do the naming? On the same assignment, Ray's special place was a river near the town called Sarazin in Haiti. Ray's English vocabulary was not always up to the task he set for himself, but he was a witty, warm person and a witty, warm writer. He had a strong sense of audience, and of where he was coming from, and where his writing was going. He described an idyllic scene with a human-voiced parrot in a mango tree; when a mango would drop, Ray wrote, "the green Perot sat on the mango's branch saying that '*mango a pa bon,*' which means 'the mango is not good.' We repeated back to him, '*Ou manti,*' which means, 'You are liar.'"

This essay delighted me. I was emphasizing writing using the senses, and Ray had certainly brought the sounds of his childhood into his essay and made them accessible to me—my Creole is not so good. Later, he described his favorite game, which he called "*Ennemie*," in which two equal groups on either side of the river pull against each other on a "cord." (We went around and around on whether or when a *cord* is a *rope* or a *string*. There's nothing like working with an ESL student to "home" your vocabulary.) I asked a couple of questions to clarify his description and then I said, casually, "We call this game 'Tug of War.'" In his next draft, "*ennemie*" had disappeared, and now Haitian children were playing "tug of war." This gave me and my English more authority than was warranted, and I pointed out to Ray how he had handled the parrot/mango section, and suggested that he do the same here. "*Ennemie*" is the real word, I explained, and using "tug of war" would help explain the game for the American reader. Use them both, I advised. Yet it remained "tug of war" until the very last draft, when it reverted to "*ennemie*." The two never got together. It might have been time and forgetfulness that kept the words apart, but I fear that Ray wanted to get the right word for his teacher.

The complexity of vocabulary acquisition discouraged me from the more typical paths such as word lists or instruction by morphology—analysis of prefix, root, and suffix. I teach a little vocabulary explicitly, and students may learn more in the college preparatory reading courses that many of them also take. However, my preferred path is by "word consciousness": I want my students to stop at words, to be fascinated at them—to fight their way to meaning, rather than fighting against what is strange and different and outside their experience.

Here is the strategy I adopted and am constantly adapting. I have always used two personal accounting sheets in Introductory Writing—one for spelling and one for frequent surface errors. I added a vocabulary page to my syllabus. Required input is minimal: write down unfamiliar words or words used in new senses; provide a hint of context; and devise a key to meaning and how to remember it. Some students have used their sheets responsibly and even delightedly, others not at all. But the sheet tells students that words matter. Also, once a student knows that a word exists, the student is likely to "see" this word recurring and come to know it better. I urge them to list two words from the vocabulary section of my self-published text on their page: "context" and "etymology." The word list is checked but not graded. Some students compile long lists but may or may not learn from them. Others avoid the exercise. The words become meaningful when they are encountered outside my class.

I assign relatively few readings, but for each reading, I develop word lists that predict new or strange vocabulary in the readings, and I ask students to add any words that they struggle with. I also ask for **their** words for similar concepts, as much to help with mutual understanding as for vocabulary development. I introduce terms that may help them to think about their process of learning, such as "receptive" and "productive" vocabulary, and oppositional pairs such as "implicit/explicit" and "intrinsic/extrinsic." I explore etymology (because how words get and change meaning is so interesting to me) and the history of the English language, which I argue can be seen as a Creole of Old English and Old French. I try to convey my interest in my language and in their language.

Through my research and my renewed attention to the role of vocabulary among my students who came out of my seminar, I attempted these changes in my teaching: put more emphasis on vocabulary. Teach some of the specialized vocabulary of the educational process. Consciously integrate words from the academic frequency list. Celebrate the conscious use of language wherever it appears. All I can report is that by the end of the semester, some students seemed to be using some new words, and they reported that they were noticing words more in more places. Other professors have helped me to locate more words that surprise us with their hollowness—an accounting professor in our seminar told me that her students did not understand "miscellaneous." All of this is a work in progress.

At the end of my Introductory Writing class, I have students put together a portfolio of their work, including a cover letter/essay with a narration of their semester, some assessment of their writing, and most painfully, an argument for a grade for their writing based on the departmental rubric. Diane was a student from Haiti, struggling with English to a greater degree than Alberto and Ray. At the beginning of the semester, I have students write an essay in class, which I read but do not mark up. I make notes in my grade book, grading from 1 to 4. A student with a 4 should think about switching up to English Composition; a student with a 1 will struggle and often has severe language issues of one sort or another. I return these first writings to students for their portfolio at the end of the semester, so they can see if there are any improvements. Diane had been scored at 2, the average score for new students, which means, we can do this, but there's a lot of work to be done. Diane began her cover letter by telling how, by looking at her first paper, she realized that at first she didn't know a lot about writing. Her sentence, and I quote approximately, read like this: "Looking back, I can see that I had a *lacuna* [my italics] in my understanding."

She had a lacuna, and of course so did I; during the length of a semester, I had no idea that Diane used words such as "lacuna." She said she used it in French, or maybe it was Latin, and she thought it was an English word, too. What else did she know? What other knowledge and thoughts did she have access to that I never tapped? What lagoons of meaning had I failed to explore? Was it just this one? Is there more? How would I know? Did my stupid authority as a teacher prevent her from saying to me: I can do more than this? Or was I, after all, in just the right place? How do I use vocabulary to investigate **my** lacunae about my students?

My seminar of Spring 2005 had as its overarching theme "Bridging Two Worlds"—the worlds of the instructor and the student—which evolved toward "becoming a welcoming classroom." But I found myself with many chasms and ravines, as well as gurgling streams, all to be crossed, all to be worked with together. My investigation into the literature of vocabulary acquisition helped me to understand issues facing English language learners, students with learning disabilities, and students from vocabulary-poor backgrounds, in addition to those disaffected students with rich but rarely applied vocabulary. I know more about working with the slipperiness of language, the power of naming, the potential richness of mixing languages in writing, and the exploration of the untapped vocabulary of my students. I am working to use vocabulary development as a means of inclusion for my diverse classes and as a means to empowerment. A useful academic vocabulary is, after all, a prerequisite to academic success, and although I cannot provide that much of it by direct instruction, I hope that I can learn to accelerate vocabulary acquisition by creating interest, understanding, and even magic around words. I trust that, as students enter into their fields of study and encounter more and more language incidentally and seek out specific instruction when needed, they will become more proficient in the language of their field, and that despite their different backgrounds, diversity and inclusion will come together, and their vocabularies and their learning will increase and multiply. But it won't come all at once. They'll just have to be a little patient.

Note

1. Most of what follows in regard to reading research comes from two documents: Scott K. Baker, Deborah C. Simmons, and Edward J. Kameenui (1995), Vocabulary acquisition: Synthesis of the research, National Center to Improve the Tools of Educators, funded by the US Office of Special Education Programs, http://idea.uoregon.edu/~ncite/documents/techrep/tech13.html; and Fran Lehr, Jean Osborn, and Elfrieda H. Hiebert (2001), A focus on vocabulary. Pacific Resources for Education and Learning, http://www.prel.org/products/re_/ES0419.htm (accessed November 17, 2007).

References

Abu-Lughod, L. 2002. Do Muslim women really need saving? Anthropological reflections on cultural relativism and its others. *American Anthropologist* 104: 783–90.

Adams, Maurianne. 1997. Pedagogical frameworks for social justice education. In *Teaching for diversity and social justice*, ed. Maurianne Adams, LeeAnn Bell, and Pat Griffin, 30–43. New York: Routledge.

Adams, Natalie G., and Pamela Jean Bettis. 2003. *Cheerleader! An American Icon*. New York: Palgrave Macmillan.

Adnan, Etel. 1982. *Sitt Marie Rose*. Sausalito, CA: Post-Apollo Press.

Akerlund, Mark, and Monit Cheung. 2000. Teaching beyond the deficit model: Gay and lesbian issues among African-Americans, Latinos, and Asian Americans. *Journal of Social Work Education* 36 (2): 279–93.

Allison, Dorothy. 1993. *Bastard Out of Carolina*. New York: Penguin.

Alternative Education Program, Inc. 2004. *Alternative Educational Program Description*. Providence, RI: College Readiness Program, URI Providence Campus.

Angelou, Maya. 1983. *I Know Why the Caged Bird Sings*. New York: Bantam.

Anyon, Jean. 1980. Social class and the hidden curriculum of work. *Journal of Education* 162: 67–92.

———. 1981. Social class and school knowledge. *Curriculum Inquiry* 11 (1): 3–42.

Anzaldúa, Gloria E., ed. 2002. *This Bridge We Call Home: Radical Visions for Transformation*. New York: Routledge.

Atwood, Margaret. 1998. *The Handmaid's Tale*. New York: Anchor.

Baca, Judith. 2004. The art of the mural. http://www.pbs.org/americanfamily/mural.html (accessed August 14, 2007).

Backer, Tamara, Jane Chang, Amanda Crawford, Teresa Ferraguto, Denise Tioseco, and Nicole Woodson. 2002. Case study and analysis: The Center for the Improvement of Teaching, University of Massachusetts Boston (unpublished manuscript). Cambridge, MA: Harvard University Graduate School of Education.

Baker, Ella. 2009. We need group centered leadership. In *Let nobody turn us around: Voices of resistance, reform, and renewal—An African American anthology*, ed. Manning Marable and Leith Mullings, 398–400. Lanham, MD: Rowman & Littlefield.

Baker, Scott K., Deborah C. Simmons, and Edward J. Kameenui. 1995. *Vocabulary acquisition: Synthesis of the research.* Technical Report No. 13. Eugene, Oregon: National Center to Improve the Tools for Educators, University of Oregon.

Bakhtin, M.M. 1981. *The Dialogic Imagination.* Ed. Michael Holquist. Austin: University of Texas press.

Baumann, J.F. and E.J. Kameenui. 1991. "Research on vocabulary instruction: Ode to Voltaire," In *Handbook of research on teaching the English language arts*, eds. J. Flood, J.J. Lapp, and J.R. Squire, 604-632. NewYork: Macmillan.

Baumann, John. 1995. General service list. http://jbauman.com/aboutgsl.html (accessed January 2, 2007).

Berger, Maurice. 2001. "Viewing the Invisible: Fred Wilson's Allegories of Absence and Loss" In *Fred Wilson: Objects and installations 1979–2000*, ed. Maurice Berger and Fred Wilson, 8–21. Baltimore: Center for Art and Visual Culture University of Maryland.

Bérubé, Michael. 2006. *What's Liberal about the Liberal Arts?: Classroom Politics and "Bias" in American Education.* New York: W.W. Norton and Company.

Bleich, D. 1995. Collaboration and the pedagogy of disclosure. *College English* 57: 43–61.

Bose, Sugata. 2006. *A Hundred Horizons: The Indian Ocean in the Age of Global Empire.* Cambridge, MA: Harvard University Press.

Bourdieu, Pierre. 1973/2000. Social reproduction and cultural reproduction. In *The structure of schooling*, ed. Richard Arum and Irene Beattie, 55–68. London: Mayfield Publishing Company.

———. 1984. *Distinction: A Social Critique of the Judgment of Taste.* Cambridge, MA: Harvard University Press.

———. 1986. Forms of capital. In *Handbook of theory and research for the sociology of education*, ed. John G. Richardson, 241–258. New York: Greenwood Press.

Brafman, Ori, and Rod A. Beckstrom. 2006. *The Starfish and the Spider: The Unstoppable Power of Leaderless Organizations.* New York: Portfolio/Penguin.

Brookfield, Stephen D. 1995. *Becoming a Critically Reflective Teacher.* San Francisco, CA: Jossey-Bass.

Brown, Caroline, and Alexia Pollack. 2004. Reconstructing the paradigm: Teaching across the disciplines. *The Journal of Undergraduate Neuroscience Education* 3 (1): A9–A15.

Cahan, Susan, and Zoya Kocur, eds. 1996. *Contemporary Art and Multicultural Education.* New York: Routledge.

Carey, S. 1978. "The child as word learner". In *Linguistic theory and psychological reality*, ed. M. Halle et al. 264–293. Cambridge: MIT press.

Casey, Janet C. 2005. Diversity, discourse, and the working-class student. *Academe Online* 91 (4). http://www.aaup.org/AAUP/pubsres/academe/2005/JA/Feat/case. htm (accessed November 27, 2005).

Castenada, Carmelita Rosie. 2004. *Teaching and Learning in Diverse Classrooms: Faculty Reflections on their Experiences and Pedagogical Practice of Teaching Diverse Populations.* New York: Routledge.

Chow, Esther N., and Catherine Berheide, eds. 1994. *Women, the Family and Policy: A Global Perspective.* Albany: SUNY Press.

Collins, Patricia H. 1986. Learning from the outsider within: The sociological significance of black feminist thought. *Social Problems* 336: 14–32.

———. 1990. *Black Feminist Thought: Knowledge, Consciousness, and the Politics of Empowerment.* Boston: Unwin Hyman.

Corrin, Lisa, ed. 1994. *Mining the Museum: An Installation by Fred Wilson.* New York: The New Press and Norton & Company.

Coxhead, Averill. 2007. Massey University School of Language Studies: Headwords of the academic word list. http://language.massey.ac.nz/staff/awl/headwords.shtml (accessed January 2, 2007).

Cross, William. 1991. *Shades of Black: Diversity in African-American Identity.* Philadelphia, PA: Temple University Press.

Daloz, Laurent A. 1999. *Effective Teaching and Mentoring.* San Francisco, CA: Jossey-Bass.

Dancis, Jerome. 2008. Alternative learning environment helps minority students excel in calculus at UC-Berkeley: A pedagogical analysis. http://www-users.math.umd.edu/~jnd/Treisman.txt (accessed January 15, 2008).

D'Arrigo, Diane. 2004. Higher education in the 1960s: The origins of the University of Massachusetts Boston (MA Thesis). Boston: University of Massachusetts Boston, American Studies Program.

Darwish, Mahmoud. 1995. *Memory for Forgetfulness.* Berkeley: University of California Press.

Day-Vines, Norma L., Susannah M. Wood, Tim Grothaus, Laurie Craigen, Angela Holman, Kylie Dotson-Blake, and Marcy J. Douglass. 2007. Broaching the subjects of race, ethnicity, and culture during the counseling process. *Journal of Counseling and Development* 85 (4): 401–9.

Delpit, Lisa. 1995. *Other People's Children.* New York: The New Press.

DeRosa, Patti, and Ulric Johnson. 2003. The 10Cs: A model of diversity awareness and social change (unpublished paper). Change Works Consulting. http://www.lesley.edu/academic_centers/peace/content/10cs.pdf (accessed November 14, 2010).

Dewey, John. 1910/1991. *How We Think.* Buffalo, NY: Prometheus Books.

Disch, Estelle. 1999. Encouraging participation in the classroom. In *Coming into her own: Educational success in girls and women,* ed. Sara N. Davis, Mary Crawford, and Jadwiga Sebrechts, 139–54. San Francisco, CA: Jossey-Bass.

Elias, Karen, and Judith C. Jones. 2002. Two voices from the front lines: A conversation about race in the classroom. In *Race in the college classroom: Pedagogy and politics,* ed. Bonnie TuSmith and Maureen T. Reddy, 7–18. New Brunswick, NJ: Rutgers University Press.

Enloe, Cynthia. 1990. *Bananas, Beaches and Bases: Making Feminist Sense of International Politics.* Berkeley and Los Angeles: University of California Press.

Espada, Martin. 1999. *Zapata's Disciples*. New York: South End Press.

Felman, Jill L. 2001. *Never a Dull Moment: Teaching and the Art of Performance Feminism Takes Center Stage*. New York: Routledge.

Filene, Peter. 2005. *The Joy of Teaching*. Chapel Hill, NC: University of North Carolina Press.

Fine, Michelle, B. Anand, C. Jordan, and D. Sherman. 2000. Before the bleach gets us all. In *Construction sites: Excavating race, class and gender among urban youth*, ed. Lois Weis and Michelle Fine, 161–79. New York: Teachers College Press.

Finkel, Donald F. 2000. *Teaching with Your Mouth Shut*. Portsmouth, NH: Boynton/Cook-Heinemann.

Finn, Patrick. 1999. *Literacy with an Attitude: Educating Working-Class Children in Their Own Self-Interest*. Albany, NY: SUNY Press.

Fobes, C., and P. Kaufman. 2008. Critical pedagogy in the sociology classroom: Challenges and concerns. *Teaching Sociology* 36: 26–33.

Freeland, Richard M. 1992. *Academia's Golden Age: Universities in Massachusetts 1945–1970*. New York: Oxford University Press.

Freire, Paulo. 1970. *Pedagogy of the Oppressed*. Trans. Myrna B. Ramos. New York: Continuum.

———. 1993. *Pedagogy of the City*. Trans. Donaldo Macedo. New York: Continuum.

———. 1998a. *Pedagogy of Freedom: Ethics, Democracy and Civic Courage*. Lanham, MD: Rowman and Littlefield.

———. 1998b. *Teachers as Cultural Workers: Letters to Those Who Dare to Teach*. Trans. Donaldo Macedo, Dale Koike, and Alexandre Oliveira. Boulder, CO: Westview.

Freire, Paulo and Donaldo Macedo. 1987. *Literacy: Reading the Word and the World*. South Hadley, MA: Bergin & Garvey.

Freud, Anna. 1966. *The Ego and the Mechanisms of Defense, American Edition*. New York: International Universities Press.

———. 1969. The writings of Anna Freud. In *Volume 5: Research at the Hampstead Child-Therapy Clinic and other papers, 1956–1965*, 221–41. New York: International Universities Press.

Gallavan, Nancy P. 1998. Why aren't teachers using effective multicultural education practices? Five major insights from experienced teachers. *Equity and Excellence in Education* 31 (2): 20–7.

García, Mildred, Cynthia Hudgins, Caryn M. Musil, Michael T. Nettles, William E. Sedlacek, and Daryl G. Smith. 2002. *Assessing Campus Diversity Initiatives*. Washington, DC: Association of American Colleges and Universities.

Gee, James P. 2005. *Introduction to Discourse Analysis*. 2nd ed. New York: Routledge.

Gettinger, Maribeth, and Jill Seibert. 2002. Contributions of study skills to academic competence. *School Psychology Review* 31 (3): 350. http://lesley.ezproxy.blackboard.com/login?url=http://search.ebscohost.com (accessed February 18, 2007).

Ghosh, Amitav. 1992. *In an Antique Land: History in the Guise of a Traveler's Tale.* New York: Vintage Books.

Gil, David G. 1992. *Unraveling Social Policy: Theory, Analysis, and Political Action toward Social Equality.* 5th ed. Rochester, VT: Schenkman Press.

Giroux, Henry A. 1995. Animating youth: The disneyfication of children's culture. *Socialist Review* 24 (3): 23–9.

———. 2000. Insurgent multiculturalism and the promise of pedagogy. In *Sources: Notable selections in multicultural education,* ed. Jana Noel, 176–84. Guilford, CT: Dushkin/McGraw Hill.

Goss, Jon, and Bruce Lindquist. 2000. Placing movers: An overview of the Asia-Pacific migration system. *The Contemporary Pacific* 12 (2): 385–414.

Gramsci, Antonio. 1992. *Prison Notebooks.* New York: Columbia University Press.

Grant, Joanne. 1998. *Ella Baker: Freedom Unbound.* New York: John Wiley.

Greene, Maxine. 1993. Diversity and inclusion: Toward a curriculum for human beings. *Teachers College Record* 95: 211–21.

———. 2000. *Releasing the Imagination: Essays on Education, the Arts and Social Change.* San Francisco, CA: Jossey-Bass.

Hall, Edward T. 1972. *The Silent Language.* New York: Anchor/Doubleday.

Hall, Nancy Lee. 1990. *A True Story of a Drunken Mother.* Boston: South End Press.

———. 1994. *A True Story of a Single Mother.* Boston: South End Press.

Haraway, D. 1988. Situated knowledges: The science question in feminism and the privilege of partial perspective. *Feminist Studies* 14: 575–99.

Havas, Eva, and Janel Lucas. 1994. Modeling diversity in the classroom. *Equity and Excellence in the Classroom* 27 (3): 43–7.

Heath, Shirley B. 1983. *Ways With Words.* New York: Cambridge University Press.

Helms, Janet. 1990. *Black and White Racial Identity.* New York: Greenwood Press.

———. 1994. The conceptualization of racial identity and other "racial" constructs. In *Human diversity: perspectives of people in context,* ed. Edison J. Trickett, Roderick J. Watts, and Dina Birman, 285–311. San Francisco: Jossey Bass.

Henriksen, Richard C., and Jerry Trusty. 2005. Ethics and values as major factors related to multicultural aspects of counselor preparation. *Counseling and Values* 49: 180–92.

hooks, bell. 1994. *Teaching to Transgress.* New York: Routledge.

———. 2003. *Teaching Community: a Pedagogy of Hope.* New York: Routledge.

Huggan, Graham. 2002. Postcolonial studies and the anxiety of interdisciplinarity. *Postcolonial Studies* 5 (3): 245–75.

Jasanoff, Maya. 2005. Cosmopolitan: A tale of identity from Ottoman Alexandria. *Common Knowledge* 11 (3): 393–409.

Johnson, Genevieve. 1999. Inclusive education: Fundamental instructional strategies and considerations. *Preventing School Failure* 43 (2): 72–8. http://lesley.ezproxy.blackboard.com/login?url=http://search.ebscohost.com (accessed February 17, 2007).

Johnson, Alan. 2001. *Privilege, Power and Difference*. London: Mayfield Publishing.

Johnson, Robert. 2005. The decline of the Ottoman Empire. *History Review*. http://www.highbeam.com/doc/1G1-141293898.html (accessed November 4, 2010).

Jones, Marjorie, and Cheryl Smith. 2003. Value-added: The impact of faculty of color on students in higher education. In *23rd Annual Adult Higher Education Alliance Conference: Extending the Boundaries of Adult Learning*, 181–96. http://ahea.org/files/pro2003jones.pdf (accessed April 5, 2011.

Kanafani, Ghassan. 1999. *Men in the Sun and Other Palestinian Stories*. Boulder, CO: Lynne Rienner.

Kawaja, Jennifer. 1999. *Under One Sky: Arab Women in North America Talk about the Hijab*. Montreal: National Film Board of Canada.

Khater, Akram F. 2004. *The Modern Middle East*. Boston: Houghton Mifflin.

Kingston-Mann, Esther. 1992. Multiculturalism without political correctness: The University of Massachusetts Boston model. *Boston Review of Books* 17: 30.

———, ed. 1999. *Building a Diversity Research Initiative: How Diverse Undergraduate Students Become Researchers, Change Agents, and Members of a Research Community*. Boston: Center for the Improvement of Teaching, University of Massachusetts Boston.

———. 2001. Three steps forward, one step back: Dilemmas of upward mobility. In *Achieving against the odds: How academics become teachers of diverse students*, ed. Esther Kingston-Mann and Tim Sieber, 36–54. Philadelphia: Temple University Press.

Kingston-Mann, Esther, and Tim Sieber. 2001. Introduction: Achieving against the odds. In *Achieving against the odds: How academics become teachers of diverse students*, ed. Esther Kingston-Mann and Tim Sieber, 1–18. Philadelphia: Temple University Press.

Kiser, Pamela. 2008. *The Human Services Internship: Getting the Most from Your Experience*. Belmont, CA: Thomson Brooks/Cole.

Kocet, Michael M. 2006. Ethical challenges in a complex world: Highlights of the 2005 ACA code of ethics. *Journal of Counseling & Development* 84: 228–34.

Kolb, D. 2006. David A. Kolb on experiential learning. Infed Encyclopedia. Retrieved April 18, 2006, from http://www.infed.org/biblio.

Ladson-Billings, Gloria. 2001. *Crossing over to Canaan: The Journey of New Teachers in Diverse Classrooms*. San Francisco, CA: Jossey-Bass.

Lamott, Anne. 1994. *Bird by Bird*. New York: Pantheon.

Lehr, Fran, Jean Osborn, and Elfrieda H. Hiebert. 2001. A focus on vocabulary. Pacific resources for education and learning. http://www.prel.org/products/re_/ES0419.htm (accessed November 5, 2010).

Leonard, Karen Isaksen. 2005. South Asians in the Indian Ocean world: Language, policing, and gender practices in Kuwait and the United Arab Emirates. *Comparative Studies of South Asia, Africa, and the Middle East* 25 (3): 677–86.

Leong, Karen J. 2002. Strategies for surviving race in the classroom. In *Race in the college classroom: Pedagogy and politics*, ed. Bonnie TuSmith and Maureen T. Reddy, 189–99. New Brunswick, NJ: Rutgers University Press.

Linek, Wayne, Charlene Fleener, Michelle Fazio, LaVerne Raine, and Kimberely Klakamp. 2003. The impact of shifting from how teachers teach to how children learn. *Journal of Educational Research* 97 (2): 78–89. http://lesley.ezproxy.black-board.com/login?url=http://search.ebscohost.com (accessed March 23, 2007).

Ludlow, Jeannie, Laurie A. Rodgers, and Mary G. Wrighten. 2005. Students' perceptions of instructors' identities: Effects and interventions. http://www.unco.edu/AE-Extra/2005/3/Art-2.html (accessed May 17, 2007).

Luria, Aleksandr R. 1976. *Cognitive Development: its Cultural and Social Foundations*. Cambridge, MA: Harvard University Press.

McIntyre, Alice. 1977. *Making Meaning of Whiteness: Exploring Racial Identity with White Teachers*. Albany: State University of New York Press.

Memmi, Albert. 2006. Assigning value to difference. In *Beyond borders: Thinking critically about global issues*, ed. Paula S. Rothenberg, 244–9. New York: Worth Publishers.

Mernissi, Fatima. 1994. *Dreams of Trespass: Tales of a Harem Girlhood*. Reading: Adison Wesley Publishing Company.

Miller, Arthur. 2003/1952. *The Crucible*. New York: Penguin Classics.

Mills, Charles W. 2000. *The Sociological Imagination: Fortieth Anniversary Edition*. New York: Oxford University Press.

Minh-ha, Trinh. 1989. *Woman, Native, Other: Writing Postcoloniality and Feminism*. Purdue: Indiana University Press.

Mohanty, Chandra T. 1991. Under western eyes: Feminist scholarship and colonial discourses. In *Third world women and the politics of feminism*, ed. Chandra T. Mohanty, A. Russo, and L. Torres, 51–80. Indianapolis: Indiana University Press.

———. 2002. Under western eyes revisited: Feminist solidarity through anticapitalist struggles. *Signs: Journal of Women in Culture and Society* 23: 499–535.

Moody, JoAnn. 2004. *Faculty Diversity: Problems and Solutions*. New York: Routledge.

Nieto, Sonia. 2000. Multicultural education and school reform. In *Notable selections in multicultural education*, ed. Jana Noel. Guilford. 2nd ed. 299–307. CT: Dushkin/McGraw-Hill.

Norgaard, Rolf. 2007. *Composing Knowledge: Readings for College Writers*. Boston: Bedford/St. Martin.

Oakes, Jeannie. 2005. *Keeping Track: How Schools Structure Inequality*. 2nd ed. New Haven: Yale University Press.

Ortner, Sherry B. 1999. Thick resistance: Death and the cultural construction of agency in Himalayan mountaineering. In *The fate of culture: Geertz and beyond*, ed. Sherry B. Ortner, 136–64. Berkeley: University of California Press.

Palmer, Parker. 2007. *A Tenth Anniversary Celebration of The Courage to Teach and the Work of Parker Palmer*. San Francisco, CA: Jossey-Bass.

Payne, Ruby K. 1996. *A Framework for Understanding Poverty*. 3rd rev. ed. Highland, TX: aha! Process, Inc.

Peterson, V. Spike, and Ann S. Runyan. 1999. *Global Gender Issues: Dilemmas in World Politics*. Boulder, CO: Westview.

Poey, Vivian M. 2003. On fictional grounds and culinary maps. *Journal for Pedagogy, Pluralism and Practice*. http://www.lesley.edu/journals/jppp/7/poey1.html (accessed January 23, 2007).

Ponterotto, Joseph G., and Brent Mallinckrodt. 2007. Introduction to the special section on racial and ethnic identity in counseling psychology: Conceptual and methodological challenges and proposed solutions. *Journal of Counseling Psychology* 54 (3): 219–23.

Powers, Peter Kerry. 2002. A ghost in the collaborative machine: The white male teacher in the multicultural classroom. In *Race in the college classroom: Pedagogy and politics*, ed. Bonnie TuSmith and Maureen T. Reddy, 28–39. New Brunswick, NJ: Rutgers University Press.

Prashad, Vijay. 2007. *The Darker Nations: A People's History of the Third World*. New York: The New Press.

Quindlen, Anna. 2000. *Black and Blue*. New York: Random House.

Ransby, Barbara. 2003. *Ella Baker and the Black Freedom Movement: A Radical Democratic Vision*. Chapel Hill: University of North Carolina Press.

Rios, Francisco. 1996. *Teaching Thinking in Cultural Contexts*. Albany, NY: SUNY Press.

Robinson, Robin A. 1996. Bearing witness to teen motherhood: the politics of violations of girlhood. In *For crying out loud: Women's poverty in the United States*, ed. Diane Dujon and Ann Withorn, 107–21. Boston: South End Press.

———. 2004. "Crystal virtues": Seeking reconciliation between ideals and violations of girlhood. *Contemporary Justice Review* 8 (1): 59–73.

———. 2007. "It's not easy to know who I am": Gender salience and cultural place in the treatment of a "delinquent" adolescent mother. *Feminist Criminology* 2 (1): 31–56.

Roffman, Eleanor. 2005. Roadblocks to learning: Studying under fire in Israel. *Radical Teacher* 74: 23–8.

Said, Edward. 1979. *Orientalism*. New York: Vintage Books.

———. 2002. Impossible histories: Why the many Islams cannot be simplified. *Harper's Magazine*. http://www.harpers.org/archive/2002/07/0079248 (accessed November 7, 2010).

Savage, Georgia. 1991. *The House Tibet*. Minneapolis: Graywolf Press.

Savery, Pancho. 2001. Odd man out. In *Achieving against the odds: How academics become teachers of diverse students*, ed. Esther Kingston-Mann and Tim Sieber, 204–14. Philadelphia: Temple University Press.

Shah, Saeeda. 2004. The researcher/interviewer in intercultural context: A social intruder! *British Educational Research Journal* 30 (4): 549–76.

Sieber, Tim. 2001. Learning to listen to students and oneself. In *Achieving against the odds: How academics become teachers of diverse students*, ed. Esther Kingston-Mann and Tim Sieber, 54–77. Philadelphia: Temple University Press.

———. 2006. Knowledge, learning and teaching: Striving for *conocimiento*. *Human Architecture: Journal of the Sociology of Self-Knowledge* 4: 355–8.

Smith, Dorothy E. 1987. *The Everyday World as Problematic: A Feminist Sociology*. Boston: Northeastern University Press.

Smith, Mark K. 2006. David A. Kolb on Experiential Learning. Infed Encyclopedia. http://www.infed.org/biblio/b-explrn.htm (accessed April 18, 2006).

Spivak, Gayatri Chakravorty. 1988. *In Other Worlds: Essays in Cultural Politics*. New York: Routledge.

Srikanth, Rajini. 2002. Gift wrapped or paper gagged?: Packaging race for the classroom. In *Race in the college classroom: Pedagogy and politics*, ed. Bonnie TuSmith and Maureen T. Reddy, 140–52. New Brunswick, NJ: Rutgers University Press.

———. 2007. Overwhelmed by the world: Teaching literature and the "difference" of nations. *Pedagogy: Critical Approaches to Teaching Literature, Language, Composition, and Culture* 7 (2): 192–207.

———. 2009. Why the solidarity? South Asian activism for Palestine. *Human Architecture: Journal of the Sociology of Self-Knowledge* 7: 105–10.

———. 2010. Collecting and translating the non-western other: The perils and possibilities of a world literature website. *The Comparatist* 34: 127–53.

Sue, Derald W., and David Sue. 1999. *Counseling the Culturally Different: Theory and Practice*. 3rd ed. New York: John Wiley.

Takaki, Ronald. 1993. *In a Different Mirror: A History of Multicultural America*. San Francisco, CA: Back Bay Books.

Taraporevala, Sooni. 2004. *Parsis: The Zoroastrians of India—A Photographic Journey*. Mumbai: Good Books.

Tatum, Beverly. 2003. *Why Are All the Black Kids Sitting Together in the Cafeteria? And Other Conversations about Race*. New York: Basic Books.

The Institute for Habits of Mind. 2009. http://www.habits-of-mind.net (accessed November 8, 2010).

Thompson, Cooper, Emmett Schaefer, and Harry Brod, eds. 2002. *White Men Challenging Racism*. Durham, NC: Duke University Press.

Trickett, E.J., R.J. Watts, D. Birman, eds. 1994. *Human Diversity*. San Fransico, CA: Jossey-Bass.

TuSmith, Bonnie, and Maureen T. Reddy, eds. 2002. *Race in the College Classroom: Pedagogy and Politics*. New Brunswick, NJ: Rutgers University Press.

Vella, Jane. 2002. *Learning to Listen Learning to Teach: The Power of Dialogue in Educating Adults*. San Francisco, CA: Jossey-Bass.

Vygotsky, Lev. S. 1978. *Mind in Society: The Development of Higher Cognitive Processes*. Cambridge, MA: Harvard University Press.

Watt, Sherry K., Tracey L. Robinson, and Helen Lupton-Smith. 2002. Building ego and racial identity: Preliminary perspectives on counselors-in-training. *Journal of Counseling and Development* 80 (1): 94–100.

Wink, Joan. 1997. *Critical Pedagogy: Notes from the Real World*. White Plains, NY: Addison, Wesley Longman, Inc.

Zamel, Vivian, and Ruth Spack, eds. 2004. *Crossing the Curriculum: Teaching Multilingual Learners in College Classrooms*. New York: Lawrence Erlbaum.

Contributors

Arlene Dallalfar is professor of sociology and women's studies at Lesley University, teaching in the Social Science Division in Lesley College and the Intercultural Relations Program in the Graduate School of Arts and Social Sciences. Her areas of specialization include visual sociology, gender, immigration and diaspora, and globalization and gender inequality. Since 2003, she has been the lead coordinator and faculty development seminar leader at Lesley and has for many years been committed to inclusive pedagogy and faculty development initiatives. Recent publications include "Negotiated Alliances: Contemporary Iranian Jewish Identities," in *Contemporary Studies of South Asia, Africa, and the Middle East* (2010); "Fragments of Home: Identity and Empowerment from the Margin," in *Crossing Borders, Making Homes: Stories of Resilient Women*, edited by D. Llera, D. Cathcart, and E. Roffman (2009); and "North America: Economics Informal Sector," in the *Encyclopedia of Women and Islamic Cultures* (2006).

Carolyn P. Panofsky is a professor of educational studies at Rhode Island College. Her teaching and research address cultural and social issues in education, with a particular focus on literacy, learning, and discourse, and framed in the tradition of cultural historical activity theory. She began her career as a literacy educator, working with students from historically underserved backgrounds, before turning primarily to the education of teachers and other educators at all levels.

Denise Patmon teaches in the Curriculum & Instruction Department of the College of Education & Human Development at the University of Massachusetts Boston. Her doctoral research was entitled *Japanese Literature and the Teaching of Writing: Multiple Frames for Knowing*. She is the author of three books for children and several monographs and articles. Pedagogy is her passion; she has received numerous Teacher of the Year awards and honors from a variety of institutions in the Greater Boston area.

Esther Kingston-Mann is a professor of history at the University of Massachusetts Boston of working-class origin. A scholar, writer, and teacher of Russian/Soviet history, she has published three books that integrate historically marginalized groups into the master narratives of Soviet/Russian history (peasants and women, in particular). Current research interests are in the history of women, property rights, and privatization. Contributions to the scholarship of teaching include "Three Steps Forward and One Step Back: Dilemmas of Upward Mobility," in *Achieving against the Odds: How Academics Become Teachers of Diverse Students* (2000) and "Teaching, Learning, Diversity: Just Don't Call It Epistemology!" in *Discourse of Sociological Practice* (2006).

Hubie Jones is former dean of the Boston University School of Social Work (1977–1993), former president of Roxbury Community College, and a board member of many other foundations and nonprofit organizations, including Roxbury Youthworks, the Community Fellows Program at Massachusetts Institute of Technology, City Year, and the Conservation Law Foundation.

Janel Lucas, Ph.D., LICSW, is a faculty member in the Social Sciences Division of Lesley University. She is also a practicing clinician who works with adults facing a variety of mental health challenges. Her research interests and previous publications have focused on enhancing multiculturalism, student and professional development, and the relationships between individuals and their environments.

Lesley Bogad teaches in the Department of Educational Studies at Rhode Island College. She teaches undergraduate and graduate courses in sociology of education, qualitative research methods, and women's studies. Her research focuses on schooling for social justice, media literacy, and the educational lives of underrepresented students in higher education.

Marjorie Jones is professor in the Division of Education, Lesley College. She also teaches courses in the Division of Social Sciences and the Center for the Adult Learner and serves as a senior advisor in the Ph.D. in Educational Studies Program. She has taught English at the secondary level and has worked in higher education training teachers and principals and has developed curricula used nationally and internationally. Her work with adults, youth, and families, with women as a specific focus, addresses their holistic development and has taken place in both community-based organizations and universities.

Phyllis C. Brown is an adjunct assistant professor in curriculum and instruction and technology and education in the School of Education of

Lesley University. Most recently, Dr. Brown was the program director of elementary education at Keiser University in Sarasota, Florida. She has also coordinated several research projects and evaluation efforts. Dr. Brown is a graduate of the University of Rhode Island (BA), the Heller School at Brandeis University (Master's), and the University of Massachusetts Amherst (Ed.D). Dr. Brown is a diversity consultant for Sarasota Government in Sarasota, Florida. Her seminars include "Managing a Diversity Force and Managing with Emotional Intelligence." Most recently, she created the Phyllis Charlotte Brown Scholarship for Youth at the Art Center Sarasota in Sarasota, Florida.

Rajini Srikanth, originally from India, teaches a wide variety of courses at the University of Massachusetts Boston. They include American literature and literatures from South Asia, South Africa, and the Middle East (in translation). Her research interests focus on the internationalizing of American Studies; her book *The World Next Door: South Asian American Literature and the Idea of America* (2004) won the Cultural Studies Book Award for the Association for Asian American Studies. Her forthcoming book is titled *Constructing the Enemy: Antipathy/Empathy in U. S. Literature and Law.*

Richard Pepp taught courses in writing and literature in the English Department at Massasoit Community College, a comprehensive community college in Brockton, Massachusetts. His students are diverse in backgrounds, ages, abilities, nationalities, and languages. His leadership of a faculty development seminar entitled "Bridging Two Worlds: Professors and Students" led to the writing of this essay. He is currently a faculty member in the English Department at Suffolk University in Boston.

Robin A. Robinson is associate professor in sociology and crime & justice studies at the University of Massachusetts Dartmouth. She earned the Ph.D. in Social Policy from Brandeis University, and the Psy.D. in Clinical Psychology from The George Washington University. Her scholarly and activist work considers, generally, women and girls in social context, focused on social constructions of female deviance, violence and trauma, social policy and criminology, psychological perspectives on crime and deviance, and social justice and crime in historical context.

Sunanda K. Sanyal, originally from India, is associate professor of art history and critical studies at the Art Institute of Boston at Lesley University, where he has been teaching since 1999. He has an MFA in visual arts (painting and installation) from University of California, San Diego (1990); an MFA in art history from Ohio University (1993); and a Ph.D. in art history from Emory University (2000). He is interested in politics of representation and identity; representation and otherness; contemporary artists from former colonies in global discourses; and art pedagogy in nineteenth-century Europe and its colonies. Sanyal has published on contemporary artists of color and chaired panels at various conferences.

Tim Sieber, professor of anthropology at the University of Massachusetts Boston, is an urban anthropologist who teaches and writes about cities in Portugal and the United States, focusing on immigration, public culture, urban planning, and education. Recent publications are "Public Architecture in a Postimperial Capital: The Portuguese Pavilion at the 1998 Lisbon's World's Fair," in *Visual Anthropology Review* (2010) and "Working Across Difference to Build Community, Democracy, and Immigrant Integration," in *The Trotter Review* (2010). He is also the author of a number of works that deal with university teaching, including coeditorship of *Achieving Against the Odds: How Academics Become Teachers of Diverse Students* (2001).

Vivian Poey is associate professor in the Creative Arts and Learning Division of the School of Education at Lesley University. She earned an MFA from the Rhode Island School of Design and has worked as a mentor at the Manchester Craftsmen's Guild, as an artist in residence in Pittsburgh Public High Schools, and as artist teacher in the Children's Studio Public Charter School in Washington, D.C. Her photographic work, which has been widely exhibited, examines issues ranging from nationalism and cultural assimilation to uncertainty and the passing of time.

Index

collaboration—*Continued*
  and student expectations, 63
  among students, 203
  see also administrators, faculty,
    mentoring, power
Collins, Patricia Hill, 17, 44, 117, 126,
  131
community
  building in the classroom, 176–8
  of faculty of color, 167–8
  learning, ix–x, 183, 217–18
  and pedagogy, 176–7
  of reflective faculty, 45
  see also classroom, collaboration,
    faculty
community college, 229–40
counseling, 165, 170, 174
  close relation to teaching, 166
  and empathy in human services, 147–8
  and teaching human services, 170
culture
  academic views of, 22
  and authenticity, 84, 131–2
  and border crossing, 84–5, 96, 132, 187
  of the classroom, 194
  critiquing media representations of,
    122
  cultural competence and ethics,
    172–4
  and difference, 128
  higher education institutional,
    184–5
  and literary texts, 99
  teachers as mediators of, 65–6
  and teaching, 92
  of warfare, 126
  see also identity, images of "the
    Other"
curriculum
  political choice, 120
  see also interdisciplinary, syllabus

Delpit, Lisa, 185, 191–2, 193, 194
diversity, ix–x, 3

curriculum requirement, 22
  and difference, 26–7
  Diversity Research Initiative (DRI),
    24–9
  and faculty training, 23, 42–5
  and identity, 77–9
  invisible types, 114–15, 172
  students, 114–15
  see also class, gender, identity,
    images of "the Other," race and
    ethnicity, sexuality

empathy, teaching of, 143–56
Enloe, Cynthia, 117–18
epistemology, 1, 7, 60, 114, 120, 125, 126

faculty
  as activists in curriculum change,
    21, 52–3
  changing role of, 53, 210
  childhood experiences of, and 17, 43,
    58–9, 113, 126, 144–7, 185–7,
    211, 213–14, 231
  of color:
    dilemmas, 167–70, 198, 209–211
    invisibility and hypervisibility, 3,
      137, 198, 209–10
    issues of race, 165–7, 175, 198
    mentoring other faculty of color,
      169–70
    and politics of representation, 131–2
    see also images of "the Other," race
      and ethnicity
  and the Cross Cultural Odyssey, 7
  and identity, 78, 82, 113–14
  importance of reflection for, 2
  leadership, 20, 30–1
  learning about students, 115, 237–40
  learning from students, 209–10
  organizing of, 23
  and race, 165–7, 175, 198
  respecting students, 91
  as role models, 81, 113, 119, 167,
    178–9

CPSIA information can be obtained at www.ICGtesting.com
Printed in the USA
LVOW10*1513010414

379810LV00013B/255/P